STRUGG PURPOSES OF SCHOOLING IN A DEMOCRATIC STATE

Selected Readings in the History of American Education

Lynn King
978 452-5885

Edited by

Richard G. Lyons
Juan C. Rodriguez
John Catallozzi
Norman Benson

University Press of America,® Inc.
Lanham • New York • Oxford

Copyright © 1998
University Press of America,® Inc.
4720 Boston Way
Lanham, Maryland 20706

12 Hid's Copse Rd.
Cummor Hill, Oxford OX2 9JJ

Library of Congress Cataloging-in-Publication Data

Struggles over the purposes of schooling in a democratic state :
selected readings in the history of American education / edited by
Richard G. Lyons . . . (et al.).
p.   cm.
1. Education—United States—History. 2. Education—Social
aspects—United States—History. 3. Education—Aims and
objectives—United States. I. Lyons, Richard.
LA205.S76 1998   370'.973—dc21   98-23782 CIP

ISBN 0-7618-1174-5 (cloth: alk. ppr.)
ISBN 0-7618-1175-3 (pbk: alk. ppr.)

♾™ The paper used in this publication meet the minimum
requirements of American National Standard for information
Sciences—Permanence of Paper for Printed Library Materials,
ANSI Z39.48—1984

To Our Parents
Our First Teachers

———————————————

Maurice & Abby Lyons
Florencio & Isabel Rodriguez
Alfred & Esther Catallozzi
Frank & Norma Benson

Contents —————————————————————

v

Preface ─────────────────────────────────

This book of readings is designed to help students clarify their understanding of the ongoing debate concerning the role of schools in contemporary society. This struggle centers on the goals of schooling and the means of achieving them within a democratic society. The book offers a variety of views defining the purposes of schools including theories that focus on the importance of transmitting community values - as well as readings that center on developing the capacities of people. Add to this dialogue the issue of whether schools can command social change that leads toward equality, and we find still another dimension of the debate. The ebb and flow of these arguments may be better understood by examining both the historical and contemporary debate over the objectives of teacher education.

Initially, the education of teachers was driven by forces that emphasized the transmitting of traditional values. A concern with methodology, school management, and child development was their defining mark. Subsequently, colleges of education not only maintained their conservative voice but also argued that traditional values could be scientifically justified. Educators tried to quantify intelligence by gender, race, and ethnicity. Our social place had a certain inevitability given our genetic equipment. These ideas, however, found critics within teacher education who argued for more humanistic concerns. Teacher education, they claimed, should emphasize historical and philosophical sensitivities especially as they relate to social inequality. Students were encouraged to take more liberal arts courses, and colleges of education began to strengthen their faculties in the humanistic areas. Students became aware of how schools uncritically reflected political, sexual, racial and religious preferences. Discussions on the power of the school to correct inequality and to become more sensitive to personal development while also paying respect to community values became common.

This humanistic trend, however, was short lived. For unrelated reasons student achievement scores declined. Moreover, the public believed that students were generally undisciplined, had too many electives, and were being exposed to controversial subjects. Teacher education responded. They again focused on the primacy of competence, technique and evaluation. Newspaper ads for Deans emphasized school experience over vision. The humanistic areas were renamed policy studies to give the impression that they had a more practical bent.

In this atmosphere, there developed a renewed emphasis on the scientific understanding of children and the skills needed within the economy. Knowledge or scientific understanding was regarded as much more significant than a historical and philosophical exposure to the possibilities of schooling. Knowledge, however, has a serious limitation. It does not inform us on how to judge a society, nor what to encourage in child development, nor the value changes that would make for a more livable world. Knowledge in many ways focused on transmitting community values. Humanists have long drawn upon an old distinction as a means of demonstrating the serious limitation of basing teacher education entirely on the acquisition of knowledge. Knowledge places no obvious value on the world. We must supplement our knowledge with meaning. This distinction was made by medieval philosophers when they drew a distinction between faith (meaning) and reason (knowledge). Meaning poses questions about the normative dimensions of life. What type of government is best, how to address inequality, and most importantly, how to educate people. If issues on meaning are regarded as knowledge bound then we end up with a technology of schooling. It is equally incorrect, on the other hand, to deny facts when they do not square with our beliefs on meaning. Nevertheless, if forced by some demon to base teacher education on science and knowledge as opposed to faith and meaning we would choose the latter. This choice would at least distinguish colleges of education from colleges of engineering.

When we consider issues of human meaning, we raise questions about the values we wish to foster and the nature of schools that would promote these values. The school must always balance three potentially conflicting goals in a democratic society. The first views the school as transmitting traditional values and aspirations of the community, especially as they relate to adult work roles. The second involves a commitment towards fair play and equality, while the third urges personal development.

William T. Harris and John Dewey sought a creative synthesis to the potentially conflicting demands of equality, personal development and socialization. Harris thought that the protection of private property allowed individuals to attain the widest possible expression of personality while maintaining reasonable community restraints and fair play. The development of basic skills, hard work, competition, and the value of private property was the key to fully developed individuals who could also be effective citizens and workers. Dewey, on the other hand, felt that the school was fairly autonomous and could influence social change. Schools would be critical of social norms when those norms become ineffective in dealing with inequality. For Dewey, the schools created values and skills that made for a more effective democratic community while liberating personality.

Jill Conway and Samual Bowles and Herbert Gintis argue that gender and class are impediments to equality. They go into great detail on the inability of schooling to correct flaws in the social fabric. They argue that the school plays a small role in the battle for equality. In their view, this issue is crucial. If we assume, for example, that the fight for racial equality can be forged with effective schooling and the school is ineffective then we have wasted our time. In fact, to put our efforts into schooling when schooling is powerless is a way to maintain the status quo. Juan Rodriguez, however, sees the school as offering some small help with its programs in areas such as bilingual education. Some minority students do make it and this can be partially attributed to their schooling. According to Rodriguez, schooling offers the best hope for the acquisition of literacy and power. George Counts is much more radical in terms as his menu for change. He regards schools as the engine for social reform, where a focus on equality will bring about the greatest amount of personal growth.

All the writers are aware that the school must face the task of socializing developing people while addressing the problem of equality. They wish to avoid excessive individualism and recognize that the community has reasonable powers over people. Yet, they also want to restrict the powers of community. The problem of whether to focus on socializing or liberating people is compounded when we add the problem of whether the school can create value which in turn improves communities and liberates the potential of its members.

In sum, Harris and Dewey emphasize personal development while Counts focuses on radical change as a condition for personal development.   Gintis and Bowles and Conway, on the other hand, look at the power of the economic structure to shape schooling, while Rodriguez is more sanguine and sees the school as partially effective in giving some students the tools to attain equality.

Researchers in the last twenty five years have focused more on the relationships between working and schooling. They still employ the traditional categories of explanation. That is to say, they use the categories of individual development, social egalitarianism, and transmitting community values, but see them as they relate to the school-work coupling. Most of the writers think that looking at the nature of work can account for the process of schooling. They argue that the transmitting of community values, rather than personal developmental and egalitarian concerns are the best historical explanations of schooling. Schools, in short, prepare students to become willing participants in the work force. Richard Lyons, Stephan Hamilton and Klaus Hurrelman, and Jean Anyon emphasize the power that work has over schooling. On the other hand, Seymour Sarason, Jane Roland Martin and Martin Conroy and Henry Levin, and Patricia Malone and Norman Benson focus more on the manner in which schools can become an effective voice for changes in the workplace. Schools are not always passive institutions since they may have some influence on how work is expressed in schools. Schools, after all, are much fairer in the allocation of rewards than the general workplace.

All of the readings are introduced with a short essay that raises the essential points of the reading. We have added a series of questions at the end of each introductory essay which we hope provokes additional questions.

Part I

Historical Perspectives on the Goals of Schooling in America

Chapter 1

Introduction to William T. Harris

William T. Harris was a founder and the only editor of the *Journal of Speculative Philosophy*, author of hundreds of articles, several books, superintendent of the St. Louis school system, and the fourth U.S. Commissioner of Education. He exercised a significant influence over the course of American education in the latter part of the nineteenth century.

He took a strong stand against business interests who wanted the public schools to take on a more vocational flavor. Businessmen predicted a new prosperity if the poor and foreign-born learned a trade. Harris, however, who was always in delicate administrative positions, disagreed. He needed and solicited business support to increase funding for free public schools but did not share their views on vocational education. Schooling, for Harris, was more than acquiring marketable skills. Reading and mathematics were important not only because they had immediate results for industry and business but also because they enabled people to better understand and live fuller lives. However, an aggressive posture by Harris toward business interests might endanger their support for the expansion of public schooling. How was it possible to have the support of the business world without that support tied to narrow vocational education? His proposal was ingenious. The school should emphasize the humanities because they would convince students that private property was the basis of human freedom. Any attack on the notion of private property would endanger the business community's existence. Harris was quick to point out that the idea of private property had implications outside the world of commerce. He pointed out that private property deals with the issue of human meaning, the essential concern of the humanities.   The humanities, argued Harris, would convince students that the basis of human life was personal freedom, and the best guarantee of that freedom was the preservation of personal and capital producing property.

His argument was timely.   Private property, especially capital producing property, was attracting criticism.   Marx, who was known in educated circles, and Engels had finally published *Das Kapital* which Harris reviewed.   Edward Bellamy's utopian novel, *Looking Backwards*, imagined the end of private ownership of capital-producing property and predicated a just distribution of wealth when property became socialized.   Furthermore, the influx of poor immigrants and considerable labor unrest could give the impression that the idea of private ownership was being seriously reexamined.   Harris brought his considerable weight to the side of business and free enterprise.   He pointed out, quite forcibly, to teachers' groups, school boards, and the reading public that the possession of private property was endangered if the great masses of people refused to believe in its significance.   The best safeguard for the existence of private property was public support, especially in a democracy, and the best instrument to ensure that support was the free public school.   A solid background in history, languages and geography would deepen and develop, in the masses, an appreciation for private ownership and its relationship to freedom and human meaning.

The following article is a reply to that portion of the business community who insisted that the study of the humanities was unimportant.   The style is less academic than what he published on the same topic in journals and books but is a good illustration of his fundamental conviction about the role of the humanities in education.   Reading the article today, one might wonder if Harris lost the argument to the belief that human progress is firmly tied to technology.   Many schools and colleges, especially in the public sector, are concerned with science and employment.   Even many universities with their historical attention to the humanities have taken on an overwhelming vocational character.   Defenders of the humanities, moreover, have forcefully argued that students with a firm foundation in the humanities make better businessmen, scientists, and service personnel.

The questions Harris raises about the humanities and their relationship to our economic and political system are as important today as when he raised these concerns over a hundred years ago.

The reader should consider three questions posed by Harris:

1. Is human freedom dependent on the existence of private property?

2. Is the private ownership of property the best way to protect ourselves from unreasonable community interference?

3. What safeguards would you develop to keep those who had a great deal of wealth from demanding their own form of conformity?

Do the Public Schools Educate Children Beyond the Position They Must Occupy in Life?

by William T. Harris

[At the State Teachers' Association, held in New Haven, October 26-28, 1882, the following address of William T. Harris, LL.D., of Concord, Massachusetts, was received with special favor, and its publication in our Report was desired by prominent members of the Association.]

Why educate the child out of his sphere? Why teach him to aspire beyond the position which the vast majority must always occupy?

These are the questions which are often asked in the days of reaction, when every established institution is saluted with the challenge *"cui bono"* and not allowed to pass on until it has given the countersign *"pro bono publico."*

Why should we educate children in common schools at public expense at all? Why should we provide opportunity for any and all children to acquire a thorough education?

We are to find the answer to this question by investigating the special conditions of society in modern civilization, and by studying the requirements of the political government under which we live.

We are accustomed to accept without dissent the proposition that, in a government founded on the ballot box, universal education is the only safeguard. It is not so obvious to the questioner, however, that the social conditions of modern civilization demand the school education of all the people. Let us therefore consider first this necessity of the nineteenth century, before we review the requirements special to our own nation.

It is agreed that this age is one of productive industry. Its active principle is invention; especially mechanic invention. Every day we hear of some new discovery that harnesses a new force of nature and compels it to work for man and assist in providing means of food, clothing, and shelter, or means of intercommunication and the spread of knowledge. Mind -- not the body -- is the inventive power; the directive power that can manage and use machines to advantage is mental and not physical skill. The growth of invention is so rapid that the increase of manufacturing power by the aid of machinery is said to double, for all the world, once in seven years. The multiplication of steam engines, and the improvement of machines, renders this possible. What unintelligent hand-labor is there that has any certainty of being in demand ten years hence? More than this, what trade is there that can count on using, ten years hence, just the kind of technical skill that it requires now?

The history of the present era of industries shows a continual shifting of vocations -- no vocation having any long lease of life. The new discovery will make the trade learned today, after a long and tedious apprenticeship, useless tomorrow. Any peculiar knack, which depends on manual dexterity, may be rendered valueless by a new application of machinery. The practical education, therefore, is not an education of the hand to the skill, but of the brain to directive intelligence. The educated man can learn to direct a new machine in three weeks, while it requires three years to learn a new manual labor. The hand trained for twenty years at one kind of labor cannot learn a new work requiring different skill, because the muscles have become set and stiffened into one form of action. An uneducated workman will be thrown aside to perish in an almshouse. Only the versatile intelligence is able to meet the demands of the age of productive industry.

We are sometimes told by political economists that the fault lies in the wisdom of the governing power. Inventions should not be permitted. The Chinese government, we are assured, is paternally watchful in this matter of protecting the laborer in his vocation. No mischievous inventions are allowed to supersede the good old ways of production. But then man can make no progress in the conquest of nature, without mechanic intervention. All but one in a thousand will be doomed to toil like slaves for a scanty pittance of food, clothing and shelter, if no aid is to be invoked from machinery.

The evil arising from the readjustment of vocations, rendered necessary by new inventions, can be relieved by two measures. First, the facilities of immigration into uninhabited borderlands offer to all peoples pressed for room in the old homes, and to all poorly paid laborers, the opportunity to remove to localities where they may till the rich soil or set up their mechanical industries for the benefit of a new population in need of their wares. Hope and courage are stimulated in the new immigrant by the spectacle of the results of his labors which convert a wilderness into a civilized country in a short time.

The second measure to remove the evil of change of vocation is to educate all laborers and thereby make them versatile and able to pass from one kind of labor to another without tedious training and waste of power.

But we are told that this education makes the common laborer aspire to become a professional man. He ought to be contented with the lot in which he is placed by the accident of birth.

The more educated intelligence, the more invention. The more conquest over nature by invention, the more aspiration in the mind of the individual. To be a drudge ought not to satisfy any human being. Perpetual growth in knowledge and wisdom, in the realization of reason, and the image of the god-like is the vocation of man. To be discontented with the real is, therefore, the lesson of civilization.

"Education makes people indolent and unwilling to get their living by honest labor," we are told. It is likely that the man who has learned the magic power of Science and Art to subdue Nature will not willingly offer himself a sacrifice to bodily wants and accept a vocation that requires mere manual labor. He will desire a position that employs his intelligence as well as his hands. For he wishes even his daily labor to recognize him as something above a beast, and as possessing reason and knowledge. But all this talk about indolence as the consequence of knowledge is without a basis of fact.

The race to which we as a people belong is not an indolent race. Look at its history and study the magnitude and quality of its achievements. Why has it done all these? What would it have done if it had not had ambition and aspiration and much heart-hunger? Have not the Anglo-Saxon and Norman races been the most discontented of races on the planet? What contented race is there that has accomplished anything for which mankind are the better?

Our civilization rewards the workman who is looking beyond the machine he is using to a better one that he has conceived in his mind.

Arkwright and Whitney, Fulton, Stephenson, Morse, and Bessemer are held in high honor as heroes in the conquest over nature.

It is clear that all the bodily wants of man -- food, clothing, and shelter, -- depending as they do upon the ownership of property for their satisfaction, are through this means elevated and spiritualized by the institution of society. For property is not the creation of the individual -- mere possession does not suffice; it is the recognition of society that makes things become property. Civil society establishes rights of property and division of labor. Through this each man labors for his fellow-men and depends upon their labor to supply him the articles of food, clothing and shelter which his own labor does not produce. His bodily wants are no longer mere immediate impulses, as animal wants, but they are converted into the instruments of realizing man's spiritual or reflected being; he is forced by hunger and cold to combine with his fellow-men and to form a community in which he is to respect their recognition far more than his animal impulses and desires. Thus, too, the institution of the family lifts man above mere sexual passion, and makes him in that respect a reflected being, a rational being. Civil society is organized for the realization of man's existence as a property owner, so that he shall be a universal or rational essence, and not a mere individual animal, dependent on his mere locality and the season of the year and his unaided might for his physical life. Through civil society each individual commands by his own feeble efforts the resources of the entire globe. The organization of civil society is so perfect that every day's labor of the wheat-grower affects the price of wheat all over the world. Every day's labor in the mills of Lowell or Lawrence affects the price of cotton cloth in Australia. The day-laborer in the streets of this city commands with his meagre wages to that extent a share in the coffee of the distant Indies, the sugar of Louisiana, the tea of China, the drugs of South America, the fruits and grains, the manufactures from all sections of the country.

The fact that conscious intelligence -- directive power -- controls the property of the world, is too obvious to need restatement. I call property a "reflected being" being it exists only through the recognition of society. Things exist, it is true, without such recognition. But things do not become property until society confirms the right of ownership. Such recognition is always an act of directive intelligence. The rights of property can be conserved only through an educated class. The higher kinds of property, such as vested rights and franchises, imply a higher intelligence in the community. Again, the possibility of possession of property by all in this country adds new validity to it here and makes it more valuable. That you can alienate your real estate makes it property in a complete sense; if it is entailed it is only part property. The free possession of property without feudal liens and tenures -- the dead hands of its past owners still clutching the symbol of their reflected being -- comes to existence only when a government of all the people, for all the people, and by all the people prevails, and when it is rendered possible through universal education. Who would own real estate in Turkey? Who would accept a Russian estate on condition that he must live on it and assume its responsibilities? No one of us, I think. The quality of property -- its intrinsic value -- depends upon the quality of the community who recognize it. The status of the reflected being is the status of those who reflect it. Property in a refined and cultivated community is raised to a high potence of value; in a barbarous community it is not worth the risks incidental to its possession. In proportion as man is educated he sees the substantial character of reflected existence, and this perception creates continually new kinds of property founded on new recognition: bodiless possessions, "incorporeal hereditaments" that receive their substance from conventional recognition. The growth of corporations is the wonder of this generation. What the individual never could do for himself and yet needs to have done in order that he may gain freedom from thralldom to nature. The individual could not afford to obtain pure water from the distant hills, or establish gas-works or own a railroad or a telegraph or express system -- corporations furnish him all these things. If corporations abuse their power sometimes, this is because society has not yet learned where to place legal restrictions upon them and is another illustration of the necessity of education in the community.

Thus not only does the culture of civilization increase the alienability of property and hence its value, but it develops into property a vast series of relations of the nature of franchises which, in a rude unpolished age, are mere rights of the strongest and non-transferable to the common people. Hence property in the highest sense, cannot exist except it be taxed for universal education. For universal education will not exist unless it is provided for by the State and unless the State supports it wholly or in part by taxation.

Macaulay in the House of Commons, in 1847, defending the Minutes of the Committee of Council on Education to which he as a member of the privy council had given consent, gave a vivid picture of the condition of Scotland, contrasting the thriftlessness of a people before education was established by law with the thrift that followed government action in behalf of schools. He said: "It was at the end of the 17th century that Fletcher of Saltoun, a brave and able man, who fought and suffered for liberty, was so overwhelmed with the spectacle of misery his country presented that he actually published a pamphlet, in which he proposed the institution of personal slavery in Scotland as the only way to compel the common people to work.

"Within two months after the appearance of the pamphlet of Fletcher, the Parliament of Scotland passed in 1696, an act for the settlement of schools.   Has the whole world given us such an instance of improvement as that which took place at the beginning of the 18th century? In a short time, in spite of the inclemency of the air and the sterility of the soil, Scotland became a country which had no reason to envy any part of the world, however richly gifted by nature; and remember that Scotchmen did this, and that wherever a Scotchman went -- and there were few places he did not go to -- he carried with him signs of the moral and intellectual cultivation he had received. If he had a shop, he had the best trade in the street; if he enlisted in the army, he soon became a non-commissioned officer. Not that the Scotchman changed; there was no change in the man; a hundred years before, Scotchmen of the lower classes were spoken of in London as you speak of the Esquimaux; but such was the difference when this system of State education had been in force for only one generation; the language of contempt was at an end and that of envy succeeded. Then the complaint was that wherever the Scotchman came he got more that his share; that when he mixed with Englishmen or Irishmen, he rose as regularly to the top as oil rises on water."

Turning from this economical aspect of the question to the political requirements that specially concern our own people, we shall discover that we, in America, have much more to urge us to establish common school education than this demand of the age of invention, for intelligent labor. We have permitted universal suffrage, and the government is of the majority. If we do not have universal education we shall all suffer for it. For we are tethered to the lowest stratum of our population, and must accept their influence in our politics. Nothing but education will ameliorate it.

The lover of his kind rejoices in the knowledge that here in America we have so organized our society that the welfare of the highest is connected, indissolubly, with the lowest, so that each and all must, in the main, see clearly that he is his brother's keeper, and realize the solidarity of the social whole. Each man is what he is, not through himself alone, but by and through the reflection thrown back upon him from the social whole in which he lives and has his being. Under monarchies and despotisms the same fact was true, but there was such a mirage created by the principle of caste that it could not be seen clearly except by deep thinkers. Here it is visible, for the common laborer is also a voter, and participates in making the laws of a free government.

We say therefore to the aristocrat who grudges his contribution to the common schools, or who looks askance and asks, "Why educate the children of the common laborers?" -- for your own well-being and the well-being of your children, the children of all must be educated. For here, all, and not the few, govern. If you wish property safe from confiscation by a majority composed of communists, you must see to it that the people are educated so that each sees the sacredness of property and its service to the world in making available to each the industry of the entire population of the earth. The study of geography in our common schools is one long lesson in the dependence of each people on all others through commerce. The industry of each nation is not the industry of individuals to supply their own immediate wants, but an industry which pours its productions into the markets of the world, and in return receives its just share of the productions of all climes and seasons. Geography is the scientific presentation of this process of producing and distributing the material blessings of civilization. How this is all accomplished is stated in a systematic exposition addressed to the thinking intelligence of the child or scholar. For geography tells us what each place produces and supplies to the rest of the world and thus exhibits the dependence of all on each and of each on all. Is there any study better calculated to interest him in the conservation of those great social institutions based on property? Not, indeed, unless it is the study of human nature as revealed in those best selections from literature contained in his school-readers. In his reading-lesson he finds the poetically-inspired expression of his deepest and purest feelings, of his subtlest insights, of his truest moral instincts. Out of the dim region of semi-conscious instinct they come forth to the light of conscious conviction and felicitous expression in words -- and all this through the study of reading in the common schools. Here he gets not only social science, but also moral culture. The soul of the child of the common laborer kindles with aspiration as he reads burning words of patriotism and immortal valor, of disinterested heroism and self-sacrifice for others. He feels his inborn divinity as he reads of the triumphs of his race, and sees in the visions of poets the lofty ideal of the future set before mankind. All this is not wanted, we are told, in the children of common laborers. If not, we are sorry for the person who does not want it. He is so blind that he does not see the shore of Charybdis when he steers away from Scylla -- he steers away from a restless and adventurous class of people but only to run into the evil alternative of a people leagued together against capital, full of communistic dreams about labor and wages, with no broad humanitarian feeling, with patriotism rooted out by international association against the rights of property. He is willing to have a proletariat elect his legislators, if only he can find cheap boot-blacks and house-servants.

It is indeed a great thing to have even one class of society educated. No doubt all profit by it, even when the education is confined to the few. But in a democracy all must be educated. The interest of property demands it, the interest of the government demands it. And one generation of well educated people in a State forces upon all adjacent States the necessity of public education as a mere war measure, as a means of the preservation of the State. So also will the existence of one successful democracy force upon the world the adoption of democratic forms of government as the condition of their continued existence. An ignorant people can be governed, but only a wise people can govern itself.

Where all are educated, and directive power exists on every hand, it finds its employment chiefly in building up the wealth of the community. The directive power required every day to manage the large banks of this country, to direct the great railroads, or the manufactories and corporations of various kinds, is infinitely more than required to direct our government. The management of the New York Central or the Pennsylvania Railroad system is as great an affair as the government of a small kingdom.

Self-directive intelligence makes for itself avenues of employment. Directive power is the only kind of power that is never wasted.

Within the past twenty-five years great strides have been taken by European governments in establishing systems of public education. It has been seen clearly that unless the laborer was educated the industrial product would be inferior and come to be discriminated against in the markets of the world. Technical education thus began at South Kensington for England as it had been before established in France and

Germany. The foresight of the great Frederick, backed by the religious dogmas of Luther, secured general education to his people. The weight of the Prussian people in war came to be seen in their Austrian and French campaigns. Since these wars, public education has received an enormous impulse but national independence itself seems dependent on the general education of the people.

The education of the people as a military necessity, although it has come to have a new meaning in Europe since the Franco-Prussian war, is not, after all, anything new. The directive power of a people has always been given the best education that the nation was able to furnish.

If we turn for a moment to the actual history of nations we shall find public education, in some sort or other, always existing. The only point is to inquire, in what does the directive power of this people exist? To find at once where the public money is used for educational purposes. In China, for instance, the schools are supported by the people in their private capacity. But the government rewards those successfully graduating, by its offices. Hence the money advanced for education is only an investment in public securities. In all countries the military education is at public expense. Where does the education and support of the nobility and royal families come from except from the public? They do no immediate work. They are going to direct and have others obey. But in our country where each is born to all the rights of mankind without distinction, all must be provided for, not by pauper schools, for that would be to burn into the plastic mind of the youth his misfortune, and he never would outgrow the stigma. Neither is it safe to leave the education of youth to religious zeal or private benevolence; for then inequalities of the most disastrous kind will slip in, and our State find elements heterogeneous to it continually growing up.

The government of a republic must educate all its people, and it must educate them so far that they are able to educate themselves in a continued process of culture extending through life. This implies the existence of higher institutions of public education. And these, not so much with the expectation that all will attend them, as that the lower schools which are more initiatory in their character and deal with mere elements, depend for their efficiency upon the organization of higher institutions for their direction and control without educating in higher institutions the teachers of lower schools, and furthermore without the possibility hovering before the pupils of ascent into the higher schools, there can be no practical effect given to primary schools.

If the monarchies of Europe think to put off the people with mere polytechnic and industrial education, they will find that they have fostered a directive power that will grope for and find the helm of State, and then attempt to administer the government. The mistake will then become visible. Man will not submit to be educated simply as a director of machines and instrumentalities of industry. He soon aspires to direct himself and be self-governed. To be sure, there is a long step from the mere hand-laborer, the one who turns a crank or carries a hod, the galley slave who works chained to his oar -- there is a long step from the mere physical laborer to the director of a machine: to the engineer, the overseer of a loom, or the manager of a telegraph; the former is all hands; his own brain is a mere hand governed by the brain of another who directs him. But when directive power develops so far as to direct and govern machine labor, nay, even when it is so far cultured as to reach the principles of natural science and be capable of applying these in mechanic inventions, even then it is not at its summit of realization. It will stop at nothing short of the spiritual culture that makes it alike directive and governing in the sphere of mind, the realm of social, moral and intellectual existence.

Human instruments, whether mere hod-carriers or locomotive engineers, will not stay contentedly as instruments; they aspire to transcend their hard limits, be they ever so near or never so far off. The higher already, the greater the aspiration. Blind aspiration, from which enlightenment is carefully shut out, leads to July revolutions and reigns of terror; over the ashes of the burnt-out volcano of popular phrensy marches Napoleonic Imperialism with cold unsympathetic step toward the return of Bourbonism and Absolutism. Not only mechanical directive power shall be taught in the people's schools, but also spiritual directive power. The snobbery that patronizingly talks of the education of the "lower classes" does not know that the industrial civilization it affects to admire is an instrument that only Democracy can wield. Leave out the humanities from that education, and you leave out the culture that can guide its course, and communism and socialism, and abstract theories will find their way quickly into the heads of the laboring classes. No merely industrial education can prevent the mind of the people from being fly-blown with crazy political and social theories, destructive to the State. Not merely natural philosophy, chemistry, mathematics and biology must be studied, but likewise the science of society and the State, of art, religion, and philosophy, in all their phases. The great educators of the race -- Homer, Dante, Shakespeare, and Goethe, Plato, Aristotle, Leibnitz, and Newton -- these must be made accessible to the people. Each child must be waited on by the institutions of man, and invited to see the spectacle spread out before him from the lofty summit of civilization; his human brothers that have added a cubit to the world's stature by their heroic labors, must be pointed out to him; the methods and results of their attainments must be revealed to him; noblest aspiration and earnest self-sacrificing endeavor must be aroused in him as the means of achieving his individual task in life. The whole world of the past and present is made, by education, the auxiliary of each man, woman, and child.

Is it not the duty of the State to make the practice of the good possible? This is the definition which a western statesman has suggested as a substitute for that other definition which says that the State exits for the protection of property. "The State exists in order to make the practice of the good possible."

Says Macaulay in the speech I have already quoted:

" I hold that it is the right and duty of the State to provide for the education of the common people . . . I say that the education of the people ought to be the first concern of a State, not only because it is an efficient means of promoting and obtaining that which all allow to be the main end of government, but because it is the most efficient, the most humane, the most civilized, and in all respects the best means of attaining that end . . . Sir, it is the opinion of all the greatest champions of civil and religious liberty in the old world and in the new. [Here he refers to the Pilgrim Fathers and their insight into the necessity of popular education.] Those men forever illustrious in history, were the founders of the Commonwealth of Massachusetts. But though their love of freedom of conscience was illimitable and indestructible, they could see nothing servile or degrading in the principle that the State should take upon itself the charge of the education of the people. In the year 1642 they passed their first legislative enactment on this subject, in the preamble of which they distinctly pledged themselves to this principle, that education was a matter of the deepest possible importance and the greatest possible interest to all nations and to all communities, and that as such it was, in an eminent degree, deserving of the peculiar attention of the State."

To the believer in Caste we would finally address ourselves. We would say:

"All the studies of the common school are conservative in their character, because they all open the windows of the soul and give the mind insight into the substantial character of the institutions of civilization. They all tend to produce the conviction that the well-being of man is best furthered by the very instrumentalities that have been discovered and elaborated by the race, and especially by modern civilization. Reading, writing and arithmetic, geography, history and grammar, all open the soul to light on the question of subduing nature or on the question of the character and destiny of the human mind as revealed in language, or social usages, or political forms and changes. The good school, moreover, teaches industry effectually. But its industry is that of directive intelligence, because the progress of civilization supplies more and more the machinery to perform menial service, and makes it necessary to educate all into directive intelligence. Your opposition to the system of public education may result in their loss of popular favor. Their loss of popular favor will result in stinting their support, and decrease of appropriations will drive away the best and most enterprising teachers. But the final result will be adverse to the education of the less intelligent classes. They will come by degrees to undervalue education altogether. The common schools being under the ban, there will be no pressure of public opinion to cause attendance upon them. Besides, they will be in reality inferior, because their excellence depends upon their patronage by the better classes in large measure. That school which educates all classes in it is the most wholesome in its influence, because it helps the lower social rank by association with finer manners, while it helps the higher social rank by bringing it into a better knowledge of human nature, by associating it with simpler and more direct manifestations of human nature -- the poorer classes being better studies for human nature because more impulsive and less under the control of social forms which disguise the manifestation of natural inclination and impulses. Inasmuch as the hope of civilization depends upon the elevating influence of the educated and cultured classes upon the lower and lowest State, it follows that our educational system should see to it that the cultured class should thoroughly understand and sympathize with the lower classes who lack knowledge, or wealth, or both. I say sympathize, because I take it for granted that no American deems it desirable or possible to oppress the lower classes and keep them down or exploit them. We have universal suffrage or something approaching to it. What we permit our neighbor to be, that we set up as the arbiter of our political well-being; for his ballot will determine our government. The caste principle can find no encouraging sign for it above the horizon of the world's history. The foxes indeed have holes, and the birds of the air have nests, but the advocate of the principle of social inequality as the goal of education has no place where he can lay his head on this planet and enjoy a sweet and refreshing repose. If he goes to Russia, there is the Nihilist and the boiling up of the nethermost depths in the name of revolution and negation. If we must regard civilization as necessarily implying caste and inequality, says the Nihilist, let us place dynamite under the whole structure and blow it into the air. No peace there.

If the lover of caste and inequality as the ideal goal of humanity goes to India, seeking his ideal in the country whose part in the progress of human history was to differentiate this caste principle and show it in its reality -- causes and consequences growing on the same tree -- there, too, he may no longer find the divine Brahminic code permitted in its fullest sway. It is in process of withdrawal from the face of the earth, thanks to the British administration of criminal law, and the conceded right to freedom of conscience. For the British aristocrat does not believe in the divine right of the Brahmin descended from Brahma's head, but finds the warrior's caste and the merchant's caste of equal or superior right, and he feels the necessity of recognizing the new avatara -- the eleventh avatara of Vishnu, under the form of the steam engine -- the avatara of productive industry; and so he confers knighthood on great inventors and manufacturers -- as on Sir Henry Bessemer. As for the exclusiveness of the Brahman caste, as it exists in England or Boston, why, anyone may become a Brahmin or a Pundit by sacrificing with midnight oil to the knowledge of the modern Vedas; namely to literature, science, or history. In India the believer in caste wavers, and then goes over to Mohammedanism or at least over to Buddhism, which is the Nihilism of ancient times. For the Buddhist placed the dynamite of his doctrine of Nirvana under the caste system of India 2300 years ago. Those Nihilists were then driven out of India, but they can now have all their rights and privileges under British rule.

Shall the lover of caste go to China? Alas, no! In China there is the possibility of ascending to any position short of that of Emperor, by success in passing the fourfold system of examinations which are established underneath the national system of education. There is no rigidity to the caste system of China, seeing that it permits all to ascend, even from the lowest, and leaves it to each to determine his status by his scholastic triumph over the difficulties in the Chinese alphabet and the classics of Confucius and Mencius.

Does the critic of our school system who believes in caste and asks: "Is it wise or best to educate our children beyond the position which the vast majority of them must always occupy?" -- suppose that reading, writing and arithmetic are studies too high for the lowest mechanic or day laborer in a country where his vote counts as much as that of the wisest and richest man? Or does he, perhaps, suppose that all the people are already past the three R's, and briskly advancing into the intricacies of philology and classical archeology? Who has told him this? The Census for our country for 1870 said: "Of the population over ten years of age, 5,658,144 cannot write; 4,880,271 are native born, and 777,873 are of foreign birth; 2,750,000 of these illiterates are colored. The total population of the Nation over ten years of age is 28,228,945." Hence 20 percent of the population over ten years of age could not write in 1870. In Massachusetts even, there were 97,742 who could not write -- 89,380 of these being of foreign birth, and only 7,912 being natives. Seven thousand is a large number for a State like Massachusetts. Twenty-three thousand illiterates were in Boston. The Census of 1880 tells us again that there are 6,239,958 persons unable to write out of a total population of 36,761,607 persons of ten years of age and upwards. Of these 28,424 are in Connecticut.

The number in our common schools who are studying reading, writing, and arithmetic chiefly, with a little geography and much less grammar, is so large that the balance who are studying the higher branches is pitiably small in comparison. In the great cities, the number engaged in high school and college studies is only one in ten in the most advanced of cities, and only one in fifty in the average of cities. And yet our dreamer of caste and inequality mutters in his sleep: "The cruel suspicion is forced upon us that our present educational system largely unfits young people to deal with the actual necessities of those who are to earn their own living. It takes away self-reliance, begets conceit, and draws attention to what is ornamental rather than what is fundamental." Reading, writing, and arithmetic, it seems, are not practical enough because they are general disciplines and give directive power to all who possess them. The one in fifty who is studying algebra and Latin is grudged his privileges. A knowledge of hod-carrying is more practical than writing.

When in 1838 the English Parliament were debating whether the sum of 30,000 pounds should or should not be appropriated "for the encouragement of schools for the common people," and when they had just appropriated 60,000 pounds for the support of the Queen's horses and hounds, Thomas Carlyle, then writing his soul-stirring book on Chartism, set down in letters of fire these words on the general humanitarian aspect of the question of government support of education:

Who would suppose that education were a thing which had to be advocated on the ground of local expediency, or indeed on any grounds? As if it stood not on the basis of everlasting duty, as a prime necessity of man. It is a thing that should need no advocating; much as it does actually need. To impart the gift of thinking to those who cannot think and yet who could in that case think; this, one would imagine, was the first function a government had to set about discharging. Were it not a cruel thing to see, in any province of an empire, the inhabitants living and mutilated in their limbs, each strong man his right arm lamed? How much crueller to find the strong soul with its eyes still sealed, its eyes extinct so that it sees not. Light has come into the world, but to this poor peasant it has come in vain. For six thousand years the Sons of Adam, in sleepless effort, have been devising, doing, discovering; in mysterious infinite indissoluble communion, warring, a little band of brothers, against the great black empire of necessity and Night; they have accomplished such a conquest and conquests: and to this man it is all as if it had not been. The four and twenty letters of the alphabet are still Runic enigmas to him. He passes by on the other side; and that great Spiritual Kingdom, the toil-won conquest of his own brothers, all that his brothers have conquered, is a thing non-extant for him. An invisible empire; he knows it not, suspects it not. And is it not his withal; the conquest of his own brothers the lawfully acquired possession of all men? Baleful enchantment lies over him, from generation to generation; he knows not that such an empire is his, that such an empire is at all . . . . Heavier wrong is not done under the sun.

One voice, the voice of Christian humanitarianism, says: Teach aspiration for all that is good and noble and divine; teach it to all, even the lowest. Teach all to desire with an unquenchable hunger more wisdom, more knowledge, more command over nature, more elevation of position, more usefulness, more directive power. The other voice says: Be contented to remain at the bottom, and quench all aspiration. All talk about perpetual growth in knowledge and wisdom is nonsense and worse when addressed to the children of common laborers.

The reason that the first voice gives for its creed is that its faith teaches the divine origin and destiny of the soul, and that the goal of civilization is the emancipation of each and from all debasing servitude of body and mind, and that it is the Christian duty of all to help their fellow men to rise. The reason given by the other voice is the necessity which it feels that there shall be a class of society perfectly contented to be menial servants and fitted for nothing above that office.

The critics of our educational system are never done with telling us that its results are to make the rising generation discontented with its lot. As if this were a defect rather than the greatest glory of an educational system. What place is there in our system for a drone who is utterly devoid of aspiration? To be like dumb, driven cattle -- is this permitted or encouraged in a Christian civilization? Man is immortal, and has an infinite destiny -- this is the burden of Christian teaching. In consequence of his, Christian civilization strives toward the heavens; it subdues nature, and makes natural forces toil for it and procure food, clothing and shelter for the body. It continually turns out the drudge from his vocation and says to him: "I do not want your mere bodily toil at any price; I have a machine that can do such work better than the like of you can, and at less than what you would call starvation wages. Up, therefore, and acquire directive intelligence so that you may manage and direct this machine, and other machines; for presently we shall need no more mere hand labor, but require all to be intelligent and directive."

As made in the image of God, and as destined for his eternal kingdom, is it possible to look upon any education that schools may give as too high for the position to which a human being is called to occupy in life? In view of the necessity for educated directive power in an age of productive industry, when the superintendence of machines is the chief industrial business, is a general education that gives one insight into nature and insight into the human mind too much? In a representative democracy in which the laws that govern property and personal rights are made by the representatives elected by all people, including the humblest citizens of the country, is any education too good for the people?

The American people answer, No.

Chapter 2

Introduction to John Dewey

John Dewey wrote scores of books and articles on philosophy, education, politics, and art. He is regarded as one of America's most significant and influential thinkers. He was a liberal activist who became involved in the political struggles of women and teachers. He served as the first president of the American Association of University Professors and was a founding member of the American Federation of Teachers.

Dewey helped initiate numerous school reforms. He argued for a more flexible attitude toward the wide range of skills and dispositions which children brought to schools. He insisted that the democratic ideal had far-reaching and fundamental implications for our notion of education. Dewey adopted Darwin's claim that people, along with other animal species, had their own evolutionary history of adaptation and change. The biological world provided a model which hinted that the social world was also in the process of change and adaptation. Human history, he argued, was filled with examples of the failure of societies to form new habits toward their changing environment.

However, schools treated children in the early part of this century as if the world were static. They emphasized drill, memorization, obedience, silence, and punctuality, and an ability to work in an authoritative world. Dewey argued that the schools did not reflect the realities of life. America was evolving as a democracy, inventing new methods of production, and moving from a rural farming society to an urban technological society. He believed we needed a school policy which empowered children to move successfully in a changing and fluid world. Power over the world was not merely information about the world but also a way to inquire, an approach and attitude toward problem solving.

A simple device that the reader might find helpful in reading Dewey is to see him trying to weave a synthesis between what appear to be conflicting positions. The titles of some of his books reflect this tactic. Consider: *Individualism Old and New, School and Society,* and *The Child and the Curriculum.*

The following selection examines three concerns of education in a reasonable community. The first is the community's need to integrate the young into its way of life. The second is the obligation to match young people with jobs which reflect their abilities and capacities. The third is the commitment to promote the psychological health of people. These three fundamental concerns are characterized as the integrative, the egalitarian, and the developmental dimensions of education. This topography raises this question: What type of community best promotes human growth conceived in terms of the developmental, egalitarian, and integrative aspects of culture?   Dewey sketches three models: the Platonic, and two examples from the eighteenth and nineteenth century, respectively.

Plato suggests that if we emphasize the egalitarian and integrative aspects of education, the developmental needs of people would be satisfied. Society is more efficient and people more fulfilled if people are working in jobs which reflect their intellectual and moral talents. The community leaders simply delineate what jobs are needed while the school develops a curriculum designed to promote job competence.

Dewey cites Rousseau as an example of an eighteenth century model of education.   Here the developmental concern of education is emphasized with little attention given to the integrative and egalitarian dimensions.   The goal of education is the development of the individual's personality, even if such development conflicts with integration into society. This model of education is a reaction against a repressive community with a low tolerance for small differences among people.   That is to say, when the community becomes intolerant of human diversity, a distinct possibility in Plato's model according to Dewey, then people are apt to react by constructing models of education which give people more choices.   Such schools would cater to the "natural" inclinations of students and would be non-structured, open, and give students a large measure of choice.

While the eighteenth century model emphasized the uniqueness of people, the nineteenth century model focused on the importance of the state. Here the integration of the young into society became the main objective.   Education was concerned with the good citizen and patriotism while the school was concerned with respect for authority, conformity, and a common curriculum. Dewey suggests a democratic model of education as appropriate for the twentieth century. This model pays due consideration to the integrative, egalitarian, and developmental aspects of education. It provides for personal development by giving people the widest range of experiences, the power to experiment with their capacities and, at the same time, the opportunity to become integrated into a critical community.

The reader should consider the following questions raised in Dewey's essay:

1. Should we emphasize at certain times the developmental dimension of education while at other times the integrative dimension?

2. Does schooling in America help students to find work which reflects their capacities and abilities rather than their class standing and social background?

3. How could teachers help students to balance two qualities of a healthy person, namely the need for a sense of connection and community with the need for a sense of self and privacy?

The Democratic Conception in Education

by John Dewey

Originally published in *The Collected Works of John Dewey, Middle Works, 1899-1924,* Volume 9, 1916, pp. 87-106, edited by JoAnn Boydston. Copyright © 1980 by the Board of Trustees, Southern Illinios University.

To say that education is a social function, securing direction and development in the immature through their participation in the life of the group to which they belong, is to say in effect that education will vary with the quality of life which prevails in a group. Particularly is it true that a society which not only changes but which has the ideal of such change as will improve it, will have different standards and methods of education from one which aims simply at the perpetuation of its own customs. To make the general ideas set forth applicable to our own educational practice, it is, therefore, necessary to come to closer quarters with the nature of present social life.

1. The Implications of Human Association

Society is one word, but many things. Men associate together in all kinds of ways and for all kinds of purposes. One man is concerned in a multitude of diverse groups, in which his associates may be quite different. It often seems as if they had nothing in common except that they are modes of associated life. Within every larger social organization there are numerous minor groups: not only political subdivisions, but industrial, scientific, religious, associations. There are political parties with differing aims, social sets, cliques, gangs, corporations, partnerships, groups bound closely together by ties of blood, and so on in endless variety. In many modern states and in some ancient, there is great diversity of populations, of varying languages, religions, moral codes, and traditions. From this standpoint, many a minor political unit, one of our large cities, for example, is a congeries of loosely associated societies, rather than an inclusive and permeating community of action and thought.

The terms society, community, are thus ambiguous. They have both a eulogistic or normative sense, and a descriptive sense; a meaning *de jure* and a meaning *de facto*. In social philosophy, the former connotation is almost always uppermost. Society is conceived as one by its very nature. The qualities which accompany this unity, praiseworthy community of purpose and welfare, loyalty to public ends, mutuality of sympathy, are emphasized. But when we look at the facts which the term *denotes* instead of confining our attention to its intrinsic *connotation*, we find not unity, but a plurality of societies, good and bad. Men banded together in a criminal conspiracy, business aggregations that prey upon the public while serving it, political machines held together by the interest of plunder, are included. If it is said that such organizations are not societies because they do not meet the ideal requirements of the notion of society, the answer, in part, is that the conception of society is then made so "ideal" as to be of no use, having no reference to facts; and in part, that each of these organizations, no matter how opposed to the interests of other groups, has something of the praiseworthy qualities of "Society" which hold it together. There is honor among thieves, and a band of robbers has a common interest as respects its members. Gangs are marked by fraternal feeling, and narrow cliques by intense loyalty to their own codes. Family life may be marked by exclusiveness, suspicion, and jealousy as to those without, and yet be a model of amity and mutual aid within. Any education given by a group tends to socialize its members, but the quality and value of the socialization depends upon the habits and aims of the group.

Hence, once more, the need of a measure for the worth of any given mode of social life. In seeking this measure, we have to avoid two extremes. We cannot set up, out of our heads, something we regard as an ideal society. We must base our conception upon societies which actually exist, in order to have any assurance that our ideal is a practicable one. But, as we have just seen, the ideal cannot simply repeat the traits which are actually found. The problem is to extract the desirable traits of forms of community life which actually exist, and employ them to criticize undesirable features and suggest improvement. Now in any social group whatever, even in a gang of thieves, we find some interest held in common, and we find a certain amount of interaction and cooperative intercourse with other groups. From these two traits we derive our standard. How numerous and varied are the interests which are consciously shared? How full and free is the interplay with other forms of association? If we apply these considerations to, say, a criminal band, we find that the ties which consciously hold the members together are few in number, reducible almost to a common interest in plunder; and that they are of such a nature as to isolate the group from other groups with respect to give and take of the values of life. Hence, the education such a society gives is partial and distorted. If we take, on the other hand, the kind of family life which illustrates the standard, we find that there are material, intellectual, aesthetic interests in which all participate and that the progress of one member has worth for the experience of other members -- it is readily communicable -- and that the family is not an isolated whole, but enters intimately into relationships with business groups, with schools, with all the agencies of culture, as well as with other similar groups, and that it plays a due part in the political organization and in return receives support from it. In short, there are many interests consciously communicated and shared; and there are varied and free points of contact with other modes of association.

I. Let us apply the first element in this criterion to a despotically governed state. It is not true there is no common interest in such an organization between governed and governors. The authorities in command must make some appeal to the native activities of the subjects, must call some of their powers into play. Talleyrand said that a government could do everything with bayonets except sit on them. This cynical declaration is at least a recognition that the bond of union is not merely one of coercive force. It may be said, however, that the activities appealed to are themselves unworthy and degrading -- that such a government calls into functioning activity simply capacity for fear. In a way, this statement is true. But it overlooks the fact that fear need not be an undesirable factor in experience. Caution, circumspection, prudence, desire to foresee future events so as to avert what is harmful, these desirable traits are as much a product of calling the impulse of fear into play as is cowardice and abject submission. The real difficulty is that the appeal to fear is *isolated*. In evoking dread and hope of specific tangible reward -- say comfort and ease -- many other capacities are left untouched. Or rather, they are affected, but in such a way as to pervert them. Instead of operating on their own account they are reduced to mere servants of attaining pleasure and avoiding pain.

This is equivalent to saying that there is no extensive number of common interests; there is no free play back and forth among the members of the social group. Stimulation and response are exceedingly one-sided. In order to have a large number of values in common, all the members of the group must have an equable opportunity to receive and take from others. There must be a large variety of shared undertakings and experiences. Otherwise, the influences which educate some into masters, educate others into slaves. And the experience of each party loses in meaning, when the free interchange of varying modes of life-experience is arrested. A separation into a privileged and a subject-class prevents social endosmosis. The evils thereby affecting the superior class are less material and less perceptible, but equally real. Their culture tends to be sterile, to be turned back to feed on itself; their art becomes a showy display and artificial; their wealth luxurious; their knowledge overspecialized; their manners fastidious rather than humane.

Lack of the free and equitable intercourse which springs from a variety of shared interests makes intellectual stimulation unbalanced. Diversity of stimulation means novelty, and novelty means challenge to thought. The more activity is restricted to a few definite lines -- as it is when there are rigid class lines preventing adequate interplay of experiences -- the more action tends to become routine on the part of the class at a disadvantage, and capricious, aimless, and explosive on the part of the class having the materially fortunate position. Plato defined a slave as one who accepts from another the purposes which control his conduct. This condition obtains even where there is no slavery in the legal sense. It is found wherever men are engaged in activity which is socially serviceable, but whose service they do not understand and have no personal interest in. Much is said about scientific management of work. It is a narrow view which restricts the science which secures efficiency of operation to movements of the muscles. The chief opportunity for science is the discovery of the relations of a man to his work -- including his relations to others who take part -- which will enlist his intelligent interest in what he is doing.

Efficiency in production often demands division of labor. But it is reduced to a mechanical routine unless workers see the technical, intellectual, and social relationships involved in what they do, and engage in their work because of the motivation furnished by such perceptions. The tendency to reduce such things as efficiency of activity and scientific management to purely technical externals is evidence of the one-sided stimulation of thought given to those in control of industry -- those who supply its aims. Because of their lack of all-round and well-balanced social interest, there is not sufficient stimulus for attention to the human factors and relationships in industry. Intelligence is narrowed to the factors concerned with technical production and marketing of goods. No doubt, a very acute and intense intelligence in these narrow lines can be developed, but the failure to take into account the significant social factors means nonetheless an absence of mind, and a corresponding distortion of emotional life.

II. This illustration (whose point is to be extended to all associations lacking reciprocity of interest) brings us to our second point. The isolation and exclusiveness of a gang or clique brings its antisocial spirit into relief. But this same spirit is found wherever one group has interests "of its own" which shut it out from full interaction with other groups, so that its prevailing purpose is the protection of what it has got, instead of reorganization and progress through wider relationships. It marks nations in their isolation from one another; families which seclude their domestic concerns as if they had no connection with a larger life; schools when separated from the interest of home and community; the divisions of rich and poor; learned and unlearned. The essential point is that isolation makes for rigidity and formal institutionalizing of life, for static and selfish ideals within the group. That savage tribes regard aliens and enemies as synonymous is not accidental. It springs from the fact that they have identified their experience with rigid adherence to their past customs. On such a basis it is wholly logical to fear intercourse with others, for such contact might dissolve custom. It would certainly occasion reconstruction. It is a commonplace that an alert and expanding mental life depends upon an enlarging range of contact with the physical environment. But the principle applies even more significantly to the field where we are apt to ignore it -- the sphere of social contacts.

Every expansive era in the history of mankind has coincided with the operation of factors which have tended to eliminate distance between peoples and classes previously hemmed off from one another. Even the alleged benefits of war, so far as more than alleged, spring from the fact that conflict of peoples at least enforces intercourse between them and thus accidentally enables them to learn from one another, and thereby to expand their horizons. Travel, economic and commercial tendencies, have at present gone far to break down external barriers; to bring peoples and classes into closer and more perceptible connection with one another. It remains for the most part to secure the intellectual and emotional significance of this physical annihilation of space.

2. *The Democratic Ideal*

The two elements in our criterion both point to democracy. The first signifies not only more numerous and more varied points of shared common interest, but greater reliance upon the recognition of mutual interests as a factor in social control. The second means not only freer interaction between social groups (once isolated so far as intention could keep up a separation) but change in social habit -- its continuous readjustment through meeting the new situations produced by varied intercourse. And these two traits are precisely what characterize the democratically constituted society.

Upon the educational side, we note first that the realization of a form of social life in which interests are mutually interpenetrating and where progress, or readjustment, is an important consideration, makes a democratic community more interested than other communities have cause to be in deliberate and systematic education. The devotion of democracy to education is a familiar fact. The superficial explanation is that a government resting upon popular suffrage cannot be successful unless those who elect and who obey their governors are educated. Since a democratic society repudiates the principle of external authority, it must find a substitute in voluntary disposition and interest; these can be created only by education. But there is a deeper explanation. A democracy is more than a form of government; it is primarily a mode of associated living, of conjoint communicated experience. The extension in space of the number of individuals who participate in an interest so that each has to refer his own action to that of others, and to consider the action of others to give point and direction to his own, is equivalent to the breaking down of those barriers of class, race, and national territory which kept men from perceiving the full import of their activity. These more numerous and more varied points of contact denote a greater diversity of stimuli to which an individual has to respond; they consequently put a premium on variation in his action. They secure a liberation of powers which remain suppressed as long as the incitations to action are partial, as they must be in a group which in its exclusiveness shuts out many interests.

The widening of the area of shared concerns, and the liberation of a greater diversity of personal capacities which characterize a democracy, are not, of course, the product of deliberation and conscious effort. On the contrary, they were caused by the development of modes of manufacture and commerce, travel, migration, and intercommunication which flowed from the command of science over natural energy. But after greater individualization on one hand and a broader community of interest on the other have come into existence, it is a matter of deliberate effort to sustain and extend them. Obviously a society, to which stratification into separate classes would be fatal, must see to it that intellectual opportunities are accessible to all on equable and easy terms. A society marked off into classes need be specially attentive only to the education of its ruling elements. A society which is mobile, which is full of channels for the distribution of a change occurring anywhere, must see to it that its members are educated to personal initiative and adaptability. Otherwise, they will be overwhelmed by the changes in which they are caught and whose significance or connections they do not perceive. The result will be a confusion in which a few will appropriate to themselves the results of the blind and externally directed activities of others.

3. *The Platonic Educational Philosophy.*

In the remaining portions of this chapter, we shall consider the educational theories which have been evolved in three epochs when the social import of education was especially conspicuous. The first one to be considered is that of Plato. No one could better express than did he the fact that a society is stably organized when each individual is doing that for which he has aptitude by nature in such a way as to be useful to others (or to contribute to the whole to which he belongs); and that it is the business of education to discover these aptitudes and progressively to train them for social use. Much which has been said so far is borrowed from what Plato first consciously taught the world. But conditions which he could not intellectually control led him to restrict these ideas in their application. He never got any conception of the indefinite plurality of activities which may characterize an individual and a social group, and consequently limited his view to a limited number of *classes* of capacities and of social arrangements.

Plato's starting point is that the organization of society depends ultimately upon knowledge of the end of existence. If we do not know its end, we shall be at the mercy of accident and caprice. Unless we know the end, the good, we shall have no criterion for rationality deciding what the possibilities are which should be promoted, nor how social arrangements are to be ordered. We shall have no conception of the proper limits and distribution of activities -- what he called justice -- as a trait of both individual and social organization. But how is the knowledge of the final and permanent good to be achieved? In dealing with this question we come upon the seemingly insuperable obstacle that such knowledge is not possible save in a just and harmonious social order. Everywhere else the mind is distracted and misled by false valuations and false perspectives. A disorganized and factional society sets up a number of different models and standards. Under such conditions it is impossible for the individual to attain consistency of mind. Only a complete whole is fully self-consistent. A society which rests upon the supremacy of some factor over another, irrespective of its rational or proportionate claims, inevitably leads thought astray. It puts a premium on certain things and slurs over others, and creates a mind whose seeming unity is forced and distorted. Education proceeds ultimately from the patterns furnished by institutions, customs, and laws. Only in a just state will these be such as to give the right education; and only those who have rightly trained minds will be able to recognize the end, and ordering principle of things. We seen to be caught in a hopeless circle. However, Plato suggested a way out. A few men, philosophers or lovers of wisdom -- or truth -- may by study learn, at least in outline, the proper patterns of true existence. If a powerful ruler should form a state after these patterns, then its regulations could be preserved. An education could be given which would sift individuals, discovering what they were good for, and supplying a method of assigning each to the work in life for which his nature fits him. Each doing his own part, and never transgressing, the order and unity of the whole would be maintained.

It would be impossible to find in any scheme of philosophic thought a more adequate recognition on one hand of the educational significance of social arrangements and, on the other, of the dependence of those arrangements upon the means used to educate the young. It would be impossible to find a deeper sense of the function of education in discovering and developing personal capacities, and training them so that they would connect with the activities of others. Yet the society in which the theory was propounded was so undemocratic that Plato could not work out a solution for the problem whose terms he clearly saw.

While he affirmed with emphasis that the place of the individual in society should not be determined by birth or wealth or any conventional status, but by his own nature as discovered in the process of education, he had no perception of the uniqueness of individuals. For him they fall by nature into classes, and into a very small number of classes at that. Consequently the testing and sifting function of education only shows to which one of three classes an individual belongs. There being no recognition that each individual constitutes his own class, there could be no recognition of the infinite diversity of active tendencies and combinations of tendencies of which an individual is capable. There were only three types of faculties or powers in the individual's constitution. Hence education would soon reach a static limit in each class, for only diversity makes change and progress.

In some individuals, appetites naturally dominate; they are assigned to the laboring and trading class, which expresses and supplies human wants. Others reveal, upon education, that over and above appetites, they have a generous, outgoing, assertively courageous disposition. They become the citizen-subjects of the state; its defenders in war; its internal guardians in peace. But their limit is fixed by their lack of reason, which is a capacity to grasp the universal. Those who possess this are capable of the highest kind of education, and become in time the legislators of the state -- for laws are the universals which control the particulars of experience. Thus it is not true that, in intent, Plato subordinated the individual to the social whole. But it is true that, lacking the perception of the uniqueness of every individual, his incommensurability with others, and consequently not recognizing that a society might change and yet be stable, his doctrine of limited powers and classes came in net effect to the idea of the subordination of individuality.

We cannot better Plato's conviction that an individual is happy and society well organized when each individual engages in those activities for which he has a natural equipment, nor his conviction that it is the primary office of education to discover this equipment to its possessor and train him for its effective use. But progress in knowledge has made us aware of the superficiality of Plato's lumping of individuals and their original powers into a few sharply marked-off classes; it has taught us that original capacities are indefinitely numerous and variable. It is but the other side of this fact to say that, in the degree to which society has become democratic, social organization means utilization of the specific and variable qualities of individuals, not stratification by classes. Although his educational philosophy was revolutionary, it was nonetheless in bondage to static ideals. He thought that change or alteration was evidence of lawless flux; that true reality was unchangeable. Hence while he would radically change the existing state of society, his aim was to construct a state in which change would subsequently have no place. The final end of life is fixed; given a state framed with this end in view, not even minor details are to be altered. Though they might not be inherently important, yet if permitted they would inure the minds of men to the idea of change, and hence be dissolving and anarchic. The breakdown of his philosophy is made apparent in the fact that he could not trust to gradual improvements in education to bring about a better society which should then improve education, and so on indefinitely. Correct education could not come into existence until an ideal state existed, and after that education would be devoted simply to its conservation. For the existence of this state he was obliged to trust to some happy accident by which philosophic wisdom should happen to coincide with possession of ruling power in the state.

4. The "Individualistic" Ideal of the Eighteenth Century

In the eighteenth-century philosophy we find ourselves in a very different circle of ideas. "Nature" still means something antithetical to existing social organization; Plato exercised a great influence upon Rousseau. But the voice of nature now speaks for the diversity of individual talent and for the need of free development of individuality in all its variety. Education in accord with nature furnishes the goal and the method of instruction and discipline. Moreover, the native or original endowment was conceived, in extreme cases, as nonsocial or even as antisocial. Social arrangements were thought of as mere external expedients by which these nonsocial individuals might secure a greater amount of private happiness for themselves. Nevertheless, these statements convey only an inadequate idea of the true significance of the movement. In reality its chief interest was in progress and in social progress. The seeming antisocial philosophy was a somewhat transparent mask for an impetus toward a wider and freer society -- toward cosmopolitanism. The positive ideal was humanity. In membership in humanity, as distinct from a state, man's capacities would be liberated; while in existing political organizations his powers were hampered and distorted to meet the requirements and selfish interests of the rulers of the state. The doctrine of extreme individualism was but the counterpart, the obverse, of ideals of the indefinite perfectibility of man and of a social organization having a scope as wide as humanity. The emancipated individual was to become the organ and agent of a comprehensive and progressive society.

The heralds of this gospel were acutely conscious of the evils of the social estate in which they found themselves. They attributed these evils to the limitations imposed upon the free powers of man. Such limitation was both distorting and corrupting. Their impassioned devotion to emancipation of life from external restrictions which operated to the exclusive advantage of the class to whom a past feudal system consigned power, found intellectual formulation in a worship of nature. To give "nature" full swing was to replace an artificial, corrupt, and inequitable social order by a new and better kingdom of humanity. Unrestrained faith in Nature as both a model and a working power was strengthened by the advances of natural science. Inquiry freed from prejudice and artificial restraints of church and state had revealed that the world is a scene of law. The Newtonian solar system, which expressed the reign of natural law, was a scene of wonderful harmony, where every force balanced with every other. Natural law would accomplish the same result in human relations, if men would only get rid of the artificial man-imposed coercive restrictions.

Education in accord with nature was thought to be the first step in ensuring this more social society. It was plainly seen that economic and political limitations were ultimately dependent upon limitations of thought and feeling. The first step in freeing men from external chains was to emancipate them from the internal chains of false beliefs and ideals. What was called social life, existing institutions, were too false and corrupt to be entrusted with this work. How could it be expected to undertake it when the undertaking meant its own destruction? "Nature" must then be the power to which the enterprise was to be left. Even the extreme sensationalistic theory of knowledge which was current derived itself from this conception. To insist that mind is originally passive and empty was one way of glorifying the possibilities of education. If the mind was a wax tablet to be written upon by objects, there were no limits to the possibility of education by means of the natural environment. And since the natural world of objects is a scene of harmonious "truth," this education would infallibly produce minds filled with the truth.

5. *Education as National and as Social*

As soon as the first enthusiasm for freedom waned, the weakness of the theory upon the constructive side became obvious. Merely to leave everything to nature was, after all, but to negate the very idea of education; it was to trust to the accidents of circumstance. Not only was some method required but also some positive organ, some administrative agency for carrying on the process of instruction. The "complete and harmonious development of all powers," having as its social counterpart an enlightened and progressive humanity, required definite organization for its realization. Private individuals here and there could proclaim the gospel; they could not execute the work. A Pestalozzi could try experiments and exhort philanthropically inclined persons having wealth and power to follow his example. But even Pestalozzi saw that any effective pursuit of the new educational ideal required the support of the state. The realization of the new education destined to produce a new society was, after all, dependent upon the activities of existing states. The movement for the democratic idea inevitably became a movement for publicly conducted and administered schools.

So far as Europe was concerned, the historic situation identified the movement for a state-supported education with the nationalistic movement in political life -- a fact of incalculable significance for subsequent movements. Under the influence of German thought in particular, education became a civic function, and the civic function was identified with the realization of the ideal of the national state. The "state" was substituted for humanity; cosmopolitanism gave way to nationalism. To form the citizen, not the "man," became the aim of education.[1] The historic situation to which reference is made is the after-effects of the Napoleonic conquests, especially in Germany. The German states felt (and subsequent events demonstrate the correctness of the belief) that systematic attention to education was the best means of recovering and maintaining their political integrity and power. Externally they were weak and divided. Under the leadership of Prussian statesmen they made this condition a stimulus to the development of an extensive and thoroughly grounded system of public education.

This change in practice necessarily brought about a change in theory. The individualistic theory receded into the background. The state furnished not only the instrumentalities of public education but also its goal. When the actual practice was such that the school system, from the elementary grades through the university faculties, supplied the patriotic citizen and soldier and the future state official and administrator, and furnished the means for military, industrial, and political defense and expansion, it was impossible for theory not to emphasize the aim of social efficiency. And with the immense importance attached to the nationalistic state, surrounded by other competing and more or less hostile states, it was equally impossible to interpret social efficiency in terms of a vague cosmopolitan humanitarianism. Since the maintenance of a particular national sovereignty required subordination of individuals to the superior interests of the state, both in military defense and in struggles for international supremacy in commerce, social efficiency was understood to imply a like subordination. The educational process was taken to be one of disciplinary training rather than of personal development. Since, however, the ideal of culture as complete development of personality persisted, educational philosophy attempted a reconciliation of the two ideas. The reconciliation took the form of the conception of the "organic" character of the state. The individual in his isolation is nothing; only in and through an absorption of the aims and meaning of organized institutions does he attain true personality. What appears to be his subordination to political authority and the demand for sacrifice of himself to the commands of his superiors is in reality but making his own the objective reason manifested in the state -- the only way in which he can become truly rational. The notion of development which we have seen to be characteristic of institutional idealism (as in the Hegelian philosophy) was just such a deliberate effort to combine the two ideas of complete realization of personality and thoroughgoing "disciplinary" subordination to existing institutions.

The extent of the transformation of educational philosophy which occurred in Germany in the generation occupied by the struggle against Napoleon for national independence, may be gathered from Kant, who well expresses the earlier individual-cosmopolitan ideal. In his treatise on Pedagogics, consisting of lectures given in the later years of the eighteenth century, he defines education as the process by which man becomes man. Mankind begins its history submerged in nature -- not as Man who is a creature of reason, while nature furnishes only instinct and appetite. Nature offers simply the germs which education is to develop and perfect. The peculiarity of truly human life is that man has to create himself by his own voluntary efforts; he has to make himself a truly moral, rational, and free being. This creative effort is carried on by the educational activities of slow generations. Its acceleration depends upon men consciously striving to educate their successors not for the existing state of affairs but so as to make possible a future better humanity. But there is the great difficulty. Each generation is inclined to educate its young so as to get along in the present world instead of with a view to the proper end of education: the promotion of the best possible realization of humanity as humanity. Parents educate their children so that they may get on; princes educate their subjects as instruments of their own purposes.

Who, then, shall conduct education so that humanity may improve? We must depend upon the efforts of enlightened men in their private capacity. "All culture begins with private men and spreads outward from them. Simply through the efforts of persons of enlarged inclinations, who are capable of grasping the ideal of a future better condition, is the gradual approximation of human nature to its end possible. . . . Rulers are simply interested in such training as will make their subjects better tools for their own intentions." Even the subsidy by rulers of privately conducted schools must be carefully safeguarded. For the rulers' interest in the welfare of their own nation instead of in what is best for humanity will make them, if they give money for the schools, wish to draw their plans. We have in this view an express statement of the points characteristic of the eighteenth century individualistic cosmopolitanism. The full development of private personality is identified with the aims of humanity as a whole and with the idea of progress. In addition we have an explicit fear of the hampering influence of a state-conducted and state-regulated education upon the attainment of these ideas. But in less than two decades after this time, Kant's philosophic successors, Fichte and Hegel, elaborated the idea that the chief function of the state is educational; that in particular the regeneration of Germany is to be accomplished by an education carried on in the interests of the state, and that the private individual is of necessity an egoistic, irrational being, enslaved to his appetites and to circumstances unless he submits voluntarily to the educative discipline of state institutions and laws. In this spirit, Germany was the first country to undertake a public, universal, and compulsory system of education extending from the primary school through the university, and to submit to jealous state regulation and supervision all private educational enterprises.

Two results should stand out from this brief historical survey. The first is that such terms as the individual and the social conceptions of education are quite meaningless taken at large, or apart from their context. Plato had the ideal of an education which should equate individual realization and social coherency and stability. His situation forced his ideal into the notion of a society organized in stratified classes, losing the individual in the class. The eighteenth century educational philosophy was highly individualistic in form, but this form was inspired by a noble and generous social ideal: that of a society organized to include humanity, and providing for the indefinite perfectibility of mankind. The idealistic philosophy of Germany in the early nineteenth century endeavored again to equate the ideals of a free and complete development of cultured personality with social discipline and political subordination. It made the national state an intermediary between the realization of private personality on one side and of humanity on the other. Consequently, it is equally possible to state its animating principle with equal truth, either in the classic terms of "harmonious development of all the powers of personality" or in the more recent terminology of "social efficiency." All this reinforces the statement which opens this chapter: The conception of education as a social process and function has no definite meaning until we define the kind of society we have in mind.

These considerations pave the way for our second conclusion. One of the fundamental problems of education in and for a democratic society is set by the conflict of a nationalistic and a wider social aim. The earlier cosmopolitan and "humanitarian" conception suffered from both vagueness and from lack of definite organs of execution and agencies of administration. In Europe, in the Continental states particularly, the new idea of the importance of education for human welfare and progress was captured by national interests and harnessed to do a work whose social aim was definitely narrow and exclusive. The social aim of education and its national aim were identified, and the result was a marked obscuring of the meaning of a social aim.

This confusion corresponds to the existing situation of human intercourse. On the one hand, science, commerce, and art transcend national boundaries. They are largely international in quality and method. They involve interdependencies and cooperation among the peoples inhabiting different countries. At the same time, the idea of national sovereignty has never been as accentuated in politics as it is at the present time. Each nation lives in a state of suppressed hostility and incipient war with its neighbors. Each is supposed to be the supreme judge of its own interests which are exclusively its own. To question this is to question the very idea of national sovereignty which is assumed to be basic to political practice and political science. This contradiction (for it is nothing less) between the wider sphere of associated and mutually helpful social life and the narrower sphere of exclusive and hence potentially hostile pursuits and purposes, exacts of educational theory a clearer conception of the meaning of "social" as a function and test of education than has yet been attained.

Is it possible for an educational system to be conducted by a national state and yet the full social ends of the educative process not be restricted, constrained, and corrupted? Internally, the question has to face the tendencies, due to present economic conditions, which split society into classes, some of which are made merely tools for the higher culture of others. Externally, the question is concerned with the reconciliation of national loyalty, of patriotism, with superior devotion to the things which unite men in common ends, irrespective of national political boundaries. Neither phase of the problem can be worked out by merely negative means. It is not enough to see to it that education is not actively used as an instrument to make easier the exploitation of one class by another. School facilities must be secured of such amplitude and efficiency as will in fact and not simply in name discount the effects of economic inequalities, and secure to all the wards of the nation equality of equipment for their future careers. Accomplishment of this end demands not only adequate administrative provision of school facilities, and such supplementation of family resources as will enable youth to take advantage of them, but also such modification of traditional ideals of culture, traditional subjects of study, and traditional methods of teaching and discipline as will retain all the youth under educational influences until they are equipped to be masters of their own economic and social careers. The ideal may seem remote of execution, but the democratic ideal of education is a farcical yet tragic delusion except as the ideal more and more dominates our public system of education.

The same principle has application on the side of the considerations which concern the relations of one nation to another. It is not enough to teach the horrors of war and to avoid everything which would stimulate international jealousy and animosity. The emphasis must be put upon whatever binds people together in cooperative human pursuits and results, apart from geographical limitations. The secondary and provisional character of national sovereignty in respect to the fuller, freer, and more fruitful association and intercourse of all human beings with one another must be instilled as a working disposition of mind. If these applications seem to be remote from a consideration of the philosophy of education, the impression shows that the meaning of the idea of education previously developed has not been adequately grasped. This conclusion is bound up with the very idea of education as a freeing of individual capacity in a progressive growth directed to social aims. Otherwise a democratic criterion of education can only be inconsistently applied.

Summary

Since education is a social process, and there are many kinds of societies, a criterion for educational criticism and construction implies a *particular* social ideal. The two points selected by which to measure the worth of a form of social life are the extent in which the interests of a group are shared by all its members, and the fullness and freedom with which it interacts with other groups. An undesirable society, in other words, is one which internally and externally sets up barriers to free intercourse and communication of experience. A society which makes provision for participation in its good of all its members on equal terms and which secures flexible readjustment of its institutions through interaction of the different forms of associated life is in so far democratic. Such a society must have a type of education which gives individuals a personal interest in social relationships and control, and the habits of mind which secure social changes without introducing disorder.

Three typical historic philosophies of education were considered from this point of view. The Platonic was found to have an ideal formally quite similar to that stated, but which was compromised in its working out by making a class rather than an individual the social unit. The so-called individualism of the eighteenth-century enlightenment was found to involve the notion of a society as broad as humanity, of whose progress the individual was to be the organ. But it lacked any agency for securing the development of its ideal as was evidenced in its falling back upon Nature. The institutional idealistic philosophies of the nineteenth century supplied this lack by making the national state the agency, but in so doing narrowed the conception of the social aim to those who were members of the same political unit, and reintroduced the idea of the subordination of the individual to the institution.

Notes

1. There is a much neglected strain in Rousseau tending intellectually in this direction. He opposed the existing state of affairs on the ground that it formed *neither* the citizen nor the man. Under existing conditions, he preferred to try for the latter rather than for the former. But there are many sayings of his which point to the formation of the citizen as ideally the higher, and which indicate that his own endeavor, as embodied in the *Emile*, was simply the best makeshift the corruption of the times permitted him to sketch.

Chapter 3

Introduction to Jill Conway

Jill Conway presents an analysis of the history of women in the teaching profession in the United States which challenges the traditional interpretation of women's presence in large numbers in this profession as evidence of an increasingly enlightened attitude toward the employment of women in American social history. In this essay, she contends that the conventional, one-dimensional view of teaching as the first *women's* profession was uninformed by an appreciation of the psychological and political understandings held by both men and women regarding the connections between the gender of the new female recruits and its implications for curriculum and the control and motivation of students.

Conway alleges that these basic assumptions about the gender of teachers allowed school boards to create working conditions which gave women teachers a marginal social status while they were employed as teachers, and to force teachers to resign their positions when they married. Both of these factors were influential in depriving female teachers of leadership positions in schools. Since female teachers were also deprived of the right to vote until 1919, their social and political marginality combined to prevent them from persuading political elites that their services were valuable, as did other professional groups who aspired to achieving recognition as high status professionals. Conway believes that the social and political isolation resulting from assumptions about their gender was a key factor in the alliance of teachers with organized labor in their struggle for economic rights.

Conway also raises profound questions concerning the effects of the over-representation of one gender in the early stages of schooling on American intellectual creativity, and also on the culture of higher education which has sought to be "tough minded" and therefore has often sought to distance itself from education in elementary and secondary schools.

Consider the following issues which Conway confronts in her essay:

on
Exam

1. To what extent is Conway correct in challenging the liberal view that teaching significantly advanced the social and economic status of women in the nineteenth century?

2. Did the decision to affiliate with labor unions contribute significantly to teachers' groups choosing to focus on economic issues rather than on professional issues such as curriculum and instruction?

3. What evidence can be cited to support Conway's thesis that policymakers in the nineteenth century were able to avoid a profound political conflict over the intellectual aims of the public schools by employing women who had limited academic training and who could be relied upon to control students through their ability to motivate the young through emotional appeals? Were there other significant factors which made American public schools less "academic" in orientation than European schools?

4. Would the progressive schools designed to implement Dewey's pedagogy have been different if most of the teachers had been male?

Politics, Pedagogy, and Gender

by Jill K. Conway

"Politics, Pedagogy, and Gender" reprinted by permission of *Dædalus*, Journal of the American Academy of Arts and Sciences, from the issue entitled, "Learning About Women: Gender, Politics, and Power," Fall 1987, Vol. 116, No.4.

In the mid-nineteenth century the public education system of the United States drew its corps of teachers from the nation's population of young women. In contrast, European public education remained a male-dominated enterprise until well into the twentieth century. Traditionally, the United States' early and extensive recruitment of female teachers has been interpreted as a sign of enlightened attitudes about women and their place in society. Horace Mann's innovative Massachusetts normal schools, which trained young women to be teachers, are customarily cited as examples of feminism in action. So, until recently, was the career of Catherine Beecher, the archetypal proselytizer for the female teaching profession. The development of a public elementary school system before the Civil War and the extension of that system through the establishment of secondary schools in the last quarter of the nineteenth century provide a happy ending to the traditional story of the establishment of the first "women's" profession.[1]

Underlying this popular history of women in teaching is the assumption that access to new work opportunities has the same meaning for everyone. If we stop to ask what gender meant for the nineteenth century founders of American public education, however, the story takes on new levels of meaning. Some of its themes speak directly to our educational dilemmas today. Its interest lies not in the sex of the teachers who staffed America's one-room schools but in the political and psychological images that men and women held regarding the gender of those teachers. The story of women's opportunities to enter teaching as a respectable occupation for single women outside the home is a case study in the meaning of access. Examination of the case of women teachers' recruitment in the mid-nineteenth century should make us rethink the incremental model of change that is presumed to characterize the liberal state.

The number of women involved in this recruitment is certainly striking. By 1848 women greatly outnumbered men as annual entrants to the teaching profession; in absolute numbers their predominance was established. In that year 2,424 men taught in the public (or common) schools of America beside 5,510 women.[2] During the 1850s the same pattern was replicated in the Midwest. After 1864 one of the impositions of the victorious North on the southern states during Reconstruction was the establishment of a predominantly female cadre of elementary school teachers. In the last three decades of the nineteenth century the same pattern emerged in the public high schools. By 1890, 65 percent of all teachers in the United States were women. Members of the new female profession were remarkably youthful, averaging from twenty-one to twenty-five years of age in different regions of the country.

Popular attitudes encouraged single women to become teachers but discouraged their presence in the schools once they married. The country's teachers were predominantly daughters of the native-born, from rural families. In comparison with European teachers, American teachers were not well educated. As late as the 1930s only 12 percent of elementary teachers in the United States had earned bachelor's degrees.[3] In the nineteenth century many entrants to the profession had not even completed high school. Because so many teachers were drawn from rural farm families, most had not traveled more than 100 miles from their place of birth. Their experience of high culture was minimal. Surveys carried out at the turn of the century recorded that most teachers had never seen reproductions of works of art during their own schooling. As adults their only reading was an occasional novel and the standard popular magazines of the day. To compensate for these deficiencies, the normal schools offered teaching programs that were largely remedial.[4]

The woman teacher, whether rural or urban, earned about 60 percent of the salary paid to men in the same school system. Around 1900 the average woman teacher's salary was $350.00 per year. Higher earnings were available to women in the textile industry and in most other industrial settings. In some states mechanics and clerks earned twice the annual wages of male teachers, whose earnings were more than a third higher than those of their female counterparts. The universal custom of "boarding out" was a major factor in depressing the level of teachers' earnings: nineteenth century school districts held down the cost of elementary schools by housing teachers in rotation with families whose children were currently school pupils. This dubious hospitality was motivated partly by economic considerations and partly by the prevailing sentiment that young single women should not be allowed to live outside a family setting. The school district's room and board carried with it a censorial social control that young single women could resist only at their peril. In short, the young teacher's social status was marginal.[5]

This marginality was not borne for long; rates of turnover were very high. Most women elementary teachers taught for only three or four years. Although 90 percent of the elementary instructors by the 1920s were women, their rapid turnover meant that they did not develop as school leaders or as curriculum planners.[6] Men did not remain teachers for long either; they did not form strong bonds to the occupation of teacher as they did to the professions of medicine and engineering. Yet male teachers were seven times more likely to become school administrators than their female colleagues. Despite the social changes that have raised women's work aspirations in recent decades, these early trends have continued unaltered. Today men hold 99.4 percent of all school superintendencies. The only area of school administration in which women predominate is librarianship. Clearly gender shapes one's status within the teaching profession, even though teaching has traditionally been singled out for its supposed hospitality to women. What, then, are we to make of women's early access to teaching in the United States? What values shaped the establishment of the common schools in America, and what was the operative significance of ideas about gender in that process? To paraphrase William James, what was the meaning of the ideas being translated into action when people like Horace Mann began to recruit women for teacher training?

If we look at the political debates that preceded the establishment of the public education system in the 1830s and 1840s, we see that political forces divided over the level of intellectual aspiration desired as an outcome of state-supported education and over the place of elites of education and talent within the young republic. One thing that united Jefferson and his Federalist opponents was the value they saw in an educated elite drawn from the best talent of their new society. Jefferson wanted his elite to be democratically recruited, its education publicly supported; he expected the result to be the highest intellectual achievement.

One of the major shifts of value in the Jacksonian era was the rejection of the idea of a socially valuable elite formed by education and high culture. Instead, Americans of that era favored a popular education that was broadly accessible and limited in its intellectual goals. As Michael Katz has shown in his study of the development of public education in Massachusetts, some of the old Federalist elites found popular education attractive not so much as a means of training the mind but as a way of providing instruction in behavior.[7]   Many New England moralists who sought to control the excesses of frontier behavior thought that this goal might be achieved through the common schools.   Their intellectual aspirations for the students who were expected to attend these schools were minimal.

We know from recent studies of the legislative decisions approving the establishment of common schools that Federalists and Jacksonians alike sought to develop public education as inexpensively as possible. The compromise that led to agreement on tax-supported public education combined the older Jeffersonian ideal of wide access to public education with Federalist and Jacksonian concerns for limited education at minimal cost to the taxpayer. The goal of cost containment made the recruitment of women completely logical because all parties to the educational debate agreed that women lacked acquisitive drives and would serve at subsistence salaries. The potentially explosive conflict over the intellectual goals of public education could also be avoided by choosing women as teachers. Their access to education was slight, so that male control over the normal schools that trained teachers insured control over the content of the curriculum. Furthermore, beliefs about the female temperament promised that the pedagogical style of women teachers would be emotional and value-oriented rather than rational and critical. Thus neither Jacksonians nor Federalists needed to make resolution of their conflicts over the goals of education an explicit part of their political agenda.[8]   The resolution of fundamental contradictions about a strategic institution for the evolving society could safely be postponed as long as women teachers presented no threat to the objectives of low cost and strictly utilitarian public education.

The following three quotations demonstrate gender stereotyping at work in the public-education policy discussions of late nineteenth-century legislators and public officials. Each of the speakers favored the recruitment of women teachers. These passages illustrate the important components of the gender ideology accepted by all parties to the dispute over the goals of education.

[Women] are endowed by nature with stronger parental impulses, and this makes the society of children delightful, and turns duty into a pleasure. Their minds are less withdrawn from their employment, by the active scenes of life; and they are less intent and scheming for future honors and emoluments. As a class, they never look forward, as young men almost invariably do, to a period of legal emancipation from parental control. . . . They are also of purer morals (*Fourth Annual Report* [Boston Board of Education, 1841], pp. 45-46).

In childhood the intellectual faculties are but partially developed -- the affections much more fully. At that early age the affections are the key of the whole being. The female teacher readily possesses herself of that key, and thus having access to the heart, the mind is soon reached and operated upon (Assemblyman Hurlburd, *New York State Education Exhibit* [World's Columbian Exposition, Chicago, 1893], pp. 45-46).

At the center of the cluster of ideas that made up each writer's picture of women we see a belief in women's capacity to influence children's behavior through the emotions. Barnard's "silken cord of affection" and Hurlburd's "access to the heart" were characteristic themes in discourse about women as teachers. The writer of the Boston Board of Education's annual report associated women's ability to establish emotional links with children with women's lack of acquisitiveness and acceptance of dependence. These presumed qualities made women ideal candidates to teach in elementary schools, the purpose of which was to instill principles of behavior and convey basic literacy at a minimum cost to the public purse. Women were favored and actively recruited as elementary teachers because their presence in the schools satisfied a larger political agenda. Their perceived gender characteristics and their lack of academic preparation were positive advantages in the eyes of early public education officials; with a corps of women teachers there was no danger that investment in public education might foster the creation of new elites.

What, then, were the consequences of this congruence of ideology and economic concerns that served to give women preferred access to the teaching profession in the United States? The first consequence, extensively commented on by foreign visitors, was that discipline in American schools was very different from any known in European classrooms. As women were not thought suited to administering corporal punishment, the rod was virtually absent from America's schools. Maintaining discipline and conveying knowledge became more a matter of persuasion than an exercise of power based on authority. One learned because one liked the teacher, not out of respect for the learning that the teacher represented, as was the case in the French lycee or the German gymnasium. The climate in the American schoolroom was wholly different; the classroom was considered an extension of the home.

This should not be taken to mean that the stereotype of the steely-eyed New England schoolmarm was incorrect; there were many such outstanding women. What it did mean, however, was that maleness involved rebellion against the values for which the schoolmarm stood. Many celebrations of maleness in American culture have retained overtones of adolescent rebellion against a female cultural presence that ostensibly cannot be easily incorporated into a strong adult male identity.

We may speculate about the consequences of subsuming school and home within a maternal, domestic culture rather than having the school serve as an impersonal agent of cultural authority, much like the church or the army. How would *Huckleberry Finn* read if the journey on the raft were an escape from male institutions? Huckleberry Finn's journey raises many profound questions about American culture. One critical question is whether the overrepresentation of one gender in the early stages of schooling permits either boys or girls to develop the balanced identities we associate with creativity. For the purpose of understanding American educational institutions, another question that requires answering is this: If the school exists in opposition to male values and frontier life, how are we to understand higher education? In what ways is there a cultural imperative to redress the balance between maternal and masculine values at different levels of the system? What has that cultural requirement meant for American intellectual life?

Teaching through love made the school a setting in which many ideas about child development were played out; it was never an agency for strenuous effort to discipline and develop young intellectual talents. Thus, the traditional twelve years of schooling did not bring the young American student to the levels of learning aimed at by the lycee of the gymnasium. Instead, and increasingly, American education came to require a further four years of intellectual exploration at the college level before the young person was considered to be in a position to make adult career commitments. Moreover, because of American public schools' identification with maternal functions, colleges and universities have distanced themselves from schools and stressed the "masculine" tough-mindedness of American scholarship. This difference remains an enduring puzzle to Europeans, who see both schools and universities in a continuum of intellectual endeavor, and who value intellectual playfulness.

We may interpret this impulse to distance higher learning from schools as a natural response to some of the major nineteenth-century curricular debates. Because the schools operated as agents of maternal values, school curricula were organized along the lines of accepted models of child development. G. Stanley Hall's celebrated theories of child development, which held that the child recapitulated the various stages of human evolutionary development, required that the teacher act as a helpful director as the pupil traversed these stages. It is unlikely that Hall would have designed so unintellectual a teaching role had he assumed that most elementary school teachers would be men. His ideas about child development were revolutionary in their largely successful redefinition of childhood as a series of developmental stages rather than as a time when the "imp of Satan" had to be disciplined; however, his view of the teacher was based on earlier nineteenth-century assumptions about the female temperament.

John Dewey's Progressive schools discarded the notion of a fixed body of intellectual skills to be acquired entirely in school. Progressive pedagogy asked that the teacher help the young to discover the world through their innate intelligence. It took individuals with an almost superhuman capacity for nurturing to manage this kind of schoolroom. Few teachers could completely repress the desire to instruct, as Dewey's theories required. Many rueful survivors of Progressive schools testified to the demoralizing nature of such self-abnegation. It is reasonable to ask whether educational theorists would have designed teaching roles of such preternatural maternal patience had they expected their male colleagues to take principal responsibility for such instruction. Had the standard levels of education required for elementary school teachers been higher, educational reformers of the Progressive variety might have found earlier curricular ideals less easy to disregard. It was because the minds of young teachers were seen as *tabulae rasae* that older notions of learning could be easily ignored. Certainly if one assesses Dewey's pedagogy from the standpoint of the gender stereotypes enshrined within it, its conservatism is striking. Dewey advanced a new theory of learning and stated new political goals for American schools, but his assumptions about the temperamental and intellectual characteristics of teachers differed little from the assumptions made by Henry Barnard and his colleagues in the 1840s.[9]

While many of the goals of Progressive education were admirable, the fact that the overwhelming majority of teachers in the American elementary school system were young women was a substantial influence on the way reformers thought about the role of teacher. Because of the persistence of the idea that women related to children primarily through the emotions, reformers prescribed intellectually demeaning roles for teachers -- roles that often ignored the teacher's intellectual capacity in relation to the child's.

Similarly, the fact that most teachers did not have the right to vote affected the dynamics of the political relationship between the common schools and the larger society. From its inception the public education system operated at the center of a vortex of political forces, many of which were intrinsically unrelated to pedagogical issues. The schools were affected by political battles over such issues as patronage rights, appointments to teaching staffs and desirable jobs on maintenance staffs, which districts would be granted the economic benefits of building contracts, and which merchants should benefit from the purchasing power of students and their families. Moreover, it was taken for granted that parents, who had an abiding interest in the curriculum and its relationship to employment opportunities, and whose taxes paid teachers' salaries, had a democratic right to influence what was and was not taught to their children. These interests found expression in city and state politics, but women teachers were disenfranchised until 1919 and consequently were unable to directly participate in the political process that shaped and established priorities for public education. Fathers and men teachers could mobilize voter support for school policies through their lodges or friendly societies, or later through Rotary, Kiwanis, or Lions Clubs; women could not.

This situation affected women's status as teachers and indirectly affected the political importance of schools: an important component of professionalism in all modern societies is the degree to which would-be professionals are able to persuade economically or politically powerful elites that their services are important enough to command special rewards. Women teachers, unable to undertake this effort effectively, found their logical political allies in the ranks of organized labor.

The history that produced this logic is vividly illustrated in the disputes affecting the Chicago school system in the 1880s and 1890s. The city's total population was 500,000 and there were 59,000 pupils in the public schools, which expended a budget of over $1,000,000. The school system was the biggest employer in the city. The school board was appointed by the mayor, and it controlled or influenced three sets of resources critical to Chicago's economic future: land voted to support the public schools, contracts for school buildings, and tax abatements for corporations occupying land within the city. The major issues of concern to teachers were security of tenure, pension rights, and professional evaluation for promotion.[10] Women teachers felt considerable social distance from the exclusively male school superintendents in the city, who were themselves political appointees. In the campaign to secure teachers' pension rights, the female-led Chicago Federation of Teachers found that it carried no weight with the municipal government, so it waged battle in the courts. In her autobiography, Margaret A. Haley, the founder of the federation, records the process by which she came to conclude that, because of women's limited voting rights, her union's predominantly female membership would gain political leverage by affiliating with a strong political organization -- the Chicago Federation of Labor. She recognized that laws were only enacted in response to the political pressures of voters. "Except in a few western states," she wrote, "the women of the nation had practically no voting power."[11]

The early choice of unionization was a natural one for nonvoting workers; its consequences were profound. As early as the Chicago Federation of Teachers' 1902 decision to affiliated with the Chicago Federation of Labor, the city's elementary teachers were in a confrontational relationship with political and social elites. The male school principals and superintendents, who identified with management in the labor-versus-management model of the school and the teacher's role within it, were even more distanced from teachers. The working peers of the school administrators were the political actors who had selected and appointed them. The place of the school in political priorities reflected the fact that most of its constituency could not vote and that its spokesmen were distant from the classroom. Decisions about educational policy were usually based entirely on the budgetary priorities of individual districts and regions. Economic considerations favored the selection of women teachers and, by the late nineteenth century, women principals; women's salaries in such positions did not reflect high esteem for their professional achievements. Jessie May Short, an assistant professor of mathematics at Reed College in Portland, Oregon, described her experience in an Oregon high school in the 1920s.

> A personal experience will illustrate the discriminations that are considered normal in the smaller schools. . . . For five years I was principal of a high school in a delightful county-seat town. During the five years the high school enrollment doubled, a new building was erected, I had salary increases each year. I resigned for graduate study although I was offered a small salary increase if I would remain. The man who took my place was freely given a salary fifty percent higher than I had received. Before his first year had closed he was literally taken from the school and thrown into a snow bank. The school board asked me to return and made me what they considered a generous offer, a ten percent increase over my former salary. I suggested that I might consider the appointment at the fifty percent increase the board had willingly given the man who could not handle the situation. The idea of compensating the service without regard to the sex of the one rendering the service was, as I had anticipated, beyond their comprehension.[12]

Short's experience strikingly illustrates that the public's view of the worth of the predominantly female teaching profession and of the predominantly male management of the public schools was fundamentally shaped by the gender of those who served in the system. Because there was little popular respect for the function of the teacher, most important professional prerogatives were gained only after protracted battle. The early decades of unionizing and struggling against low social esteem focused teachers' concerns on job security to the neglect of curricular issues. The cherished right of tenure, sought since the 1880s, was not achieved until the 1950s, when the postwar baby boom and the Cold-War mentality of the Sputnik era gave schools and teachers national importance.

The public's low esteem of the profession was also related to the youthfulness of women teachers. As most of them remained teachers for no more than three or four years, it was easy for local school boards to disregard their opinions. The assumption that young women need protection gave school boards and committees ample justification to scrutinize teachers' conduct and to represent such activity to be in the teachers' best interest. The small minority of men teachers acquired the status of their women colleagues by association. Because society accorded such scant respect to the role of teacher, it was considered perfectly appropriate to pay teachers wages equivalent to those of unskilled labor. By 1900 teacher turnover was as high as 10 percent a year; every year 40,000 new recruits had to be brought into the common school system.[13] The high annual rates of change in teaching personnel throughout the first century of the profession made teachers seem much more like transient workers than career professionals (teaching was not accepted as a lifetime career for women until the Second World War). School reformers even today struggle with the consequences of Margaret Haley's accurate perception that to bargain successfully, women teachers had to unionize like industrial laborers.

If we compare the public esteem accorded to teaching in the late nineteenth century with that held for other emerging professions, we begin to see that the difference lies in the fact that most of the people recruited into public education were women. Consider, for instance, attitudes toward the engineer -- the male professional who emerged to meet national needs in transportation, communication, and industrial technology over the same one hundred years that saw the establishment of public education. In the United States the social origins of engineers were almost identical to those of teachers. Engineers, too, came from rural and blue-collar families. Initially, their training was not highly theoretical and their tasks were strictly utilitarian. Yet engineers were held in high public esteem.

Clearly, gender categories and cultural values had a tremendous influence on the process of professionalization. We have only to read Henry Adams's assessment of the new technology in his commentaries on *The Virgin and the Dynamo*, or Thorstein Veblen's description of the engineer in *The Engineers and the Price System* (1919), to see what a difference gender made. "These technological specialists," Veblen wrote, "whose constant supervision is indispensable to the due working of the industrial system, constitute the general staff of industry, whose work is to control the strategy of production at large and keep an oversight of the tactics of production in detail."[14]   During the Depression, when married women teachers were dismissed by school systems to create openings for unemployed men, Lewis Mumford wrote, "The establishment of the class of engineers in its proper characteristics is the more important because this class will, without doubt, constitute the direct and necessary instrument of coalition between men of science and industrialists, by which alone the new social order can commence."[15]   No one thought to exclaim on how much the new social order might depend on the labors of "the class of teachers." Engineers, of course, pursued their training at the college level and developed a professional culture of aggressive masculinity. Their skills were of critical and immediate importance to the business elites of American society -- but then so were the skills of teachers, although no one recognized their value.

Gender stereotypes helped to account for the differences in social mobility experienced by women and men drawn from the same social background. If we look at the gender composition of the teaching profession cross-culturally, we see that the American pattern established at the time of the creation of the public school system was unique. In 1930-31, a national survey of American teachers showed that women outnumbered men by 19 to 1 in elementary education and by 3 to 1 in secondary education. In contrast, men held 65 percent of the elementary teaching posts in Norway and 69 percent of the secondary teaching positions there. In Germany 75 percent of the primary school teachers and 71 percent of the secondary school teachers were men; the ratios for France were similar.[16]   These figures reflect the conditions that existed in societies that had had relatively stable populations when the public system of elementary and secondary education was being established, and that made strongly centralized educational planning a high national priority.

In these European countries, lifetime careers of stead progression through the different levels of the public school system were established; entry-level positions based on long and strict academic preparation were accepted as the norm. In France, for instance, completion of the baccalaureate was required to become a lycee teacher; further progress in the system required an advanced degree. Besides contributing substantially to the intellectual level of the schools, this pattern of recruitment defined the teacher as an agent of the nation's culture, not simply a representative of its maternal values. When the possibility of recruiting more men to the profession or requiring teachers to undergo more rigorous academic preparation was broached in the United States, it was generally discarded as prohibitively costly. In 1906-7, for instance, the New York City school superintendent acknowledged the desirability of having a cadre of teachers more balanced in gender composition. In a report, he commented that the achievement of this goal would require equalizing the pay scales of the gender groups and raising all salary levels. This, he calculated, was politically impossible. It would add between $8 million and $11 million to the annual school system budget. To propose such a budget increase in the absence of popular demand would be political suicide, and there was not the slightest popular sentiment for such action.[17]

Gender was a highly significant factor in the way American society mobilized its resources to develop its public education system. Assumptions about female temperament and motivation dovetailed with the often contradictory ideals and values of the public school system's creators. Stereotypes about women coincided neatly with the economic priorities that dictated how much money was appropriated for public education, and reinforced popular preferences regarding the purpose of public schooling. Assumptions about the gender and intellectual level of the typical teacher influenced successive waves of curricular reform. Culturally, these gender stereotypes had a tremendous impact on everyone involved in the schools -- teachers, pupils, principals, superintendents, school board members. These assumptions played a part in what it meant to grow up male or female in America. Their enduring power explains the continued inability of our affluent society to muster either the will or the resources to create and maintain schools that are intellectually demanding and that accord the profession of teaching sufficient dignity to engender high teacher morale.

Much has been made of the degree to which teaching offered American women the opportunity to move out of family subordination and into an independent existence. The memoirs of some of America's greatest women reformers tell us that this new life outside the family was a heady experience. Frances Willard, for example, wrote of learning to live without reliance on her parents as a very young teacher. Through her struggles with unruly children in rural one-room schools, she came to see herself as an agent for improving society. Dozens of other young women documented similar experiences. Service as teachers inspired many young women to seek other active careers. Both as individuals and as a group, women proved themselves capable of creating and sustaining demanding intellectual tasks when they were given adequate preparation and appropriate remuneration. It was not the sex of women teachers that created problems in the school system and made the status of teachers so lowly; it was the gender identity that women carried into the schools with them. It is the terms on which women enter occupations that govern their opportunities. Horace Mann and Henry Barnard, two of America's greatest educational reformers, actively admired women and thought that by employing them as teachers they could secure both a better society and important advantages for women. They bore women no ill will whatsoever. Their assumptions about women, however, established the terms on which women entered the teaching profession, and those terms were far more consequential than the great numbers of women who were invited to teach in the public schools. Those terms still matter today. So, too, does our ambivalence about the goals of public education. This piece of unfinished business from the politics of the Jacksonian era matters as much today as it did in the 1840s. We cannot conclude it satisfactorily without taking into account the unintended consequences of our assumptions about the gender of teachers. They matter not only to women but to our whole society.

Notes ────────────────────────

[1.] Horace Mann, *Eleventh Annual Report* (Massachusetts Normal Schools, 1845), 24.

[2.] Redding R. Sugg, Jr., *Motherteacher: The Feminization of American Education* (Charlottesville, VA: The University Press of Virginia, 1978), 37.

[3.] Lindley J. Stiles, ed., *The Teacher's Role in American Society* (New York: Harper & Row, 1957), 279.

[4.] Lotus D. Coffman, *The Social Composition of the Teaching Population* (New York: Bureau of Publications, Teacher's College, Columbia University, 1911), 550.

[5.] Ibid., p. 550. See also Myra H. Strober and Audri Gordon Lanford, "The Feminization of Public School Teaching: A Cross-Sectional Analysis, 1850-1880," *Signs* 11, no. 2 (1986): 212-35, and Willard S. Ellsbree, *The American Teacher: Evolution of a Profession in a Democracy* (New York: American Book Company, 1933), 281.

[6.] Ellsbree, *The American Teacher*, 206.

[7.] Michael Katz, *The Irony of Early School Reform* (Cambridge, MA: Harvard University Press, 1968).

[8.] Sugg, *Motherteacher*, 4-25.

[9.] On G. Stanley Hall's educational theories, see Dorothy Ross, *G. Stanley Hall, The Psychologist as Prophet* (Chicago: University of Chicago Press, 1972). On Dewey and Progressive education, see *John Dewey On Education* (New York: The Modern Library, 1964).

[10.] Robert J. Braun, *Teachers and Power: The Story of the American Federation of Teachers* (New York: Simon & Schuster, 1972), 21-27. See also Robert I. Reid, ed., *Battleground: The Autobiography of Margaret A Haley* (Urbana, IL: University of Illinois Press, 1982).

[11.] Reid, *Battleground*, 90.

[12.] Jessie May Short, *Women in the Teaching Profession: Or Running as Fast as You Can to Stay in the Same Place* (Portland, OR: Reed College, June 1939), 10.

[13.] B.A. Hinsdale, "The Training of Teachers," *Education in the United States: A Series of Monographs Prepared for the United States Exhibit at the Paris Exposition, 1900*, Nicholas Murray Butler, ed. (Albany: J. Lyon, 1900), 16.

[14.] Thorstein Veblen, *The Engineers and the Price System* (New York: Heubsch, 1921), 52-53.

[15.] Lewis Mumford, *Technics and Civilization* (New York: Harcourt Brace, 1934), 219-20.

[16.] Edward S. Evenden, Guy C. Gamble, and Harod G. Blue, "Teacher

Personnel in the United States," *National Survey of the Education of Teachers* 11, U.S. Department of the Interior Bulletin no. 10 (1931): 20.

17. Sugg, *Motherteacher*, 122.

Chapter 4

Introduction to Samuel Bowles and Herbert Gintis

Samuel Bowles and Herbert Gintis argue that schooling is not an effective way to promote equality of job opportunity. Contrary to popular opinion, the school, they argue, does much to insure that lower class kids find jobs similar to those of their parents. This correspondence theory holds that economic background rather than intelligence and schooling is the best predictor of the jobs we hold. Schools play an important part in preparing students for work by making sure that children develop traits that lead to their eventual occupations. The school discriminates against poor students by emphasizing traits required in low status jobs. Obedience, docility, and cooperation are marks of schools in poor communities. They report that poor parents prefer a school which promotes these traits since they are so essential to their working lives. Yet the very traits that make for success at lower status jobs are the same traits which would hinder success in college and higher status jobs. On the other hand, parents from affluent communities are critical of schools that emphasize conformity. These parents prefer schools that allow for independence, self-discipline and involvement. These, of course, are traits that have served them well in their eventual high status jobs. Most students who enter prestigious colleges come from affluent backgrounds. While some children from poor families do enter various other colleges they generally do not acquire the traits of self-discipline and autonomy which are so essential to success not only in college, but also in the acquisition of very high status jobs.

In sum, Gintis and Bowles argue that schools do little to correct inequality of job opportunity since they reflect the values of parents who prefer that schools reproduce the personality traits which meet their job requirements.

Consider the following questions when you examine this provocative paper:

1. Poor parents feel that the best opportunity for economic advancement lays with developing conforming traits. Does this belief hinder the economic advancement of their children?

2. How would the authors account for the fact that many poor children advanced economically in the fifties and sixties?

3. The authors hint that when looking for a teaching job, applicants must be sensitive to the fit between their teaching style and the economic level of the community. Explore that issue!

Education and Personal Development: The Long Shadow of Work

by *Samuel Bowles and Herbert Gintis*

> Every child born into the world should be looked upon by society as so much raw material to be manufactured. Its quality is to be tested. It is the business of society, as an intelligent economist, to make the best of it.
> Lester Frank Ward
> *Education*, c. 1872

It is not obvious why the U.S. educational system should be the way it is. Since the interpersonal relationships it fosters are so antithetical to the norms of freedom and equality prevalent in American society, the school system can hardly be viewed as a logical extension of our cultural heritage. If neither technological necessity nor the bungling mindlessness of educators explain the quality of the educational encounter, what does?

Reference to the educational system's legitimation function does not take us far toward enlightenment. For the formal, objective, and cognitively oriented aspects of schooling capture only a fragment of the day-to-day social relationships of the educational encounter. To approach an answer, we must consider schools in the light of the social relationships of economic life. In this chapter, we suggest that major aspects of educational organization replicate the relationships of dominance and subordinacy in the economic sphere. The correspondence between the social relation of schooling and work accounts for the ability of the educational system to produce an amenable and fragmented labor force. The experience of schooling, and not merely the content of formal learning, is central to this process.

In our view, it is pointless to ask if the net effect of U.S. education is to promote equality or inequality, repression or liberation. These issues pale into insignificance before the major fact: The educational system is an integral element in the reproduction of the prevailing class structure of society. The educational system certainly has a life of its own, but the experience of work and the nature of the class structure are the bases upon which educational values are formed, social justice assessed, the realm of the possible delineated in people's consciousness, and the social relations of the educational encounter historically transformed.

In short, and to return to a persistent theme of this book, the educational system's task of integrating young people into adult work roles constrains the types of personal development which it can foster in ways that are antithetical to the fulfillment of its personal developmental function.

Reproducing Consciousness

> . . . children guessed (but only a few
> and down they forgot as up they grew
> autumn winter spring summer) . . .
> e e cummings, 1940

Economic life exhibits a complex and relatively stable pattern of power and property relationships. The perpetuation of these social relationships, even over relatively short periods, is by no means automatic. As with a living organism, stability in the economic sphere is the result of explicit mechanisms constituted to maintain and extend the dominant patterns of power and privilege. We call the sum total of these mechanisms and their actions the reproduction process.

Amidst the sundry social relations experienced in daily life, a few stand out as central to our analysis of education. These are precisely the social relationships which are necessary to the security of capitalist profits and the stability of the capitalist division of labor. They include the patterns of dominance and subordinacy in the production process, the distribution of ownership of productive resources, and the degrees of social distance and solidarity among various fragments of the working population—men and women, blacks and whites, and white- and blue-collar workers, to mention some of the most salient.

What are the mechanisms of reproduction of these aspects of the social relations of production in the United States? To an extent, stability is embodied in law and backed by the coercive power of the state. Our jails are filled with individuals who have operated outside the framework of the private-ownership market system. The modern urban police force as well as the National Guard originated, in large part, in response to the fear of social upheaval evoked by militant labor action. Legal sanction, within the framework of the laws of private property, also channels the actions of groups (e.g., unions) into conformity with dominant power relationships. Similarly, force is used to stabilize the division of labor and its rewards within an enterprise: Dissenting workers are subject to dismissal and directors failing to conform to "capitalist rationality" will be replaced.

But to attribute reproduction to force alone borders on the absurd. Under normal conditions, the effectiveness of coercion depends at the very least on the inability or unwillingness of those subjected to it to join together in opposing it. Laws generally considered illegitimate tend to lose their coercive power, and undisguised force too frequently applied tends to be self-defeating. The consolidation and extension of capitalism has engendered struggles of furious intensity. Yet instances of force deployed against a united and active opposition are sporadic and have usually given way to détente in one form or another through a combination of compromise, structural change, and ideological accommodation. Thus it is clear that the consciousness of workers—beliefs, values, self-concepts, types of solidarity and fragmentation, as well as modes of personal behavior and development—are integral to the perpetuation, validation, and smooth operation of economic institutions. The reproduction of the social relations of production depends on the reproduction of consciousness.

Under what conditions will individuals accept the pattern of social relationships that frame their lives? Believing that the long-term development of the existing system holds the prospect of fulfilling their needs, individuals and groups might actively embrace these social relationships. Failing this, and lacking a vision of an alternative that might significantly improve their situation, they might fatalistically accept their condition. Even with such a vision they might passively submit to the framework of economic life and seek individual solutions to social problems if they believe that the possibilities for realizing change are remote. The issue of the reproduction of consciousness enters each of these assessments.

The economic system will be embraced when, first, the perceived needs of individuals are congruent with the types of satisfaction the economic system can objectively provide. While perceived needs may be, in part, biologically determined, for the most part needs arise through the aggregate experiences of individuals in the society. Thus the social relations of production are reproduced in part through a harmony between the needs which the social system generates and the means at its disposal for satisfying these needs.

Second, the view that fundamental social change is not feasible, unoperational, and utopian is normally supported by a complex web of ideological perspectives deeply embedded in the cultural and scientific life of the community and reflected in the consciousness of its members. But fostering the "consciousness of inevitability" is not the office of the cultural system alone. There must also exist mechanisms that systematically thwart the spontaneous development of social experiences that would contradict these beliefs.

Belief in the futility of organizing for fundamental social change is further facilitated by social distinctions which fragment the conditions of life for subordinate classes. The strategy of "divide and conquer" has enabled dominant classes to maintain their power since the dawn of civilization. Once again, the splintered consciousness of a subordinate class is not the product of cultural phenomena alone, but must be reproduced through the experiences of daily life.

Consciousness develops through the individual's direct perception of and participation in social life.[1] Indeed, everyday experience itself often acts as an inertial stabilizing force. For instance, when the working population is effectively stratified, individual needs and self-concepts develop in a correspondingly fragmented manner. Youth of different racial, sexual, ethnic, or economic characteristics directly perceive the economic positions and prerogatives of "their kind of people." By adjusting their aspiration accordingly, they not only reproduce stratification on the level of personal consciousness, but bring their needs into (at least partial) harmony with the fragmented conditions of economic life. Similarly, individuals tend to channel the development of their personal powers—cognitive, emotional, physical, aesthetic, and spiritual—in directions where they will have an opportunity to exercise them. Thus the alienated character of work, for example, leads people to guide their creative potentials to areas outside of economic activity: consumption, travel, sexuality, and family life. So needs and need-satisfaction again tend to fall into congruence and alienated labor is reproduced on the level of personal consciousness.[2]

But this congruence is continually disrupted. For the satisfaction of needs gives rise to new needs. These new needs derive from the logic of personal development as well as from the evolving structure of material life, and in turn undercut the reproduction of consciousness. For this reason the reproduction of consciousness cannot be the simple unintended byproduct of social experience. Rather, social relationships must be consciously organized to facilitate the reproduction of consciousness.

Take, for instance, the organization of the capitalist enterprise discussed in Chapter 3. Power relations and hiring criteria within the enterprise are organized so as to reproduce the workers' self-concepts, the legitimacy of their assignments within the hierarchy, a sense of the technological inevitability of the hierarchical division of labor itself, and the social distance among groups of workers in the organization. Indeed, while token gestures towards workers' self-management may be a successful motivational gimmick, any delegation of real power to workers becomes a threat to profits because it tends to undermine patterns of consciousness compatible with capitalist control. By generating new needs and possibilities, by demonstrating the feasibility of a more thoroughgoing economic democracy, by increasing worker solidarity, an integrated and politically conscious program of worker involvement in decision-making may undermine the power structure of the enterprise. Management will accede to such changes only under extreme duress of worker rebellion and rapidly disintegrating morale, if at all.

But the reproduction of consciousness cannot be insured by these direct mechanisms alone. The initiation of youth into the economic system is further facilitated by a series of institutions, including the family and the educational system, that are more immediately related to the formation of personality and consciousness. Education works primarily through the institutional relations to which students are subjected. Thus schooling fosters and rewards the development of certain capacities and the expression of certain needs, while thwarting and penalizing others. Through these institutional relationships, the educational system tailors the self-concepts, aspirations, and social class identifications of individuals to the requirements of the social division of labor.

The extent to which the educational system actually accomplishes these objectives varies considerably from one period to the next. We shall see in later chapters that recurrently through U.S. history these reproduction mechanisms have failed, sometimes quite spectacularly. In most periods—and the present is certainly no exception—efforts to use the schools to reproduce and extend capitalist production relations have been countered both by the internal dynamic of the educational system and by popular opposition.

In earlier chapters we have identified the two main objectives of dominant classes in educational policy: the production of labor power and the reproduction of those institutions and social relationships which facilitate the translation of labor power into profits. We may now be considerably more concrete about the way that educational institutions are structured to meet these objectives. First, schooling produces many of the technical and cognitive skills required for adequate job performance. Second, the educational system helps legitimate economic inequality. As we argued in the last chapter, the objective and meritocratic orientation of U.S. education, reduces discontent over both the hierarchical division of labor and the process through which individuals attain position in it. Third, the school produces, rewards, and labels personal characteristics relevant to the staffing of positions in the hierarchicy. Fourth, the educational system, through the pattern of status distinctions it fosters, reinforces the stratified consciousness on which the fragmentation of subordinate economic classes is based.

What aspects of the educational system allow it to serve these various functions? We shall suggest in the next section that the educational system's ability to reproduce the consciousness of workers lies in a straightforward correspondence principle: For the past century at least, schooling has contributed to the reproduction of the social relations of production largely through the correspondence between school and class structure.

Upon the slightest reflection, this assertion is hardly surprising. All major institutions in a "stable"social system will direct personal development in a direction compatible with its reproduction. Of course, this is not, in itself, a critique of capitalism or of U.S. education. In any conceivable society, individuals are forced to develop their capacities in one direction or another. The idea of a social system which merely allows people to develop freely according to their "inner natures" is quite unthinkable, since human nature only acquires a concrete form through the interaction of the physical world and preestablished social relationships.

Our critique of education and other aspects of human development in the United States fully recognizes the necessity of some form of socialization. The critical question is: What for? In the United States the human development experience is dominated by an undemocratic, irrational, and exploitative economic structure. Young people have no recourse from the requirements of the system but a life of poverty, dependence, and economic insecurity. Our critique, not surprisingly, centers on the structure of jobs. In the U.S. economy work has become a fact of life to which individuals must by and large submit and over which they have no control. Like the weather, work "happens" to people. A liberated, participatory, democratic, and creative alternative can hardly be imagined, much less experienced. Work under capitalism is an alienated activity.

To reproduce the social relations of production, the educational system must try to teach people to be properly subordinate and render them sufficiently fragmented in consciousness to preclude their getting together to shape their own material existence. The forms of consciousness and behavior fostered by the educational system must themselves be alienated, in the sense that they conform neither to the dictates of technology in the struggle with nature, nor to the inherent developmental capacities of individuals, but rather to the needs of the capitalist class. It is the prerogatives of capital and the imperatives of profit, not human capacities and technical realities, which render U.S. schooling what it is. This is our charge.

The Correspondence Principle

> In the social production which men carry on they
> enter into definite relations which are indispensible
> and independent of their will;
> . . . The sum total of these relations of production
> constitutes . . . the real foundation on which rise
> legal and political superstructures, and to which
> correspond definite forms of social consciousness.
> Karl Marx, *Contribution to a Critique
> of Political Economy,* 1857

The educational system helps integrate youth into the economic system, we believe, through a structural correspondence between its social relations and those of production. The structure of social relations in education not only inures the student to the discipline of the work place, but develops the types of personal demeanor, modes of self-presentation, self-image, and social-class identifications which are the crucial ingredients of job adequacy.   Specifically, the social relationships of education—the relationships between administrators and teachers, teachers and students, students and students, and students and their work—replicate the hierarchical division of labor. Hierarchical relations are reflected in the vertical authority lines from administrators to teachers to students. Alienated labor is reflected in the student's lack of control over his or her education, the alienation of the student from the curriculum content, and the motivation of school work through a system of grades and other external rewards rather than the student's integration with either the process (learning) or the outcome (knowledge) of the educational "production process." Fragmentation in work is reflected in the institutionalized and often destructive competition among students through continual and ostensibly meritocratic ranking and evaluation. By attuning young people to a set of social relationships similar to those of the work place, schooling attempts to gear the development of personal needs to its requirements.

But the correspondence of schooling with the social relations of production goes beyond this aggregate level. Different levels of education feed workers into different levels within the occupational structure and, correspondingly, tend toward an internal organization comparable to levels in the hierarchical division of labor. As we have seen, the lowest levels in the hierarchy of the enterprise emphasize rule-following, middle levels, dependability, and the capacity to operate without direct and continuous supervision while the higher levels stress the internalization of the norms of the enterprise. Similarly, in education, lower levels (junior and senior high school) tend to severely limit and channel the activities of students. Somewhat higher up the educational ladder, teacher and community colleges allow for more independent activity and less overall supervision. At the top, the elite four-year colleges emphasize social relationships conformable with the higher levels in the production hierarchy.[3] Thus schools continually maintain their hold on students. As they "master" one type of behavioral regulation, they are either allowed to progress to the next or are channeled into the corresponding level in the hierarchy of production. Even within a single school, the social relationships of different tracks tend to conform to different behavioral norms. Thus in high school, vocational and general tracks emphasize rule-following and close supervision, while the college track tends toward a more open atmosphere emphasizing the internalization of norms.

These differences in the social relationships among and within schools, in part, reflect both the social backgrounds of the student body and their likely future economic positions. Thus blacks and other minorities are concentrated in schools whose repressive, arbitrary, generally chaotic internal order, coercive authority structures, and minimal possibilities for advancement mirror the characteristics of inferior job situation. Similarly, predominantly working-class schools tend to emphasize behavioral control and rule-following, while schools in well-to-do suburbs employ relatively open systems that favor greater student participation, less direct supervision, more student electives, and, in general, a value system stressing internalized standards of control.

The differential socialization patterns of schools attended by students of different social classes do not arise by accident. Rather, they reflect the fact that the educational objectives and expectations of administrators, teachers, and parents (as well as the responsiveness of students to various patterns of teaching and control) differ for students of different social classes. At crucial turning points in the history of U.S. education, changes in the social relations of schooling have been dictated in the interests of a more harmonious reproduction of the class structure. But in the day-to-day operation of the schools, the consciousness of different occupational strata, derived from their cultural milieu and work experience, is crucial to the maintenance of the correspondences we have described.   That working-class parents seem to favor stricter educational methods is a reflection of their own work experiences, which have demonstrated that submission to authority is an essential ingredient in one's ability to get and hold a steady, well-paying job.   That professional and self-employed parents prefer a more open atmosphere and a greater emphasis on motivational control is similarly a reflection of their position in the social division of labor. When given the opportunity, higher-status parents are far more likely than their lower-status neighbors to choose "open classrooms" for their children.[4]

Differences in the social relationships of schooling are further reinforced by inequalities in financial resources.   The paucity of financial support for the education of children from minority groups and low-income families leaves more resources to be devoted to the children of those with more commanding roles in the economy; it also forces upon the teachers and school administrators in the working-class schools a type of social relationships that fairly closely mirrors that of the factory.   Financial considerations in poorly supported schools militate against small intimate classes, multiple elective courses, and specialized teachers (except for disciplinary personnel).   They preclude the amounts of free time for teachers and free space required for a more open, flexible educational environment.   The well-financed schools attended by the children of the rich can offer much greater opportunities for the development of the capacity for sustained independent work and all the other characteristics required for adequate job performance in the upper levels of the occupational hierarchy.

Much of this description will most likely be familiar to the reader and has been documented many times.[5]   But only recently has there been an attempt at statistical verification.   We will review a number of excellent studies, covering both higher and secondary education.   Jeanne Binstock investigated the different patterns of social relations of higher education by analyzing the college handbooks covering rules, regulations, and norms of fifty-two public junior colleges, state universities, teacher-training colleges, and private, secular, denominational, and Catholic colleges.   Binstock rated each school along a host of dimensions,[6] including the looseness or strictness of academic structure, the extent of regulations governing personal and social conduct, and the degree of control of the students over their cultural affairs and extracurricular activities.   Her general conclusion is quite simple:

The major variations of college experiences are linked to basic psychological differences in work perception and aspiration among the major social class (occupational) groups who are its major consumers. Each social class is different in its beliefs as to which technical and interpersonal skills, character traits, and work values are most valuable for economic survival (stability) or to gain economic advantage (mobility). Each class (with subvariations based on religion and level of urban-ness) has its own economic consciousness, based on its own work experiences and its own ideas (correct or not) of the expectations appropriate to positions on the economic ladder above their own. . . . Colleges compete over the various social class markets by specializing their offerings. Each different type of undergraduate college survives by providing circumscribed sets of "soft" and "hard" skill training that generally corresponds both to the expectations of a particular social class group of customers and to specific needs for sets of "soft" and "hard" skills at particular layers of the industrial system.[7]

Binstock isolated several organizational traits consistently related to the various educational institutions she studied. First, she distinguished between behavioral control which involves rules over the student's behavior rather than intentions and stresses external compliance rather than internalized norms, and motivational control which emphasizes unspecified, variable, and highly flexible task-orientation, and seeks to promote value systems that stress ambiguity and innovation over certainty, tradition, and conformity. Second, Binstock isolated a leader-versus-follower orientation with some schools stressing the future subordinate positions of its charges and teaching docility, and other stressing the need to develop "leadership" self-concepts.

Binstock found that institutions that enroll working-class students and are geared to staff lower-level jobs in the production hierarchy emphasize followership and behavioral control, while the more elite schools that tend to staff the higher-level jobs emphasize leadership and motivational control. Her conclusion is:

Although constantly in the process of reformation, the college industry remains a ranked hierarchy of goals and practices, responding to social class pressures, with graded access to the technical equipment, organizational skills, emotional perspectives and class (work) values needed for each stratified level of the industrial system.[8]

The evidence for the correspondence between the social relations of production and education, however, goes well beyond this structural level and also sheds light on the communality of motivational patterns fostered by these two spheres of social life. Juxtaposing the recent research of Gene Smith, Richard Edwards, Peter Meyer, and ourselves, the same types of behavior can be shown to be rewarded in both education and work. In an attempt to quantify aspects of personality and motivation, Gene Smith has employed a relatively sensitive testing procedure, which he has shown in a series of well-executed studies[9] to be an excellent predictor of educational success (grade-point average). Noting that personality inventories traditionally suffer because of their abstraction from real-life environments and their use of a single evaluative instrument, Smith turned to student-peer ratings of forty-two common personality traits, based on each student's observation of the actual classroom behavior of his or her classmates. A statistical technique called factor analysis then allowed for the identification of five general traits—agreeableness, extroversion, work orientation, emotionality, and helpfulness—that proved stable across different samples. Of these five traits, only the work-orientation factor, which Smith calls "strength of character"—including such traits as ". . . not a quitter, conscientious, responsible, insistently orderly, not prone to daydreaming, determined, persevering . . ."—was related to school success. Smith then proceeded to show that, in several samples, this work-orientation trait was three times more successful in predicting post-high-school academic performance than any combination of thirteen cognitive variables, including SAT verbal, SAT mathematical, and high school class rank.

Our colleague Richard C. Edwards has further refined Smith's procedure. As part of his Ph.D. dissertation on the nature of the hierarchical division of labor, he prepared a set of sixteen pairs of personality measures relevant to work performance.[10] Edwards argued that since supervisor ratings of employees are a basic determinant of hirings, firings, and promotions, they are the best measure of job adequacy and, indeed, are the implements of the organization's motivational system. Edwards, therefore, compared supervisor ratings of worker performance with the set of sixteen personality measures as rated by the workers' peers. In a sample of several hundred Boston area workers, he found a cluster of three personality traits—summarized as rules orientation, dependability, and internalization of the norms of the firm—strongly predicting supervisor ratings of workers in the same work group. This result, moreover, holds up even when the correlation of these traits with such attributes as age, sex, social class background, education, and IQ is corrected for by linear regression analysis. In conformance with our analysis in Chapter 3, Edwards found that rules orientation was relatively more important at the lowest levels of the hierarchy of production, internalization of norms was predominant at the highest level, while dependability was salient at intermediate levels.[11]

Edwards' success with this test in predicting supervisor ratings of workers convinced us that applying the same forms to high school students would provide a fairly direct link between personality development in school and the requirements of job performance.

This task we carried out with our colleague Peter Meyer.[12] He chose as his sample the 237 members of the senior class of a single New York State high school.[13] Following Edwards, he created sixteen pairs of personality traits,[14] and obtained individual grade-point averages, IQ scores, and college-entrance-examination SAT-verbal and SAT-mathematical scores from the official school records.[15]

As we expected, the cognitive scores provided the best single predictor of grade-point average—indeed, that grading is based significantly on cognitive performance is perhaps the most valid element in the "meritocratic ideology." But the sixteen personality measures possessed nearly comparable predictive value, having a multiple correlation of 0.63 compared to 0.77 for the cognitive variables.[16] More important than the overall predictive value of the personality traits, however, was the pattern of their contribution to grades. To reveal this pattern, we first eliminated the effect of differences in cognitive performance in individual grades and then calculated the correlation between grades and the personality traits.[17] The results are presented in Figure 4—1.

The pattern of resulting associations clearly supports the correspondence principle and strongly replicates our initial empirical study of grading presented in Chapter 2. The only significant penalized traits are precisely those which are incompatible with conformity to the hierarchical division of labor—creativity, independence, and aggressivity. On the other hand, all the personality traits which we would expect to be rewarded are, and significantly so. Finally, a glance at Figure 4—2 shows a truly remarkable correspondence between the

FIGURE 4—1

Personality Traits Rewarded and Penalized (in a New York High School)

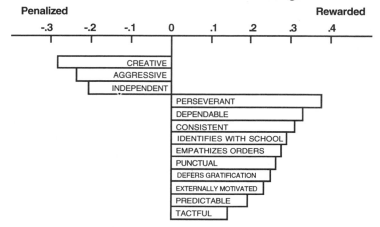

NOTES: Each bar shows the partial correlation between grade-point average and the indicated personality trait, controlling for IQ, SAT-Verbal, and SAT-Mathematical. The penalized traits (left) indicate creativity and autonomy, while the rewarded traits (right) indicate subordinacy and discipline. The data are from Samuel Bowles, Herbert Gintis, and Peter Meyer, "The Long Shadow of Work: Education, the Family, and the Reproduction of the Social Division of Labor," *The Insurgent Sociologist*, Summer 1975, and is described in Appendix B (see Bibliography Appendix B). All partial correlations are statistically significant at the 1 percent level. The results for English grades alone, and for a teacher-attitude rating in place of grade-point average, are similar and are presented in Appendix B.

personality traits rewarded or penalized by grades in Meyer's study and the pattern of traits which Edwards found indicative of high or low supervisor ratings in industry.

As a second stage in our analysis of Meyer's data, we used factor analysis to consolidate the sixteen personality measures into three "personality factors." Factor analysis allows us to group together those measured traits which are normally associated with one another among all individuals in the sample. The first factor, which we call "submission to authority," includes these traits: consistent, identifies with school, punctual, dependable, externally motivated, and persistent. In addition, it includes independent and creative weighted negatively. The second, which we call temperament, includes: not aggressive, not

FIGURE 4—2

Personality Traits Approved by Supervisors

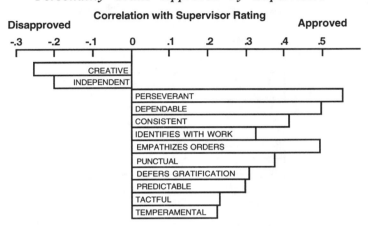

Correlation with Supervisor Rating

Disapproved   **Approved**

NOTES: The pattern of personality traits indicative of supervisor approval correspond to those rewarded in high school. Each bar shows the correlation between supervisor rating and the indicated personality trait. The results are similar to Figure 4-1, except that aggressive is insignificant and temperamental significant in the sample of workers. The data are from Richard C. Edwards, "Personal Traits and 'Success' in Schooling and Work," *Educational and Psychological Measurement*, in Press, 1976; "Individual Traits and Organizational Incentives: What Makes a 'Good Worker'" *Journal of Human Resources*, Spring 1976, and are based on a sample of 240 workers in several government offices in the Boston area. All correlations are significant at the 1 percent level.

temperamental, not frank, predictable, tactful, and not creative. The third we call internalized control, and it includes: empathizes orders and defers gratification.[18]

These three factors are not perfectly comparable to Edwards' three factors. Thus our submission to authority seems to combine Edwards' rules and dependability factors, while our internalized control is comparable to Edwards' internalization factor. In the case of the latter, both Edwards' and Meyer's data depict an individual who sensitively interprets the desires of his or her superior and operates adequately without direct supervision over considerable periods of time.

Our theory would predict that at the high school level submission to authority would be the best predictor of grades among personality traits, while internalization would be less important. (The temperament factor is essentially irrelevant to our theory and might be expected to be

FIGURE 4-3

Predicting Job Performance and Grades in School from the same Personality Traits

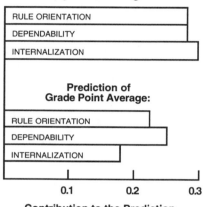

**Prediction of
Supervisor Ratings:**

RULE ORIENTATION

DEPENDABILITY

INTERNALIZATION

**Prediction of
Grade Point Average:**

RULE ORIENTATION

DEPENDABILITY

INTERNALIZATION

0.1   0.2   0.3

Contribution to the Prediction

NOTES: The top three bars show the estimated normalized regression coefficients of the personality factors in an equation predicting supervisor ratings. The bottom three bars show the coefficients of the same three factors in an equation predicting high-school grade-point average. All factors are significant at the 1 percent level. The regression equations are presented in our Appendix B.
SOURCES: Bowles, Gintis, and Meyer (1975); Edwards (See full citations in Figures 4-1 and 4-2).

unimportant.)   This prediction was confirmed.   Assessing the independent contributions of both cognitive measures and personality factors to the prediction of grades, we found that SAT-math were the most important, followed by submission to authority and SAT-verbal scores (each equally important).   Internalized control proved to be significantly less important as predictors.   The temperament and IQ variables made no independent contribution.

Thus, at least for this sample, the personality traits rewarded in schools seem to be rather similar to those indicative of good job performance in the capitalist economy. Since moreover both Edwards and Meyer used essentially the same measures of personality traits, we can test this assertion in yet another way. We can take the three general traits extracted by Edwards in his study of workers—rules orientation, dependability, and internalization of norms—and find the relationship between those traits and grades in Meyer's school study. The results shown in Figure 4—3, exhibit a remarkable congruence.[19] While the correspondence principle stands up well in the light of grading practices, we must stress that the empirical data on grading must not be regarded as fully revealing the inner workings of the educational system's reproduction of the social division of labor. In the first place, it is the overall structure of social relations of the educational encounter which reproduces consciousness, not just grading practices. Nor are personality traits the only relevant personal attributes captured in this data; others are modes of self-presentation, self-image, aspirations, and class identifications. The measuring of personality traits moreover is complex and difficult, and these studies probably capture only a small part of the relevant dimensions. Finally, both traits rewarded in schools and relevant to job performance differ by educational level, class composition of schools, and the student's particular educational track. These subtleties are not reflected in this data.

For all these reasons, we would not expect student grades to be a good predictor of economic success. In addition, grades are clearly dominated by the cognitive performance of students, which we have seen is not highly relevant to economic success. Still, we might expect that in an adequately controlled study in which work performances of individuals on the same job and with comparable educational experience are compared, grades will be good predictors. We have managed to find only one study even approaching these requirements—a study which clearly supports our position, and is sufficiently interesting to present in some detail.[20] Marshall S. Brenner studied one hundred employees who had joined the Lockheed-California Company after obtaining a high school diploma in the Los Angeles City school districts. From the employees' high school transcripts, he obtained their grade-point averages, school absence rates, a teacher's "work habits" evaluation, and a teacher's "cooperation" evaluation. In addition to this data, he gathered three evaluations of job performance by employees' supervisors: a supervisors' "ability rating," "conduct rating," and "productivity rating." Brenner found a significant correlation between grades and all measures of supervisor evaluation.

We have reanalyzed Brenner's data to uncover the source of this correlation. One possibility is that grades measure cognitive performance and cognitive performance determines job performance.

However, when the high school teachers' work habits and cooperation evaluations as well as school absences were controlled for by linear regression, grades had no power to predict either worker conduct or worker productivity. Hence, we may draw two conclusions: First, grades predict job adequacy only through their noncognitive component; and second, teachers' evaluations of behavior in the classroom are strikingly similar to supervisors' ratings of behavior on the job. The cognitive component of grades predicts only the supervisors' ability rating—which is not surprising in view of the probability that both are related to employee IQ.[21]

Why then the association between more schooling and higher incomes? In Chapter 3, we indicated the importance of four sets of noncognitive worker traits—work-related personality characteristics, modes of self-presentation, racial, sexual, and ethnic characteristics, and credentials. We believe that all of these traits are involved in the association between educational level and economic success. We have already shown how personality traits conducive to performance at different hierarchical levels are fostered and rewarded by the school system. A similar, but simpler, argument can be made with respect to modes of self-presentation. Individuals who have attained a certain educational level tend to identify with one another socially and to differentiate themselves from their "inferiors." They tend to adjust their aspirations and self-concepts accordingly, while acquiring manners of speech and demeanor more or less socially acceptable and appropriate to their level.[22] As such, they are correspondingly valuable to employers interested in preserving and reproducing the status differences on which the legitimacy and stability of the hierarchical division of labor is based. Moreover, insofar as educational credentials are an independent determinant of hiring and promotion, they will directly account for a portion of this association.[23]

Finally, family background also accounts for a significant portion of the association between schooling and economic attainment. Indeed, for white males, about a third of the correlation between education and income is due to the common association of both variables with socioeconomic background, even holding constant childhood IQ.[24] That is, people whose parents have higher-status economic positions tend to achieve more income themselves independent of their education, but they also tend to get more education. Hence the observed association is reinforced.

Indeed, there is a strong independent association between family background and economic success, illustrated in Figure 4—4. For the large national sample represented there, children of the poorest tenth of families have roughly a third the likelihood of winding up well-off as the children of the most well-to-do tenth, even if they have the same educational attainments and childhood IQ's. What is the origin of this effect? The inheritance of wealth, family connections, and other more or less direct advantages play an important role here. But there are more subtle if no less important influences at work here as well. We shall argue in the following section that the experiences of parents on the job tend to be reflected in the social relations of family life. Thus, through family socialization, children tend to acquire orientations toward work, aspirations, and self-concepts, preparing them for similar economic positions themselves.

Family Structure and Job Structure

> According to the materialist conception, the determining factor in history is, in the last resort, the production and reproduction of immediate life. But this itself is of a two-fold character. On the one hand, the production of the means of subsistence, of food, clothing, and shelter and the tools requisite therefore; on the other, the production of human beings themselves, the propagation of the species. The social institutions under which people of a particular historical epoch and a particular country live are conditioned by both kinds of production; by the stage of development of labor, on the one hand, and of the family on the other.
>
> Friedrich Engels, *The Origin of the Family, Private Property, and the State*, 1884

Family experience has a significant impact on the well-being, behavior, and personal consciousness of individuals, both during maturation and in their daily adult lives. The social relationships of family life—relationships between husband and wife as well as between parents and children and among children—have undergone important changes in the course of U.S. economic development. The prospect for future changes is of crucial importance in the process of social transformation.[25]

FIGURE 4—4

The Effect of Socioeconomic Background on Economic Successis Strong even for Individuals with Equal Education and I.Q.

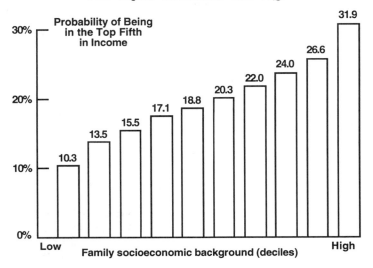

NOTES: Each bar shows the estimated probability that a man is in the top fifth of the income distribution if he is from the given decile of socioeconomic background (as a weighted average of his father's education, occupation status, and his parents' income), and is he has an average childhood IQ and average number of years of schooling. That is, it measures the effect of socioeconomic background on income, independent of any effects caused by education or IQ differences.[24]

SAMPLE: Non-Negro males from nonfarm backgrounds, aged 35-44.

SOURCE: Samuel Bowles and Valerie Nelson, "The 'Inheritance of IQ' and the Intergenerational Reproduction of Economic Inequality," *The Review of Economics and Statistics* 56, no. 1 (February 1974).

Rather than attempt a broad analysis of family life, we shall limit our discussion to a few issues directly linked to our central concern: the reproduction of the social relations of production. Like the educational system, the family plays a major role in preparing the young for economic and social roles. Thus, the family's impact on the reproduction of the sexual division of labor, for example, is distinctly greater than that of the educational system.

This reproduction of consciousness is facilitated by a rough correspondence between the social relations of production and the social relations of family life, a correspondence that is greatly affected by the experiences of parents in the social division of labor. There is a tendency for families to reproduce in their offspring not only a consciousness tailored to the objective nature of the work world, but to prepare them for economic positions roughly comparable to their own. Although these tendencies can be countered by other social forces (schooling, media, shifts in aggregate occupational structure), they continue to account for a significant part of the observed intergenerational status-transmission processes.

This is particularly clear with respect to sexual division of labor. The social division of labor promotes the separation between wage and household labor, the latter being unpaid and performed almost exclusively by women. This separation is reflected within the family as a nearly complete division of labor between husband and wife. The occupational emphasis on full-time work, the dependence of promotion upon seniority, the career-oriented commitment of the worker, and the active discrimination against working women conspire to shackle the woman to the home while minimizing the likelihood of a joint sharing of domestic duties between husband and wife.

But how does the family help reproduce the sexual division of labor? First, wives and mothers themselves normally embrace their self-concepts as household workers. They then pass these onto their children through the differential sex role-typing of boys and girls within the family. Second, and perhaps more important, children tend to develop self-concepts based on the sexual divisions which they observe around them. Even families which attempt to treat boys and girls equally cannot avoid sex role-typing when the male parent is tangentially involved in household labor and child-rearing. In short, the family as a social as well as biological reproduction unit cannot but reflect its division of labor as a production unit. This sex-typing, unless countered by other social forces, then facilitates the submission of the next generation of women to their inferior status in the wage-labor system and lends its alternative—child-rearing and domesticity—an aura of inevitability, if not desirability.

However, in essential respects, the family exhibits social patterns that are quite uncharacteristic of the social relations of production. The close personal and emotional relationships of family life are remote from the impersonal bureaucracy of the wage-labor system. Indeed, the family is often esteemed as a refuge from the alienation and psychic poverty of work life. Indeed, it is precisely because family structure and the capitalist relations of production differ in essential respects that our analysis sees schooling as performing such a necessary role in the integration of young people into the wage-labor system. We will return to this point in the next chapter.

Despite the tremendous structural disparity between family and economy—one which is never really overcome in capitalist society- —there is a significant correspondence between the authority relationships in capitalist production and family child-rearing. In part, this is true of family life common at all social levels. The male-dominated family, with its characteristically age-graded patterns of power and privilege, replicates many aspects of the hierarchy of production in the firm. Yet here we shall be more concerned with the difference among families whose income-earners hold distinct positions in this hierarchy.

As we have seen, successful job performance at low hierarchical levels requires the worker's orientation toward rule-following and conformity to external authority, while successful performance at higher levels requires behavior according to internalized norms. It would be surprising, indeed, if these general orientations did not manifest themselves in parental priorities for the rearing of their children. Melvin Kohn's massive, ten-year study at the National Institute of Mental Health has documented important correspondences between authority in the social relationships of work and the social relationships of the family precisely of this type.

Kohn, in a series of papers and in his book, *Class and Conformity*, has advanced and tested the following hypothesis: Personality traits and values of individuals affect the economic positions they attain and, conversely, their job experiences strongly affect their personalities and values.[26] The most important values and behavior patterns in this interaction are those relating to self-direction and conformity,[27] with individuals of higher economic status more likely to value internal motivation and those of lower status more likely to value behavior that conforms with external authority. Thus, Kohn argues, individuals in higher-status jobs tend to value curiosity and self-reliance, to emphasize the intrinsic aspects of jobs such as freedom and choice, and to exhibit a high level of internalized motivation and a high degree of trust in interpersonal relationships. Conversely, people in lower-status jobs tend to value personal responsibility and the extrinsic aspects of jobs such as security, pay, and working conditions. Moreover, they exhibit more external motivations, a greater conformity to explicit social rules and they are less trustful of others.[28]

Kohn goes on to inquire which aspects of jobs produce these results and concludes that the statistically relevant job characteristic is the degree of occupational self-direction, including freedom from close supervision, the degree of initiative and independent judgment allowed, and the complexity and variety of the job.[29] Thus no matter what their economic status, whether white or blue collar, individuals with the same degree of occupational self-direction, tend to have similar values and traits. Self-direction versus close supervision and routinization on the job account for most of the status-related differences in personal preferences for self-direction, degree of internalized morality, trustfulness, self-confidence, self-esteem, and idea conformity.[30] He concludes:

In industrial society, where occupation is central to men's lives, occupational experiences that facilitate or deter the exercise of self-direction come to permeate men's views, not only of work and their role in work, but of the world and of self. The conditions of occupational life at higher social class levels facilitate interest in the intrinsic qualities of the job, foster a view of self and society that is conducive to believing in the possibilities of rational action toward purposeful goals, and promote the valuation of self-direction. The conditions of occupational life at lower social class levels limit men's view of the job primarily to the extrinsic benefits it provides, foster a narrowly circumscribed conception of self and society, and promote the positive valuation of conformity to authority.[31]

There remains, however, an important discrepancy between our interpretation and Kohn's. What Kohn calls "self-direction" we feel is usually better expressed as "internalized norms." That is, the vast majority of workers in higher levels of the hierarchy of production are by no means autonomous, self-actualizing, and creatively self-directed. Rather, they are probably supersocialized so as to internalize authority and act without direct and continuous supervision to implement goals and objectives relatively alienated from their own personal needs. This distinction must be kept clearly in mind to avoid the error of attributing "superior" values and behavior traits to higher strata in the capitalist division of labor.

Kohn then went on to investigate the impact of work-related values on child-rearing. He began, in 1956, with a sample of 339 white mothers of children in the fifth grade, whose husbands held middle-class and working-class jobs.[32] He inquired into the values parents would most like to see in their children's behavior. He found that parents of lower-status children value obedience, neatness, and honesty in their children, while higher-status parents emphasize curiosity, self-control, consideration, and happiness. The fathers of these children who were interviewed showed a similar pattern of values. Kohn says:

> Middle class parents are more likely to emphasize children's *self-direction*, and working class parents to emphasize their *conformity to external authority*. . . . The essential difference between the terms, as we use them, is that self-direction focuses on *internal* standards of direction for behavior; conformity focuses on *externally* imposed rules.[33]

Kohn further emphasized that these values translate directly into corresponding authority relationships between parents and children, with higher-status parents punishing breakdowns of internalized norms, and lower-status parents punishing transgression of rules:

> The principal difference between the classes is in the *specific conditions* under which parents—particularly mothers—punish children's misbehavior. Working class parents are more likely to punish or refrain from punishing on the basis of the direct and immediate consequences of children's actions, middle class parents on the basis of their interpretation of children's intent in acting as they do. . . . If self-direction is valued, transgressions must be judged in terms of the reasons why the children misbehave. If conformity is valued, transgressions must be judged in terms of whether or not the actions violate externally imposed proscriptions.[34]

In 1964, Kohn undertook to validate his findings with a national sample of 3,100 males, representative of the employed, male civilian labor force. His results clearly support his earlier interpretation: Higher-job-status fathers prefer consideration, curiosity, responsibility, and self-control in their children; low-status fathers prefer good manners, neatness, honesty, and obedience. Moreover, Kohn showed that about two-thirds of these social status-related differences are directly related to the extent of occupational self-direction. As a predictor of child-rearing values, the structure of work life clearly overshadows the other correlates of status such as occupational prestige or educational level.[35] He concludes:

> Whether consciously or not parents tend to impact to their children lessons derived from the conditions of life of the their own social class—and this helps to prepare their children for a similar class position. . . .
> Class differences in parental values and child rearing practices influence the development of the capacities that children will someday need. . . . The family, then, functions as a mechanism for perpetuating inequality.[36]

Kohn's analysis provides a careful and compelling elucidation of one facet of what we consider to be a generalized social phenomenon: the reflection of economic life in all major spheres of social activity. The hierarchical division of labor, with the fragmentation of the work force which it engenders, is merely reflected in family life. The distinct quality of social relationships at different hierarchical levels in production are reflected in corresponding social relationships in the family. Families, in turn, reproduce the forms of consciousness required for the integration of a new generation into the economic system. Such differential patterns of childrearing affect more than the worker's personality, as is exemplified in Kohn's study. They also pattern self-concepts, personal aspirations, styles of self-presentation, class loyalties, and modes of speech, dress, and interpersonal behavior. While such traits are by no means fixed into adulthood and must be reinforced at the workplace, their stability over the life cycle appears sufficient to account for a major portion of the observed degree of intergenerational status transmission.

Conclusion

> You will still be here tomorrow,
> but your dreams may not.
> Cat Stevens

The economic system is stable only if the consciousness of the strata and classes which compose it remains compatible with the social relations which characterize it as a mode of production. The perpetuation of the class structure requires that the hierarchical division of labor be reproduced in the consciousness of its participants. The educational system is one of the several reproduction mechanisms through which dominant elites seek to achieve this objective. By providing skills, legitimating inequalities in economic positions, and facilitating certain types of social intercourse among individuals, U.S. education patterns personal development around the requirements of alienated work. The educational system reproduces the capitalist social division of labor, in part, through a correspondence between its own internal social relationships and those of the workplace.

The tendency of the social relationships of economic life to be replicated in the educational system and in family life lies at the heart of the failure of the liberal educational creed. This fact must form the basis of a viable program for social change. Patterns of inequality, repression, and forms of class domination cannot be restricted to a single sphere of life, but reappear in substantially altered, yet structurally comparable, form in all spheres. Power and privilege in economic life surface not only in the core social institutions which pattern the formation of consciousness (e.g., school and family), but even in face-to-face personal encounters, leisure activities, cultural life, sexual relationships, and philosophies of the world. In particular, the liberal goal of employing the educational system as a corrective device for overcoming the "inadequacies" of the economic system is vain indeed. We will argue in our concluding chapter that the transformation of the educational system and the pattern of class relationships, power, and privilege in the economic sphere must go hand in hand as part of an integrated program for action.

Notes

[1.] Herbert Gintis, "Welfare Criteria with Endogenous Preferences: The Economics of Education," *International Economic Review*, June 1974; Alfred Schutz and Thomas Luckmann, *The Structure of the Life-World* (Evanston, IL: Northwestern University Press, 1973); and Peter L. Berger and Thomas Luckmann, the *Social Construction of Reality: A Treatise in the Sociology of Knowledge* (Garden City, NY: Doubleday and Co., 1966).

[2.] For an extended treatment of theses issues, see Herbert Gintis, "Alienation and Power," in *The Review of Radical Political Economics* 4, no. 5 (fall 1972).

[3.] Jeanne Binstock, "Survival in the American College Industry," unpublished Ph.D. dissertation, Brandeis University, 1970.

[4.] Burton Rosenthal, "Education Investments in Human Capital: The Significance of Stratification in the Labor Market," unpublished honors thesis, Harvard University, 1972; and Edgar Z. Friedenberg, *Coming of Age in America* (New York: Random House, 1965).

[5.] Florence Howe and Paul Lauter, "The Schools Are Rigged for Failure," *New York Review of Books* (June 20, 1970); James Herndon, *The Way It Spozed to Be* (New York: Simon and Schuster, 1968); and Ray C. Rist, "Student Social Class and Teacher Expectations: The Self-Fulfilling Prophesy in Ghetto Education," *Harvard Educational Review* (August 1970).

[6.] Binstock, 103-106, "Survival."

[7.] *Ibid.*, 3-4.

[8.] *Ibid.*, 3-4.

[9.] Gene M. Smith, "Usefulness of Peer Ratings of Personality in Educational Research," *Educational and Psychological Measurement* (1967); "Personality Correlates of Academic Performance in Three Dissimilar Populations," Proceedings of the 77th Annual Convention, American Psychological Association (1967); and "Nonintelligence Correlates of Academic Performance," mimeo (1970).

[10.] Richard C. Edwards, "Alienation and Inequality: Capitalist Relations of Production in a Bureaucratic Enterprise," Ph.D. dissertation, Harvard University (July 1972).

[11.] Richard C. Edwards, "Personal Traits and 'Success' in Schooling and Work," *Educational and Psychological Measurement* (in press, 1975); and "Individual Traits and Organizational Incentives: What Makes a 'Good' Worker?" *Journal of Human Resources* (in press, 1976).

[12.] Peter J. Meyer, "Schooling and the Reproduction of the Social Division of Labor," unpublished honors thesis, Harvard University (March 1972).

[13.] Personality data was collected for 97 per cent of the sample. Grade-point average and test-scored data was available for 80 per cent of the sample, and family background data was available for 67 per cent. Inability to collect data was due usually to students' absences from school during test sessions.

[14.] These are described fully in Appendix B.

[15.] The school chosen was of predominantly higher income, so that most students had taken college-entrance examinations.

[16.] The multiple correlation of IQ, SAT-verbal, and SAT-math with grade-point average (GPA) was $r = 0.769$, while their correlation with the personality variables was $r = 0.25$.

[17.] That is, we created partial correlation coefficients between GPA and each personality measure, controlling for IQ, SAT-V, and SAT-M. The numerical values are presented in Appendix B.

[18.] We emphasize that these groupings are determined by a computer program on the basis of the observed pattern of association among the sixteen variables. The fact that they are so clearly interpretable, rather than being hodgepodge, is a further indicator of the correctness of our analysis. We have not grouped the personality traits in terms of our preconceived theory, but observed rather how they are naturally grouped in our data. The results of the factor analysis are presented in Appendix B.

[19.] This is taken from Table 3 of Edwards (1975) "Personal Traits and 'Success'"; and Samuel Bowles, Herbert Gintis, and Peter Meyer, "The Long Shadow of Work: Education, the Family and the Reproduction of the Social Division of Labor," *The Insurgent Sociologist* (Summer 1975).

[20.] Marshal H. Brenner, "The Use of High School Data to Predict Work Performance," *Journal of Applied Psychology* 52, no. 1 (January 1968). This study was suggested to us by Edwards, and is analyzed in Edwards "Alienation and Inequality" (1972).

[21.] The relevant regression equations are presented in Appendix B.

[22.] See Claus Offe, *Leistungsprinzip und Industrielle Arbeit* (Frankfurt: Europaische Verlaganstalt, 1970). Offe quotes Bensen and Rosenberg in Maurice Stein et al., eds., *Identity and Anxiety* (New York: The Free Press, 1960) 183-84:

> Old habits are discarded and new habits are nurtured. The would-be success learns when to simulate enthusiasm, compassion, interest, concern, modesty, confidence and mastery; when to smile and with whom to laugh and how intimate and friendly he can be with other people. He selects his home and his residential area with care; he buys his clothes and chooses styles with an eye to their probable reception in his office. He reads or pretends to have read the right books, the right magazines, and the right newspapers. All this will be reflected in the "right line of conversation" which he adapts as his own. . . . He

joins the right party and espouses the political ideology of his fellows.
[23.] See Ivar Berg, *Education and Jobs: The Great Training Robbery* (Boston: Beacon Press, 1971); and Paul Taubman and Terence Wales, *Higher Education and Earnings* (New York: McGraw-Hill, 1974).
[24.] Calculated from of an estimated normalized regression coefficient of 0.23 on socioeconomic background in an equation using background, early childhood IQ, and years of schooling to predict income for 35-44-year-old males. This is reported in Table 1 of Samuel Bowles and Valerie Nelson, "The 'Inheritance of IQ' and the Intergenerational Reproduction of Economic Inequality," *The Review of Economics and Statistics* 56, no. 1 (February 1974), and in Appendix A. The corresponding coefficients for other age groups are 0.17 for ages 25-34; 0.29 for ages 45-54; and 0.11 for ages 55-64 years.
[25.] Margaret Benston, "The Political Economy of Women's Liberation," *Monthly Review* (September 1969); Marilyn P. Goldberg, "The Economic Exploitation of Women," in David M. Gordon, ed., *Problems in Political Economy* (Lexington, MA: D.C. Heath and Co., 1971); L. Gordon, *Families* (Cambridge, MA: A. Bread and Rose Publication, 1970); Zaretsky, "Capitalism and Personal Life," *Socialist Revolution* (January-April 1973); and Juliet Mitchell, *Women's Estate* (New York: Vintage Books, 1973).
[26.] Melvin Kohn, *Class and Conformity: A Study in Values* (Homewood, IL: Dorsey Press, 1969).
[27.] Melvin Kohn and Carmi Schooler, "Occupational Experience and Cognitive Functioning: An Assessment of Reciprocal Effects," *American Sociological Review* (February 1973).
[28.] Kohn, chapters 5 and 10, *Class and Conformity*.
[29.] *Ibid.*, Chapter 10.
[30.] *Ibid.*, Table 10-7.
[31.] *Ibid.*, 192.
[32.] The occupational index used was that of Hollingshead, which correlates 0.90 with the Duncan index. Charles M. Bonjean, Richard J. Hill, and S. Dale McLemore, *Sociological Measurement: An Inventory of Scales and Indices* (San Francisco: Chandler, 1967).
[33.] Kohn, 34-35, *Class and Conformity*.
[34.] *Ibid.*, 104-105.
[35.] Two problems with the Kohn study may be noted. First, we would like to have more direct evidence of the ways in which and to what extent child-raising values are manifested in child-raising practices. And second, we would like to know more about the impact of differences in child-rearing practice upon child development.
[36.] Kohn, 200, *Class and Conformity*.

Chapter 5

Introduction to Juan C. Rodriguez

In this article the author argues that in an effort to accommodate the changing demographics of school populations, we must first study not only the cultural and language diversity that exist within school systems, but we must further make an attempt to understand how it is that these issues do in fact relate to changes within the community as a whole.

He further suggests that there must be an effort towards determining the perceptions and visions of bilingual teachers as to:

- their expectations of the school systems
- their sense of efficacy
- the dynamics of excellence within their classrooms
- the role of the schools within the newly emerging demographics

This basic knowledge about the ideologies of bilingual teachers, he concludes, would serve as an excellent starting point for determining new policies and methods for reaching and educating a culturally and linguistically diverse student population.

Questions:

    1. Do you feel that determining the sense of efficacy of bilingual teachers would help to improve the education of culturally and linguistically diverse students?

    2. Do you think that teachers who work with culturally and linguistically diverse students need to play a new

and expanded role in the schools?

3. What do you feel would be required to better educate culturally and linguistically diverse students?

4. Do you think that culturally and linguistically diverse students can achieve academic excellence?

5. Do you think that schools should make accommodations to educate this new emerging population?

The Challenge of Bilingual Teachers

by Juan C. Rodriguez

The ethnic and language composition of the students in American schools is changing radically. Large numbers of students whose native language is other than English are entering public school and presenting a new challenge for educators.[1] The dramatic encounter of language minority students with public schools came as a surprise to many people. Numerous school systems in the country, especially those located in urban areas, were caught unprepared to provide an appropriate and relevant education to this fast emerging young population.

The rapid transformation that America is facing from an autonomous European cultural tradition to one of global interdependency requires serious reflection regarding the fundamental question that all educators confront: How to better educate our children for the future, and in this case more specifically: How to better educate linguistically and culturally diverse students.

In this endeavor, if the genuine concern is the authentic teaching and learning of linguistically and culturally diverse students, we need to take a hard look at what is happening within the American school system, and particularly to understand what is going on in the public schools.

This hermeneutic inquiry must also include the community at large, because education is not a neutral enterprise[2] and schools are not only an agent for change but a reflection of what is happening in society. Environmental influences are powerful determinants in the way a school operates.[3] Ignoring what is transpiring outside the school would be a terrible mistake.

Furthermore, if the goal is to improve educational programs for non-English speaking immigrants, it is imperative to determine from bilingual teachers' expectations and sense of effectiveness when teaching linguistically and culturally diverse students. If one wants to bring out the best in teaching, it is vital to identify not only the external aspects of the profession, such as technical skills and professional experiences, but it is also necessary to unravel the internal dynamics that make teachers move beyond mere competence, to a high level of excellence, which according to Renck Jalongo is characterized by decision-making, creativity, perceptibility, and spontaneity.[4] It is also necessary to interpret the scope and function of their ideologies, attitudes, beliefs and values that drive their professional careers. It is essential to know about their perceived abilities to perform successfully in class and to understand their sense of teaching and learning and what motivates bilingual teachers to generate appropriate educational responses for their students. It is also important to look at the ways they interact day to day with students in school[5] and how they are bringing about intended outcomes.[6]

Ideologies influence everyday function[7] and, as Apple argues, they "are not only a global set of interests, things imposed by one group on another. They are embodied by our common sense, meaning and practices".[8] They are also inevitable creations that are essential and function as shared convictions of meaning for making complex social reality understandable.[9]

If the guiding principle of education is to promote learning, especially now that schools in America are confronting large contentions and new demands, teachers in this decade need to play appropriate and expanded new roles in the school. To renew and change deteriorated educational programs, as Sinclair and Nieto state,

> the basic structures of schools and the human relationships within the school personnel must be changed. This is especially true if limited interaction between teachers and students, and teachers and parents persist.[10]

All of these complexities make it urgent to learn more about what is going on within the teachers as men and women, what is the force that motivates these bilingual teachers who effectively impart education to this new type of student, considered by many as hard to educate. The research-based knowledge of these ideologies, beliefs and goals will provide the basis to point to new ways of thinking about the directions and essential roles bilingual teachers need to play in the improvement of education, as we enter the next millennium.

By traditionally focusing on external aspects of education, fundamental questions relevant to bilingual teachers' educational goals and aspirations were often neglected and overlooked. To determine the patterns of bilingual teachers' behavior and students' outcomes we need to learn about many aspects of teachers' self assessments, including: What is their conception of their teaching? What are their educational goals and priorities? What are they trying to accomplish with their students? What is their interest in change and professional growth? What is the nature of the bilingual teachers' sense of efficacy? What are the qualities that make them effective bilingual teachers? What are their perceived roles? What are the unique attributes that competent bilingual teachers have? What are the conditions that foster or inhibit their professional accomplishments? What kinds of instructional interaction takes place collegially, administratively, familially and societally, as Bandura points out, when teaching linguistically and culturally diverse students in American schools.[11]

The research-based knowledge and literature on ideologies of bilingual teachers and the conception of their teaching is scant, vague, or nonexistent, and there is little agreement as to what specific knowledge, skills, behaviors and attitudes bilingual teachers should possess for teaching effectively.[12]

Synthesis Construct of Bilingual Teachers' Conception of Teaching

Teaching to this newly emerging population requires individual talents and educational techniques different from traditional ones. Bilingual, English as a Second Language (ESL) or mainstream teachers must do more than speak the language of their students. In addition to competencies awareness, performance, knowledge and skills of what to teach, attitudes, behaviors, and ideologies are important aspects in the teaching process, especially when the emphasis is not only on students learning and teachers teaching, but in their active instructional interaction. As Garza and Barnes suggest:

New teachers need intellectual tools that provide a mindset for evaluating their teaching critically, reflecting upon their teaching, and making reasoned decisions about it. Teachers need to focus not only upon how things are to be done but also upon why.[13]

In this regard, the Center for Applied Linguistics (CAL) proposed in 1974 the specific qualities that bilingual teachers should have—in addition to cultural awareness and sensitivity—such as proper academic preparation and professional experience, and a genuine and sincere interest in the education of children, regardless of their personal qualities, or linguistic and cultural background. The CAL proposal also indicated several specific attitudes and behaviors, that bilingual teachers should have, that greatly influence the teaching of limited English proficient students "beliefs, values, traditions and rules for social behavior is shared and valued by the group and passed from one generation to the next."[14]

Teachers' sensitivity to the effects of transculturation of their students or of themselves; the significance of the socialization process in the family unit; conflict in the students' lives; and the ability to assist with student needs, are concerns of the CAL proposal. Teaching to the newly emerging linguistically and culturally diverse population, in our view, requires a new kind of teacher; one who plays particular roles, who has a perception different from the traditional ones, and who has distinct behaviors, attitudes and skills that enable the teacher to efficiently integrate educational goals into action. Teaching for the future also requires teachers who can make sense of the nature of teaching and be able to function effectively in a social setting that many times is unfamiliar to them and to their students. What teachers do in their classroom is a reflection of their conception of their role as educators. In the words of Montero-Sieburth:

> The ways teachers select knowledge, interpret and use knowledge and correct meanings in their classrooms mirror the teachers' understanding of the perspective or definition they bring to a situation, the constraints which they face, and the way such perspectives are finally played out.[15]

Bilingual teachers need to have a sense of who they are,[16] and what the professional goals, objectives and activities are. As Renck Jalongo points out, one must use reflection as the vehicle for self-perception of one's "perspectives, priorities, practices."[17]   Reflection also helps us to confront problems. In this regard Heath discerns:

when faced by a problem, we reflect, we become more aware, we search for hints or clues, we explore the consequences of our hunches. We reflect more about our feelings, values, our interpersonal styles. We try to understand why students and colleagues react as they do. Research clearly shows that the more mature person is a more reflective, self-insightful, understanding person.[18]

In other words, to promote change and to develop professionally, bilingual teachers need, on one hand, to have a sense of community that according to Battistich, Solomon, Kim, Watson, and Schaps, provides the feeling of belonging, satisfaction and meaning, where they feels accepted and valued, and without which they would feel alienation or normlessness.[19] On the other hand it is necessary to have, from within, a sense of what one is, which provides the opportunity to learn and grow not only from accomplishments but also from past mistakes. In this regard Schon says:

> When a practitioner becomes a researcher into his own practice he engages in a continuous process of self-education. The recognition of error, with its resulting uncertainty, can become a source of discovery rather than an occasion for self defense.[20]

Moreover, when teachers examine their own practices, the hermeneutic purpose becomes their focal point,[21] because there is an effort to understand what it means to be a teacher, and thus they become active learners seeking professional growth and self-direction.[22] All of these denote the quest for professional development. Educational attainment, in the mind of many, represents one of the few hopes for social mobility from generation to generation.

Traditionally in education, there is an assumption that teachers must be accountable for students' outcomes, a demand that increased when federal legislation was enacted in the 1960s, but this concern as Boorish says, is very often filtered in spirit if not in substance by local schools and teachers.[23] Also, teachers have the responsibility to create productive learning environments and bring about intended students' outcomes at any cost. This is to say according to Ashton that the main concern is teacher efficacy.[24]

But a question immediately arises: Are bilingual teachers alone and by themselves able to create this positive and productive school environment, without having a sense of community belonging, where many times there is a lack of trusting and caring environment. For those of us who have spent many years close to learners, practical experience shows that classroom teachers, especially those with students having Limited English Proficient (LEP), spend much of their time working in isolation, without much professional dialogue and lacking opportunities for participation and supportive relationships, as the Past President of the MTA Nancy Finkelstein stated:

> In thinking about the responsibility and capacity to create productive learning environments, one must recognize that over the last fifty or more years, teachers have been left standing on a drastically eroded mainland of professional discretion.[25]

This reflection is only an attempt to address some of the questions, focusing on the hermeneutic purpose as they relate specifically to role, visions, perceptions, and expectations of bilingual teachers and students, and its nexus with effective education.

Notes ───────────────────

[1.] Population Reference Bureau, Inc., Spring 1994 publication (Washington, DC).

[2.] Michael Apple, *Ideology and Curriculum* (London: Routledge & Kegan Paul, 1979).

[3.] Albert Bandura, "Reflections on Self-Efficacy," Advances in Behavioral Research and Therapy 1: 237-239.

[4.] Mary Jalongo, *The Role of the Teacher in the 21st Century* (Bloomington, IN: National Educational Service, 1991).

[5.] Bandura, "Reflections on Self-Efficacy."

[6.] Carole Ames and Russell Ames, eds., *Research On Motivation*, vol. 1-3 (Boston: Academic Press, 1989).

[7.] Brophy 1974

[8.] Michael Apple, *Cultural and Economic Reproduction in Education* (London: Routledge & Kegan Paul, 1982).

[9.] Apple, *Ideology and Curriculum.*

[10.] Robert Sinclair and Sonia Nieto, eds., *Renewing School Curriculum* (Amherst, MA: University of Massachusetts Amherst, 1988).

[11.] Bandura, "Reflections on Self-Efficacy."

[12.] Ana Garza and Carol T. Barnes, "Competencies for Bilingual Multicultural Teachers," *Journal of Educational Issues of Language Minority Students* 5 (Fall 1989): 1-20.

[13.] *Ibid.*

[14.] *Ibid.*

[15.] Martha Montero-Sieburth, "Bilingual Teachers' Ideologies in the Integration of Hispanic and Southeast Asian Immigrant Students: An Initiative Between Practitioners and Researchers," *NABE Annual Conference Journal* (1988-1989): 40.

[16.] Patricia T. Ashton and Rodman B. Webb, *Making and Difference: Teacher's Sense of Efficacy and Student Achievement* (White Plains, NY: Longman, 1986).

[17.] Jalongo, *Role of the Teacher.*

[18.] Douglas Heath, "Developing Teachers, Not Just Techniques," *Improving Teaching*, 1986 Yearbook ASCD, Association for Supervision and Curriculum Development.

[19.] V. Battistich, D. Solomon, Dong-il Kim, M. Watson and E. Schaps, "Schools as Communities, Poverty Levels of Student Populations, Students' Attitudes, Motives, and Performance: A Multilevel Analysis," *American Educational Research Journal* 32, no. 3 (fall 1995): 627-658.

[20.] Donald Schon, *The Reflective Practitioner: How Professionals Think in Action* (London: Temple Smith, 1983).

[21.] Virginia Richardson, "Conducting Research on Practice," *Educational Researcher* 23, no. 5 (June-July 1994).

[22.] Jalongo, *Role of the Teacher.*

[23.] Gary D. Borich, *The Appraisal of Teaching, Concepts and Process* (Reading, MA: Addison-Wesley, 1997), viii.

[24.] Ashton and Webb, 143, *Making a Difference.*

[25.] Nancy Finkelstein, unpublished paper delivered as President of the Massachusetts Teachers Association (1988).

Chapter 6

Introduction to George S. Counts

George Counts was an historian and man of broad experience and education that enabled him to develop an unusual view of schooling. He was at various times a secondary school teacher, a student of international educational systems, especially that of the Soviet Union, and one of the first to study the sociology of education. Counts viewed the schooling process as an integral part of the shaping of the American character.

Counts' understanding of the impact of social forces on schooling was shaped by his observances of the rise of the industrial systems in Europe and the United States in the 1920's. He was very concerned with the undemocratic features that were becoming increasingly apparent in Italy, Germany, the Soviet Union, and also in the Unites States. Counts advocated the reconstruction of American society through the establishment of democratic socialism. He continued this advocacy through a number of political campaigns and offices held, especially with the American Federation of Teachers and the American Labor Party. Counts was an outstanding example of a political activist who believed in the power of educators to change the existing social and political systems.

The "American Dream," the vision that life for the common person will get better with the passing of the years, has been sorely tested a number of times in American history. Whether is lives for most Americans today is in doubt. However, in the 1930's "the Dream" was tested as it never had been before. The 1930's were in many ways the crucial decade in American history. The American economic system seemed to have collapsed and the country suffered the Great Depression. While millions survived in poverty, the political system was unable to respond in helpful ways. The Depression, which began in 1929, did not end until the onset of World War II.

The early years of the 1930's were a time when many reformers, both leftist and rightist, advocated abandoning the democratic capitalist system and substituting something else. Communists and fascists both increased their numbers and, for a time, were perceived by many as viable alternatives to the existing political and economic structures. The programs of the New Deal and Franklin Roosevelt quite effectively destroyed the possibility that communist or fascist political groups would become popular mass movements in the United States during the 1930's. However, some of the critics of the political and economic systems in the United States, including those closer to the center of the political spectrum, also began to take a closer look at the role schools played in perpetuating societal conditions with which they were displeased. George Counts was one such critic. Counts believed that it was crucial for teachers to understand that schooling could have a significant impact on society's institutions and not just react to them. The political issues of who controlled the various forms and distribution of power were central to his argument. Counts considered teaching an inherently political act. He thought that teachers were incompetent if they did not recognize that a neutral stance toward the teaching of values was impossible. Counts believed that this imposition of values upon students was necessary and desirable if a democratic society was to be built and maintained.

Listed below are three questions that Counts asked teachers to think about and take positions on:

1. What is the best way to protect the majority of the people from the control of special interests?

2. Why can't capitalism and democracy co-exist?

3. Why is indoctrination of students necessary?

Dare the School Build a New Social Order?

by George S. Counts

Originally published in *Dare The School Build A New Social Order?*
(John Day Company, 1932), pp. 38-56. Reprinted with permission.

In *The Epic of America* James Truslow Adams contends that our chief
contribution to the heritage of the race lies not in the field of science, or
religion, or literature, or art, but rather in the creation of what he calls
the "American Dream" -- a vision of a society in which the lot of the
common man will be made easier and his life enriched an ennobled. If
this vision has been a moving force in our history, as I believe it has,
why should we not set ourselves the task of revitalizing and
reconstituting it? This would seem to be the great need of our age,
both in the realm of education and in the sphere of public life, because
men must have something for which to live. Agnosticism, skepticism,
or even experimentalism, unless the last is made flesh through the
formulation of some positive social program, constitutes an extremely
meager spiritual diet for any people. A small band of intellectuals, a
queer breed of men at best, may be satisfied with such a spare ration,
particularly if they lead the sheltered life common to their class; but the
masses, I am sure, will always demand something more solid and
substantial. Ordinary men and women crave a tangible purpose towards
which to strive and which lends richness and dignity and meaning to
life. I would consequently like to see our profession come to grips
with the problem of creating a tradition that has roots in American soil,
is in harmony with the spirit of the age, recognizes the facts of
industrialism, appeals to the most profound impulses of our people, and

takes into account the emergence of a world society.[1]

The ideal foundations on which we must build are easily discernible. Until recently the very word *America* has been synonymous throughout the world with democracy and symbolic to the oppressed classes of all lands of hope and opportunity. Child of the revolutionary ideas and impulses of the eighteenth century, the American nation became the embodiment of bold social experimentation and a champion of the power of environment to develop the capacities and redeem the souls of common men and women. And as her stature grew, her lengthening shadow reached to the four corners of the earth, and everywhere impelled the human will to rebel against ancient wrongs. Here undoubtedly is the finest jewel in our heritage and the thing that is the most worthy of preservation. If America should lose her honest devotion to democracy, or if she should lose her revolutionary temper, she will no longer be America. In that day, if it has not already arrived, her spirit will have fled and she will be known merely as the richest and most powerful of the nations. If America is not to be false to the promise of her youth, she must do more than simply perpetuate the democratic ideal of human relationships: she must make an intelligent and determined effort to fulfill it. The democracy of the past was the chance fruit of a strange conjunction of forces on the new continent; the democracy of the future can only be the intended offspring of the union of human reason, purpose, and will. The conscious and deliberate achievement of democracy under novel circumstances is the task of our generation.

Democracy, of course, should not be identified with political forms and functions -- with the federal constitution, the popular election of officials, or the practice of universal suffrage. To think in such terms is to confuse the entire issue, as it has been confused in the minds of the masses for generations. The most genuine expression of democracy in the United States has little to do with our political institutions; it is a sentiment with respect to the moral equality of men; it is an aspiration towards a society in which this sentiment will find complete fulfillment. A society fashioned in harmony with the American democratic tradition would combat all forces tending to produce social distinctions and classes; repress every form of privilege and economic parasitism; manifest a tender regard for the weak, the ignorant, and the unfortunate; place the heavier and more onerous social burdens on the backs of the strong; glory in every triumph of man in his timeless urge to express himself and to make the world more habitable; exalt human labor of hand and brain as the creator of all wealth and culture; provide adequate material and spiritual rewards for every kind of socially useful work; strive for genuine equality of opportunity among all races, sects, and occupations; regard as paramount the abiding interests of the great masses of the people; direct the powers of government to the elevation and refinement of the life of the common man; transform or destroy all conventions, institutions, and special groups inimical to the underlying principles of democracy; and finally be prepared, as a last resort, in either the defense or the realization of this purpose, to follow the method of revolution. Although these ideals have never been realized or perhaps even fully accepted anywhere in the United States, and have always had to struggle for existence with contrary forces, they nevertheless have authentic roots in the past. They are the values for which America has stood before the world during most of her history, and with which the American people have loved best to associate their country. Their power and authority are clearly revealed in the fact that selfish interests, when grasping for some special privilege, commonly wheedle and sway the masses by repeating the words and kneeling before the emblems of the democratic heritage.

It is becoming increasingly clear, however, that this tradition, if its spirit is to survive, will have to be reconstituted in the light of the great social trends of the age in which we live. Our democratic heritage was largely a product of the frontier, free land, and a simple agrarian order. Today a new and strange and closely integrated industrial economy is rapidly sweeping over the world. Although some of us in our more sentimental moments talk wistfully of retiring into the more tranquil society of the past, we could scarcely induce many of our fellow citizens to accompany us. Even the most hostile critics of industrialism would like to take with them in their retirement a few such fruits of the machine as electricity, telephones, automobiles, modern plumbing, and various labor-saving devices, or at least be assured of an abundant supply of slaves or docile and inexpensive servants. But all such talk is the most idle chatter. For better or for worse we must take industrial civilization as an enduring fact: already we have become parasitic on its institutions and products. The hands of the clock cannot be turned back.

If we accept industrialism, as we must, we are then compelled to face without equivocation the most profound issue which this new order of society has raised and settle that issue in terms of the genius of our people -- the issue of the control of the machine. In whose interests and for what purposes are the vast material riches, the unrivaled industrial equipment, and the science and technology of the nation to be used? In the light of our democratic tradition there can be but one answer to the question: all of these resources must be dedicated to the promotion of the welfare of the great masses of the people. Even the classes in our society that perpetually violate this principle are compelled by the force of public opinion to pay lip service to it and to defend their actions in its terms. No body of men, however powerful, would dare openly to flout it. Since the opening of the century the great corporations have even found it necessary to establish publicity departments or to employ extremely able men as public relations counselors in order to persuade the populace that, regardless of appearances, they are lovers of democracy and devoted servants of the people. In this they have been remarkably successful, at least until the coming of the Great Depression. For during the past generation there have been few things in America that could not be bought at a price.

If the benefits of industrialism are to accrue fully to the people, this deception must be exposed. If the machine is to serve all, and serve all equally, it cannot be the property of the few. To ask these few to have regard for the common weal, particularly when under the competitive system they are forced always to think first of themselves or perish, is to put too great a strain on human nature. With the present concentration of economic power in the hands of a small class, a condition that is likely to get worse before it gets better, the survival or development of a society that could in any sense be called democratic is unthinkable. The hypocrisy which is so characteristic of our public life today is due primarily to our failure to acknowledge the fairly obvious fact that America is the scene of an irreconcilable conflict between two opposing forces. On the one side is the democratic tradition inherited from the past; on the other is a system of economic arrangements which increasingly partakes of the nature of industrial feudalism. Both of these forces cannot survive: one or the other must give way. Unless the democratic tradition is able to organize and conduct a successful attack on the economic system, its complete destruction is inevitable.

If democracy is to survive, it must seek a new economic foundation. Our traditional democracy rested upon small-scale production in both agriculture and industry, and a rather general diffusion of the rights of property in capital and natural resources. The driving force at the root of this condition, as we have seen, was the frontier and free land. With the closing of the frontier, the exhaustion of free land, the growth of population, and the coming of large scale production, the basis of ownership was transformed. If property rights are to be diffused in industrial society, natural resources and all important forms of capital will have to be collectively owned. Obviously every citizen cannot hold title to a mine, a factory, a railroad, a department store, or even a thoroughly mechanized farm. This clearly means that, if democracy is to survive in the United States, it must abandon its individualistic affiliations in the sphere of economics. What precise form a democratic society will take in the age of science and the machine, we cannot know with any assurance today. We must, however, insist on two things: first, that technology be released from the fetters and the domination of every type of special privilege; and, second, that the resulting system of production and distribution be made to serve directly the masses of the people. Within these limits, as I see it, our democratic tradition must of necessity evolve and gradually assume an essentially collectivistic pattern. The only conceivable alternative is the abandonment of the last vestige of democracy and the frank adoption of some modern form of feudalism.

The important point is that fundamental changes in the economic system are imperative. Whatever services historic capitalism may have rendered in the past, and they have been many, its days are numbered. With its deification of the principle of selfishness, its exaltation of the profit motive, its reliance upon the forces of competition, and its placing of property above human rights, it will either have to be displaced altogether or changed so radically in form and spirit that its identity will be completely lost. In view of the fact that the urge for private gain tends to debase everything that it touches, whether business, recreation, religion, art, or friendship, the indictment against capitalism has commonly been made on moral grounds. But today the indictment can be drawn in other terms.

Capitalism is proving itself weak at the very point where its champions have thought it impregnable. It is failing to meet the pragmatic test; it no longer works; it is unable even to organize and maintain production. In its present form capitalism is not only cruel and inhuman; it is also wasteful and inefficient. It has exploited our natural resources without the slightest regard for the future needs of our society; it has forced technology to serve the interests of the few rather than the many; it has chained the engineer to the vagaries and inequities of the price system; it has plunged the great nations of the earth into a succession of wars ever more devastating and catastrophic in character; and only recently it has brought on a world crisis of such dimensions that the entire economic order is paralyzed and millions of men in all the great industrial countries are deprived of the means of livelihood. The growth of science and technology has carried us into a new age where ignorance must be replaced by knowledge, competition by cooperation, trust in providence by careful planning, and private capitalism by some form of socialized economy.

Already the individualism of the pioneer and the farmer, produced by free land, great distances, economic independence, and a largely self-sustaining family economy, is without solid foundation in either agriculture or industry. Free land has long since disappeared. Great distances have been shortened immeasurably by invention. Economic independence survives only in the traditions of our people. Self-sustaining family economy has been swallowed up in a vast society which even refuses to halt before the boundaries of nations. Already we live in an economy which in its functions is fundamentally cooperative. There remains the task of reconstructing our economic institutions and of reformulating our social ideals so that they may be in harmony with the underlying facts of life. The man who would live unto himself alone must retire from the modern world. The day of individualism in the production and distribution of goods is gone. The fact cannot be overemphasized that choice is no longer between individualism and collectivism. It is rather between two forms of collectivism: the one essentially democratic, the other feudal in spirit; the one devoted to the interests of the people, the other to the interests of a privileged class.

The objection is, of course, raised at once that a planned, coordinated, and socialized economy, managed in the interests of the people, would involve severe restrictions on personal freedom. Undoubtedly in such an economy the individual would not be permitted to do many things that he has customarily done in the past. He would not be permitted to carve a fortune out of the natural resources of the nation, to organize a business purely for the purpose of making money, to build a new factory or railroad whenever and wherever he pleased, to throw the economic system out of gear for the protection of his own private interests, to amass or to attempt to amass great riches by the corruption of the political life, the control of the organs of opinion, the manipulation of the financial machinery, the purchase of brains and knowledge, or the exploitation of ignorance, frailty, and misfortune. In exchange for such privileges as these, which only the few could ever enjoy, we would secure the complete and uninterrupted functioning of the productive system and thus lay the foundations for a measure of freedom for the many that mankind has never known in the past. Freedom without a secure economic foundation is only a word: in our society it may be freedom to beg, steal, or starve. The right to vote, if it cannot be made to ensure the right to work, is but an empty bauble. Indeed it may be less than a bauble: it may serve to drug and dull the senses of the masses. Today only the members of the plutocracy are really free, and even in their case freedom is rather precarious. If all of us could be assured of material security and abundance, we would be released from economic worries and our energies liberated to grapple with the central problems of cultural advance.

Under existing conditions, however, no champion of the democratic way of life can view the future with equanimity. If democracy is to be achieved in the industrial age, powerful classes must be persuaded to surrender their privileges, and institutions deeply rooted in popular prejudice will have to be radically modified or abolished. And according to the historical record, this process has commonly been attended by bitter struggle and even bloodshed. Ruling classes never surrender their privileges voluntarily. Rather do they cling to what they have been accustomed to regard as their rights, even though the heavens fall. Men customarily defend their property, however it may have been acquired, as tenaciously as the proverbial mother defends her young. There is little evidence from the pages of American history to support us in the hope that we may adjust our difficulties through the method of sweetness and light. Since the settlement of the first colonists along the Atlantic seaboard we have practiced and become inured to violence. This is peculiarly true wherever and whenever property rights, actual or potential, have been involved. Consider the pitiless extermination of the Indian tribes and the internecine strife over the issue of human slavery. Consider the long reign of violence in industry, from the days of the Molly Maguires in the seventies down to the strikes in the mining regions of Kentucky today. Also let those, whose memories reach back a dozen years, recall the ruthlessness with which the privileged classes put down every expression of economic or political dissent during the period immediately following the World War. When property is threatened, constitutional guarantees are but scraps of paper, and even the courts and the churches, with occasional exceptions, rush to the support of privilege and vested interest.

This is a dark picture. If we look at the future through the eyes of the past, we find little reason for optimism. If there is to be no break in our tradition of violence, if a bold and realistic program of education is not forthcoming, we can only anticipate a struggle of increasing bitterness terminating in revolution and disaster. And yet, as regards the questions of property, the present situation has no historical parallel. In earlier paragraphs I have pointed to the possibility of completely disposing of the economic problem. For the first time in history we are able to produce all the goods and services that our people can consume. The justification, or at least the rational basis, of the age-long struggle for property has been removed. This situation gives to teachers an opportunity and a responsibility unique in the annals of education.

In an economy of scarcity, where the population always tends to outstrip the food supply, any attempt to change radically the rules of the game must inevitably lead to trial by the sword. But in an economy of plenty, which the growth of technology has made entirely possible, the conditions are fundamentally altered. It is natural and understandable for men to fight when there is scarcity, whether it be over air, water, food, or women. For them to fight over the material goods of life in America today is sheer insanity. Through the courageous and intelligent reconstruction of their economic institutions, they could obtain not only physical security but also the luxuries of life and as much leisure as men could ever learn to enjoy. For those who take delight in combat, ample provision for strife could, of course, be made; but the more cruel aspects of the human struggle would be considerably softened. As the possibilities in our society begin to dawn upon us, we are all, I think, growing increasingly weary of the brutalities, the stupidities, the hypocrisies, and the gross inanities of contemporary life. We have a haunting feeling that we were born for better things and that the nation itself is falling far short of its powers. The fact that other groups refuse to deal boldly and realistically with the present situation does not justify the teachers of the country in their customary policy of hesitation and equivocation. The times are literally crying for a new vision of American destiny. The teaching profession, or at least its progressive elements, should eagerly grasp the opportunity which the fates have placed in their hands.

Such a vision of what America might become in the industrial age I would introduce into our schools as the supreme imposition, but one to which our children are entitled -- a priceless legacy which it should be the first concern of our profession to fashion and bequeath. The objection will, of course, be raised that this is asking teachers to assume unprecedented social responsibilities. But we live in difficult and dangerous times -- times when precedents lose their significance. If we are content to remain where all is safe and quiet and serene, we shall dedicate ourselves, as teachers have commonly done in the past, to a role of futility, if not of positive social reaction. Neutrality with respect to the great issues that agitate society, while perhaps theoretically possible, is practically tantamount to giving support to the forces of conservatism. As Justice Holmes has candidly said in his essay on Natural Law, "we all, whether we know it or not, are fighting to make the kind of world that we should like." If neutrality is impossible even in the dispensation of justice, whose emblem is the blindfolded goddess, how is it to be achieved in education? To ask the question is to answer it.

To refuse to face the task of creating a vision of a future America immeasurably more just and noble and beautiful than the America of today is to evade the most crucial, difficult, and important educational task. Until we have assumed this responsibility we are scarcely justified in opposing and mocking the efforts of so-called patriotic societies to introduce into the schools a tradition which, though narrow and unenlightened, nevertheless represents an honest attempt to meet a profound social and educational need. Only when we have fashioned a finer and more authentic vision than they will we be justified in our opposition to their efforts. Only then will we have discharged the age-long obligation which the older generation owes to the younger and which no amount of sophistry can obscure. Only through such a legacy of spiritual values will our children be enabled to find their place in the world, be lifted out of the present morass of moral indifference, be liberated from the senseless struggle for material success, and be challenged to high endeavor and achievement. And only thus will we as a people put ourselves on the road to the expression of our peculiar genius and to the making of our special contribution to the cultural heritage of the race.

Notes ——————————————————————

[1.] In the remainder of the argument I confine attention entirely to the domestic situation. I do this, not because I regard the question of international relations unimportant, but rather because of limitations of space. All I can say here is that any proper conception of the world society must accept the principle of the moral equality of races and nations.

Part II
_____

**Contemporary Essays on
the Goals of Schooling and
its Relationship to Work**

Chapter 1

Introduction to Richard G. Lyons

Richard G. Lyons presents a comparative essay on the theories of Sigmund Freud, Karl Marx, and Frederick Herzberg on the nature and value of work, and the implications of the three theories on schooling. He begins by outlining their divergent views, and he follows with an analysis of models of work and schooling based upon Marx's theory of unalienated labor, Herzberg's idea of satisfactory labor, and Freud's view of the healthy personality. Lyons then goes on to speculate on possible alternative work and school practices based upon the three models, and points to the similarity of school reforms which they implied. For example, he thinks that their ideas are also an argument for a general education for all.

He concludes with the suggestion that work is a vital idea for developing an understanding of school policy, and that meaningful school reform can only follow on the heels of changes in our working lives. Schools, he argues, will dramatically change only when we conceive of -- and articulate -- a work ethic which would be based upon personal growth and satisfaction, rather than productivity.

Questions:

1. According to Marx, what changes would alleviate alienating labor, and how might these changes impact traditional educational practices?

2. To what degree might you find the Freudian model of a healthy personality and a healthy society (censorship of basic instincts coupled with socially

approved substitutes) embedded in contemporary models of education?

3. What evidence might you offer as support for Herzberg's contention that within industrial societies "work continues to be viewed as an instrument not so much to eliminate scarcity and danger but as a means to over consume?"

4. Do you feel that national goals and standards should guide school reform? Why? Why not?

Karl Marx, Sigmund Freud and Frederick Herzberg and the Nature of Schooling and Working

Richard G. Lyons

Originally published in the *Journal of Thought* Volume 23, nos. 2 & 3 (Fall-Winter 1988), pp. 6-27. Reprinted with permission.

What should we expect from our work? Can work be both meaningful and productive? How are schools disciplined by our work expectations? To appreciate the parameters of this issue, an historical look at the meaning of work may be helpful. The Old Testament, for instance, presents productive work as sweaty and distasteful. Work has no intrinsic appeal and must be judged on its ability to scratch out a living in a world of permanent poverty. Karl Marx, however, ties unsatisfying work to capitalist economies. Capitalism views work as another commodity to be bought on a market. Capitalism usually finds grueling work much more productive than work which has personal appeal. Good work, for most people, simply means well-paid work. Work in other words, is judged on the return it brings to employers or by the wages it provides the employee. While the Bible and Marx connect work to our need to be productive in a world of scarcity, Sigmund Freud suggests that we suffer from instinctual as well as material scarcity. Our sexual instinct must be compromised and repressed if we wish to live in reasonable communities. Our sexual energy must be redirected in ways which benefit the community. Work for Freud absorbs anti-social sexual energy. The American psychologist, Frederick Herzberg, adds an important point for the contemporary worker. He argues that the most productive work brings a high level of satisfaction. The best way to increase productivity is to provide people with work which fulfills their emotional and intellectual capacities.

All these views insist that work must be understood as responding to some form of scarcity, yet they differ over/about our ability to alter scarcity. Freud assumes that no matter how thorough our sublimations, our instinctual gratification will always be uneasy, laden with conflict. Work from this perspective has a tragic quality. Marx and Herzberg, however, are much more optimistic. Marx forecast the elimination of scarcity when work would be directed toward personal and spiritual development. Herzberg, while not predicting the elimination of scarcity, thinks that meaningful work will increase productivity and induce us to change the way we produce.

Our evaluation of work is also related to geographical and personal factors. In industrial economies, people have high expectations about the composition of meaningful work. People from third world countries may enjoy high levels of work satisfaction if they are paid well. Work is much more than an activity—it is also what people experience while working. We must be sensitive to theories of work as well as the expectations which people bring to work. If we ignore the social and personal context of work by insisting that good work has certain universal qualities, we risk becoming authoritarian. If we regard some work as meaningful, yet its workers complain, we characterize their reaction as moral weakness or even stupidity. Members of the clergy, women or physicians should be able to complain about their work. Freud is sensitive to the diversity of criteria we bring to work evaluation and how such variations reflect our capacities, background, and the unequal opportunities societies offer us. On the other hand, when we emphasize personal and subjective norms, we may overlook our capacity to be mistaken about our judgments on work. Marx is aware of our capacity to make bad assessments of our working lives—to settle for work which should be viewed as insufferable and degrading. Herzberg, like Marx, emphasizes objective norms to evaluate work, but is surer than Marx about our ability to have reasonable standards.

This paper will compare and evaluate the norms advanced by Freud, Marx, and Herzberg to judge work. I will argue that their fundamentally different norms serve as a radical critique of contemporary work practices. The paper will conclude with some speculation on how changing criteria of work might influence schooling.

Karl Marx and Unalienated Labor

Marx's vision of work, unalienated labor, to use his term, can be achieved when we eliminate scarcity in a communist context. However, capitalism insists that toil is more productive than work or unalienated labor.[1] Alienated labor exists even when we have an abundance of goods and services. People in wealthy countries work not because of real scarcity but because of fabricated scarcity. Wealthy countries, consequently, develop an ideology which justifies a high level of consumption in exchange for alienating labor. Working conditions may differ from the mining villages of Wales to the slick manufacturing plants in Detroit, but the fundamental impression by the worker should be one of disgust. Ironically, working people may not share Marx's deep contempt for the type of work common in wealthy capitalistic societies. This evaluation may stem from the mistaken assumption that alienating labor is the price we must pay for a high living standard. Marx asks this question: What is an adequate standard of living? When we speak about a minimum standard of living, we are on fairly objective grounds. One might further assume that the standard may have some flexibility depending on availability of goods and services. Herbert Marcuse, a Marxist scholar, insists that too much flexibility is irrational. For instance, present working conditions in advanced technological societies have created a "euphoria in unhappiness"[2] where the toil-to-consume partnership has become a substitute for the development of rational human capacities. The horror story under Marcuse's standard is that most workers are dissatisfied with their jobs and suffer further debasement because consumption alone frustrates our humanity. We debase one another by engaging in work that is unsatisfying and consuming that which is unnecessary. Alienating labor makes more sense under real scarcity than under the conditions of affluence and abundance. Capitalism maintains its power by convincing people that they need more and that toil is the price we must pay.

What then makes work alienating? Alienating labor, as Marx points out in his early *Economic and Philosophic Manuscripts*,[3] is much more than disagreeable work. First, we are alienated from what we produce, the object of our toil. The object is foreign to our nature since it is motivated by the posture of capital rather than the needs of the community. In fact, a commodity could be unnecessary or even harmful to the community. Ironically, the better we produce the object, the more power we return to capital to continue its domination, since profits are turned into political power over labor. Second, the method of production reflects the need for profit rather than the need of workers for unalienating work. If production techniques take on more humane characteristics, the motivation stems from greed rather than a concern for people. Third, capital alienates people from one another simply by creating relationships that are unhealthy. Unhealthy competition and the tendency to measure people only by their possessions and their contributions prostitutes our humanity. Lastly, we are alienated from nature since nature is exploited for wealth and power rather than the needs of people. Water, air, etc., are not regarded as a way to sustain reasonable human values but a way to extend the entire process of alienated labor, consumerism and minority control of the economic and political structure.

Furthermore, it is not enough that people experience alienation but that they conclude that it is insufferable. The response that alienation is intolerable implies that we can change the circumstances that sustain alienating labor. Violence, strikes, political organization, and persuasion must have as their aim the control of the process of production for human ends, as well as the control of the entire superstructure of capital. Schools, churches, publishing outlets must all come under the power of the state. Only then, by Marx's account, will the causes of alienation terminate. What then constitutes unalienated labor? He writes:

> Supposing that we had produced in a human manner; each of us would in his production have doubly affirmed himself and his fellow men. I would have: (1) Objectified in my production my individuality and its peculiarity and thus both in my activity enjoyed an individual expression of my life and also in looking at the object have had the individual pleasure of realizing that my personality was objective, visible to the senses and thus a power raided beyond all doubt. (2) In direct enjoyment of realizing that I had both satisfied a human need by my work and also objectified the human essence and therefore fashioned for another human being the object that met his need. (3) I would have been for you the mediator between you and the species and thus been acknowledged

and felt by you as a completion of your own essence and a necessary part of yourself and have thus realized that I am confirmed both in your thought and in your love. (4) In my expression of my life I would have fashioned your expression of your life, and thus in my own activity have realized my own essence, my human, my communal essence.[4]

This description differs from Marx's notion of alienated labor as it refers not to the natural environment or to the means of production but to the relationship the worker has with the object of his labor and how that relationship extends to others. The need to realize one's creative energies is one aspect of unalienated labor. It is equally important that others appreciate such expression. The relationship between producers and consumers does not reflect an active and passive dichotomy since consumers understand how their humanity is extended by the work of the producer.

Marx's most fundamental assumption is that work cannot be gratifying to the producer if it is harmful to the consumer. Conversely, the work cannot be helpful to the consumer if it requires alienated labor. Why? Is it not possible to supply some commodity by alienated labor that saves someone's life? Yes—but the existence of any form of alienated labor, no matter how small and seemingly useful, would be characteristic of a society which discriminates between classes and emphasizes the separation of ends from means or work from its uses.

Marx has no doubt that capital will self-destruct because of its internal contradictions. For example, it justifies competition but moves toward monopoly. The movements toward socialism and communism, he predicts, may be hastened with the aid of progressive forces such as labor unions. The influence of these forces was evident to Marx in England, Holland and the United States where peaceful means could be used to reconstruct production and the distribution of wealth and power.

Equally important is Marx's open-endedness. Here his idea of praxis becomes important. Praxis, to simplify, is a self-correcting application of theory to the world we encounter. The resulting experience disciplines and corrects the initial theory. Consequently, theory and practice are not two separate worlds.[5] Marx is therefore subjected to the changes, corrections and developments that are justified by experience. Marxism, with an emphasis on praxis, is critical of the mechanistic application of Marx's works to modern problems.

Nevertheless, Marx is committed to a world of unalienated labor—the application and definition of which is disciplined by the times we occupy. The significance of Marx is suggestive rather than doctrinaire.

Sigmund Freud and the Tragedy of Work

The optimism which characterizes Marx's writing stands in sharp contrast to the tragic flavor which dominates Freud's writings, especially *Civilization and Its Discontents* and *The Future of an Illusion*. Nevertheless, they share a fundamental assumption: work must extend our humanity as well as meet material scarcity and death. Scarcity for Freud also refers to a lack of instinctual satisfaction.[6] Sexual scarcity must always prevail since it is a prerequisite for a viable community.   Work is a substitute for natural objects of sexual gratification.   What led Freud to the view that work is a coping mechanism as well as a way to meet material scarcity? Our nature, by his account, is pleasure-seeking, aggressive and antisocial. To live well in a community, we must learn to curb our instinctual expressions so that they do not harm others. If we insist on raw instinctual expression rather than socially approved substitutes like work, we suffer from guilt.   Yet by expressing our basic instincts we maintain our psychological integrity but risk societal disapproval and punishment—even death. On the other hand, when we deny our instinctual foundations and accept surrogates, we become unhealthy—even neurotic. Healthy societies must try to maintain a balance between our instincts and the demand of a civilized society. We first must learn to censor our basic instincts and second, we must find socially approved substitutes. For instance, children have strong sexual desire for the opposite gender parent. To allow for sexual relationships between parent and child would create social havoc and genetic corruption. The child, therefore, must submerge his desire for parental sex into the unconscious. Censorship can never be complete since the child must express some sort of sexual behavior in order to be healthy. Childhood play absorbs some of this sexual energy. Work for adults, serves the same kind of function that play serves for children. In Freud's terms, adults' sexual energy becomes sublimated from many sexual partners to the traditional marriage. Traditional marriage cannot satisfy our sexual needs, but marriage coupled with work is a reasonable expectation. Whether work was alienated or unalienated does not make a difference from the viewpoint of its ability to serve as a sexual surrogate. This should not imply that Freud did not make any distinction between various kinds of work but merely that all labor had the same psychological dimension. People, from this perspective, are older children driven by pleasure and restricted by social norms. Unconsciously we prefer the womb, a kind of Garden of Eden, to the responsibilities of maturity. In other words, we would prefer to remain in childhood but are driven out by the harshness of the world where reality rather than pleasure governs.

Work also serves the instinct to survive and to meet the types of scarcity which living presents. Once this minimum is met, however, work loses its instrumental quality and may serve the intrinsic interest of people. This raises the issue of the place of working competence. Under real scarcity one can understand why competence is highly valued since working productivity may mean the difference between living and dying. If scarcity is not an issue, then work satisfaction becomes more important than work competence. This assumes that one can enjoy and grow while engaging in competent work. To place the emphasis on working competence signifies the needs of society for better goods and services while placing the emphasis on work satisfaction reflects the importance of the individual. Ideal work for Freud is more like a hobby or even childhood play.

Freud preferred artistic and especially scientific hobbies to the crafts and trades. This reflects a personal bias since any kind of work could serve as a hobby, depending on the interest and talent of the person involved. Nevertheless, one would assume that highly specialized work has less intrinsic appeal. Therefore, the need for specialization, like work competence, would depend on the scarcity of goods and services, or, to be more accurate, the perceived scarcity of goods and services.

A disturbing element in Freud's work is a lack of faith in the ability of people to lead intelligent lives and to govern themselves democratically. The mind, he emphasized, was capable of justifying the most unreasonable views. Political candidates, for example, were favored not because of their programs, but because of their ability to serve as father substitutes.[7]   Racism, like our choice of political candidates, is basically the projection of our own forbidden desires onto another group. To dislike some group is a way to express our desire for the kind of life we attribute to that group. Blacks are disliked by whites because they are perceived as having sexual values, that whites repress. Fundamentally, Freud argues, the mind is an instrument for rationalization and censorship rather than reason. This explains Freud's skepticism about democracy.[8]

Freud was content with an apolitical response to widespread alienating work. He advises us to find the best possible job; take comfort in family life; develop an appreciation for the artistic and scientific dimensions of culture; free yourself from the stupid taboos. Human suffering engenders, for Freud, the courageous acceptance of the tragedy of life and the necessity of conformity.

Herzberg and the Worker-Consumer

A more recent and equally provocative theory of work has been developed by the American psychologist, Frederick Herzberg.[9] He insists that industrialized societies serve to create material overabundance at the expense of meaningful work. His criteria for meaningfulness are developed both ethically and factually.

Ethically, he argues, our fundamental concern should be the elimination of pain caused by human scarcity. That concern reflects our animal dimension and is concerned with food, shelter, clothing and a safe and congenial environment. The irony is that we are capable of being dominated by this pain-avoidance motivation while enjoying a high level of consumption. The modern preoccupation with money and things only reflects one dimension of our humanity. One advantage of pre-industrial work was its ability to be responsive to real scarcity and pain. Work was viewed as successful and meaningful only if it protected life. Work in industrial countries is viewed as having little intrinsic merit and is judged by how much it pays and the leisure it affords.[10] The disaster, at least in industrial societies, is that work continues to be viewed as an instrument not so much to eliminate real scarcity and danger but as a means to overconsume. Consequently, theories have developed to justify consumerism on the one hand and poverty on the other. For example, the idea of the religious elect grew popular among the well off because they were God's favorites who were chosen to enjoy a high level of consumption compromised by the hand of distasteful work. More importantly, from Herzberg's viewpoint, work continues to be viewed in terms of pain and avoidance criteria rather than a way to develop our moral and intellectual capacities. Human growth, like Marx's notion of unalienated labor, should be the aim of work rather than salary. Growth must be defined intellectually and emotionally and work must meet these ends.

On an intellectual level, work must provide conditions where we can get new information, see new relationships between experiences, and have an opportunity to play with ideas and to create. Work, he insists, does not provide these opportunities since it is usually boring and routine. Work must also provide for recognition, promotion, and a sense of achievement.

Further, the emotional criteria refer to our ability to enhance certain types of motivations. For example, we must be motivated by ambiguous situations which provide opportunities to be effective. We must also be motivated by a need to protect our integrity when it is in conflict with employers' expectations. Work, consequently, should produce conflict, and a certain measure of anxiety and insecurity. In other words. we must be motivated by real growth of personality rather than the symbols society uses to reward people. Thus, money, awards, and other symbols of status, must never be confused with real personality development.

Another facet of Herzberg's analysis resulted from the study he conducted to determine the factors that made work meaningful in industrial societies. The work experience, he argued, can be divided into two distinct categories—pain avoidance and growth. Work satisfaction, like life itself, must provide us with growth of personality and also help us to avoid pain. What facets of work help to avoid pain? Herzberg's study suggests that people regard the working environment, company policy, supervision, relationship with peers, and salary with the minimum standards they expect from their jobs. When people did not feel their jobs met these standards, they experienced job dissatisfaction. Yet, when these conditions were improved, the long-term experience of workers was not job satisfaction but merely no job dissatisfaction. Consequently, observes Herzberg, "the opposite of job satisfaction would not be dissatisfaction but no job satisfaction; similarly, the opposite of job dissatisfaction is no job dissatisfaction, not satisfaction with one's job."[11]   For instance, if people are dissatisfied with their salaries and subsequently get adequate salaries, the longterm effect of the increase is not work satisfaction but no work dissatisfaction. The reason, Herzberg contends, is that salary and the other minimum standards only respond to our need to survive and maintain ourselves and not to personal growth. Employers subsequently became confused when people experienced no job satisfaction since work was dull and no job dissatisfaction since it paid well. What they ignore is the other quality of meaning—namely how work should enhance growth. It is a mistake to assume that workers are one-dimensional and only motivated by the need to avoid pain and other discomforts. What if people are motivated by pain avoidance criteria while enjoying abundance? Further, what if the same people do not have any of the symptoms usually associated with unhappiness and psychological poor health? What, in other words, do we say if people are psychologically asymptomatic but are motivated by the consumption principle? Herzberg gives a straightforward reply. They are sick.[12]   These neurotics suffer from the incorrect motivation endemic to our culture. On the other hand, people who do not have jobs conducive to their own growth and are forced to settle for work which is merely instrumental to survival are healthy if they are motivated by growth criteria in areas outside their work. Minorities and women, for instance, may be denied access to work which fulfills a growth standard. Herzberg also notes that women and minorities are often denied work which meets the pain avoidance standard.

Herzberg, Marx, and Freud

Herzberg's standard for growth-oriented work is very similar to that of Marx, with one exception—Herzberg's notion of advancement as a result of doing well is not mentioned by Marx. Why? Herzberg does not invent the standard for fulfilling work but derives it from a study of workers. Professional and blue collar workers were studied to ascertain the factors in work which had a lasting effect in motivating people to work. Advancement plays a large role in industrial societies in motivating people to work. This is consequently reflected in Herzberg's study. Marx, on the other hand, has an intuitive standard for fulfilling work. Whether the majority of people are motivated by Marx's standard is irrelevant since the majority may be unduly influenced by unreasonable values. Unlike Marx, Herzberg is optimistic about our ability to evoke a human consensus which will lead to a de-emphasis on pain avoidance considerations. He appeals to management, labor and government to re-examine their partnership with consumerism and distasteful work. Unlike Freud, Herzberg has faith in persuasion, reason, and imagination as a way to deliver our culture from the worship of pain avoidance considerations. He feels that, even in less democratic countries, pain avoidance motivators will be replaced, since the inclusion of more humane motivators will result in higher production. Marx argues that capitalism is a debasement of the worker and insists, unlike Herzberg, that private property interests will fight any attempt to grant workers power over the process of production. Furthermore, Herzberg's assumption about the eventual cooperation of management and labor depends on higher production. If production dropped, but the general working population enjoyed more meaningful work, management would have some incentive to return to pain avoidance motivators and the envisioned cooperation between management and worker would be compromised.

How, then, is work improvement possible? Freud's argument seems to be the most apolitical since political activities are usually reducible to a psychological explanation. The political radical is a male who has failed to work out an authority conflict with his father. His adult political behavior reflects a childhood experience. Freud does hint that societies can be unnecessarily repressive and that some type of political activism is the only responsible response.[13]   Still he emphasizes especially for women the sexual facet of work to the exclusion of work enrichment and equality of opportunity.

For Marx, the repressiveness in capitalist society is more unfair than irrational. For example, women are generally assigned jobs with less responsibility and lower wages regardless of their ability. An unnatural division of labor exists between classes and among sexes. However, Marx insists that the only natural division of labor is sexual reproduction.[14]   Capital supports these detailed divisions of labor because of a higher profit or for economic growth. The institutions under capitalism, such as churches, schools, and the political ideology, can be models of rationality supporting the economic system's reliance on alienated labor. Change can be achieved through violence in the more repressive states, and political activism in the more progressive countries. Finally, Herzberg sees change as a realization that consumerism only relies on survival criteria; a neurotic motivation to be overcome if we only examine the qualities of our lives. He believes the current economic structure has the capacity for improvement.

Schooling and Working

Freud, Marx, and Herzberg all insist that the basis for the

understanding of schooling lies outside that institution. Freud, for example, found that the basis of schooling is the human psyche as it comes to be expressed in a rational community. A good school would be a place where we would pay homage to the need for social control yet never ignore indirect avenues of instinctual gratification. Marx argues that the foundation for understanding the school is not so much the study of psychology as a study of the modes of production. To understand schools one must look at that institution which reflects the predominant ethical principle of the community—the political economy. Nevertheless, the political economy may demand schooling objectives which make capital more efficient even as it risks undercutting its power over people. For instance, compulsory education laws in nineteenth century England reflected a need generated by capitalism for a more educated work force. Yet the laws had the potential of helping workers come to a better understanding of their powers and thus would eventually weaken the control of capitalism. Learning basic skills had the potential of liberating the worker. Herzberg also looks at the economy to discover the prevailing motivations of schooling. He maintains that the political economy is fundamentally irrational since it emphasizes the achievement of money rather than the emotional and intellectual satisfaction derived from meaningful work. Schools, for Herzberg as well as Marx, reflect the prevailing economic climate with its emphasis on consumerism. Schools, for Herzberg, are dominated by irrational goals since they are committed to pain avoidance and consumption, not health.[15]

In sum, all three thinkers view the school reflecting either basic psychological and/or economic dispositions. Working and schooling must be evaluated within some ethical framework like unalienated labor for Marx, satisfactory work for Herzberg, and the healthy personality for Freud.

Let us now turn to the examination of some school practices which directly relate to work. A prevailing characteristic of the school is grading. This practice reflects the belief in the importance of individual attainment and accomplishment. Grades and other school symbols of achievement conform fairly well with the workplace emphasis on pay, titles, and awards. Grades, like pay, reflect levels of mastering information, skills, and attitudes. The competitive model for the school, in other words, reflects a wider commitment to an economy where people compete for material scarcity and status Grading also serves as an explanation and justification for the wide range of income:

those who do well in school go to the better colleges and have the opportunity to gain entrance to better paying jobs.

When good grades open placement to high salaries and even consumerism, then the practice of grading fits very well into what Herzberg calls the pain avoidance structure of work. Marxist thinkers, on the other hand, view the schools' emphasis on grades as a sign of our belief in equality of opportunity which serves the myth that we all have a fair, if not equal, chance of high income and good jobs if we do well in school. Freud, on the other hand, is well aware that grades and other social awards reflected achievement as defined by society, which compromises our need to stay aware of our instinctual foundation. The respected person may exhibit high levels of instinctual denial when motivated by social rewards. From this perspective, the poor and unpretentious are healthier than the ambitious.

Their analysis of the workplace also explains our preference for certain types of knowledge, especially in higher education. For instance, we emphasize those natural sciences which have vocational promise. Thus physics is preferred over paleontology and psychology preferred over anthropology. Even the humanities are seen as they may relate to further graduate training or given some other vocational rationale.

This type of schooling encourages specialization and passivity and may be fit training for authoritative, specialized, and intrinsically unrewarding work. This is especially the case where management plays the central role in production. For instance, we begin with a situation which must be changed or transformed by methods communicated by management for a desired result. In other words, people are told to change situation A to desired outcome B by using method C. All three factors are preprogrammed by management. Herzberg, Marx, and to some extent, Freud, argue that if work is to fulfill intellectual criteria, one or more of the three factors must be missing from work. Satisfying work must be based on what the worker can figure out rather than what management knows.

The school model that resembles the work model of three determined areas of information is rather obvious. Usually the students learn to define the initial situation or that which needs transforming by following the lead of the teacher. Then the appropriate method which would transform the initial situation into the predetermined desired outcome is given. Thus, school, like work, is a place to learn the answers to problems determined by others. These methods give people the message that passive processing of information is the way to work and school success.[16]

Herzberg argues that stimulating work, that is, work which enables people to grow intellectually and emotionally, can be more productive than the passive application of skills and information. He raises an interesting possibility for schools. What would schools look like if the overriding demand was not the inculcation of information but the moral and intellectual growth of the student? That is to say, would students become more productive economically if the school became an institution for intellectual and moral stimulation?

When work must be productive as well as stimulating, we raise an ethical dilemma. What should we do if stimulating work is also less productive? In Sweden, workers and managers have turned away from the traditional automobile assembly line in several Volvo plants.[17] They have employed a team approach for the assembly of cars and trucks despite the fact that this method is *less* productive. Nevertheless, Volvo decided against reverting to the assembly line because workers and managers insisted that productivity should not outweigh employee's satisfaction. In other words, a tension exists between the needs for higher productivity and job satisfaction. Volvo insisted that unskilled tasks should be eliminated as much as possible and replaced by tasks which demand complexity, sharing of information and group consensus. A school which emphasized acceptance of authority, rote memory, competition and grades, would be inconsistent with a workplace which emphasized creative group processes and sharing of information and group responsibility. Needless to say, Sweden must restrict the importation of cheaper cars to keep higher priced Volvos competitive.

However, one must be rather careful in assigning to the school any mechanical consequences resulting from a changing pattern of work. Certainly the fetish we have for grades would diminish if working and living were less competitive. Nevertheless, teachers and parents may find ways in which grades could point to student potentials and abilities. The encouragement to foster one's potential by some form of evaluation rests on criteria which may range from Herzberg's growth formula to Marx's individualistic criteria under communism. To some, individualistic criteria may translate into a de-emphasis on grades since the appeal to a common standard becomes more difficult. To others, children must conform to some standard because of their immaturity. The point is that if the nature of work changes, we should begin to debate and experiment with ways in which grading meets the new concept of work. The evaluation of a new concept of work can only occur when child rearing that is consistent with the new concept of work has been experienced and debated.

The problem of work not only involves what kind of work brings human satisfaction, but also the additional problem of how to treat the young and inexperienced, given a new vision. We must also be sensitive to the possibility that what we may regard as ideal work or a prerequisite to the world of ideal work, may be regarded by students as toil. To ignore or dismiss the students' views and adopt ways which bypass their objections may establish relationships which we do not wish to foster with new concepts of work.

This essay looks at the relationship between scarcity, human meaning, and work and how that relationship disciplines schools. Work is a key idea for an understanding of school policy. If we want to change the school, we must first consider changing the ways in which we work. The effecting of radical school policy will come to nothing if we do not change our working lives. Educators are left then with a painful dilemma. If we treat children in ways which envision more humane work, we are preparing them for a working world that, for most people, does not exist. If, on the other hand, we emphasize the knowledge, skill, and attitudes which will make them acceptable to current working practices, we are preparing them for working lives which are, in many ways, quite alienating. This conclusion may be quite upsetting for teachers and educators, since they have long believed that the quality of life will dramatically improve if the quality of schools improves. This essay suggests the contrary: Schools will dramatically change when we insist that work should bring a high level of personal satisfaction and growth.

Notes ─────────────────────────────

[1] V.I. Lenin, "The Immediate Task of the Soviet Government," in *Collected Work* vol. 27 (Moscow, 1965): 259.

[2] Herbert Marcuse, *One Dimensional Man* (Boston: Beacon Press, 1964): 5.

[3] Karl Marx, *Economic and Philosophical Manuscripts*, in *Karl Marx: Selected Writings*, edited by David McLellan, (London: Oxford University Press, 1977): 80-81. All references to Marx are from this edition, unless otherwise noted.

[4] Quoted by David McLellan in "Marx's View of the Unalienated Society," *The Review of Politics* 31 (October 1969): 465.

[5] Marx, *Toward a Critique of Hegel's Philosophy of Right: Introduction*, in McLellan, 77.

[6] Sigmund Freud, *Civilization and Its Discontents*, edited and translated by James Stracheys (New York: W.W. Norton, 1961): 26. Also see Erik Erikson's account in *Identity and the Life Cycle* (New York: International Universities Press, 1960): 100.

[7] Philip Rieff, *Freud: The Mind of the Moralist* (Garden City: Doubleday and Co., 1959): 13.

[8] Freud, *Civilization*, 13.

[9] Frederick Herzberg, *Work and the Nature of Man* (New York: T.V. Crowell, 1966).

[10] Marx, *Grundrisse*, in McLellan, 363.

[11] Herzberg, *Work*, 76.

[12] *Ibid.*, 83-89.

[13] Herbert Marcuse, *Eros and Civilization* (Boston: Beacon Press, 1974): 50.

[14] Karl Marx, *The German Ideology*, in McLellan, 167.

[15] Herzberg, *Work*, 175.

[16] Martin Carnoy and Henry M. Levin, *Schooling and Work in the Democratic State* (Stanford: Stanford University Press, 1985): 110-143. They argue that schools in working class neighborhoods are much more demanding of conforming behavior than schools in affluent areas. They suggest that school practices must be seen as reflecting class distinctions. While I believe this observation to be true, I have written in more general terms and have not emphasized different levels of passivity.

[17] "Manufacturing: The Assembly Team," *Newsweek*, August 21, 1972: 69; Norman Eiger, "The Workplace as Classroom for Democracy: The Swedish Experience," *New York University Educational Quarterly* (Summer 1982): 16-23.

* I am grateful to my friend and colleague Robert A. Stein for his helpful criticism of this article.

Chapter 2

Introduction to Jane Roland Martin

Jane Roland Martin argues that Richard Rodriguez's education is mainly concerned with the development of rational powers, "disembodied minds." She describes his autobiography as a "narrative of loss," "story of alienation" and a "journey from intimacy to isolation."

To be educated, Martin argues, Rodriguez had to make the transition from a private world (Spanish) to a public world (English). In this transition he had to forget the sounds and feelings of his native home, and to learn a new language that inducted him into schools and the society at large.

What is ironic in Rodriguez's case is that his private activities and his culture do not serve his preparation for work in this culture. In fact, they are road blocks. This gives rise to what Wallace Lambert considers a subtractive bilingualism, in which it is necessary to eradicate the native language and culture so as to make room for and not interfere with the process of second language acquisition. The negative implications of this action are profusely illustrated in the autobiography.

The subtractive bilingualism, in Rodriguez's case, perhaps helped him to become "educated" yet the emotional and psychological price was too high since it produced confusion, alienation and loss of self identity.

Richard Rodriguez maintains this view because he found it difficult to live in both worlds. The liberal education that he was pursuing did not fit with his private world. Paradoxically, liberal education that tries to emancipate the individual, can also imprison and deprive them of their own cultural and linguistic heritage.

Martin redesigns the concept of education, to include both the productive and reproductive processes of society. This redefinition is of crucial importance to students who have culturally and linguistically diverse backgrounds.

If we continue endorsing the traditional concept of liberal education, while ignoring its reproductive quality, we do so at the risk of continuing to allow for the development of individuals whose biographies may also be viewed as "a narrative of loss."

After reading this article please consider the following questions:

1. What would you make of the author's redefinition of the concept of education?

2. Do you think that to be educated, language minority students need to risk transitions like Richard Rodriguez?

3. Should the language and cultural background of language minority students be part of the curriculum?

4. Do you think that the use of dual languages as a medium of instruction will benefit the education of language minority students?

Becoming Educated: A Journey of Alienation or Integration?

by *Jane Roland Martin*

"Becoming Educated: A Journey of Alienation or Integration?" Jane Roland Martin. Reprinted from *Journal of Education*, Boston University School of Education (1985), Vol. #167, with permission from the Trustees of Boston University (copyright holder) and the author.

Today's journey of becoming educated is one of the alienation of mind from body, thought from action, reason from feeling and emotion, and self from other. Education does not have to be alienating. Our contemporary journey is a function of a definition of the educational realm and an ideal of the educated person that can be rejected. For the sake of the individual and society and, indeed, of the earth itself, an integrative journey must be substituted for our alienating one. The tasks of redefinition and reconstruction can only be accomplished, however, if we acknowledge the workings of gender in educational theory and remain sensitive to them in our practice.

In his educational autobiography *Hunger of Memory*, Richard Rodriguez tells of growing up in Sacramento, California, the third of four children in a Spanish-speaking family.[1] Upon entering first grade he could understand perhaps 50 English words. Within the year his teachers convinced his parents to speak only English at home and Rodriguez soon became fluent in the language. By the time he graduated from elementary school with citations galore and entered high school, he had read hundreds of books. He went on to attend Stanford University and, 20 years after his parents' decision to abandon their native tongue, he sat in the British Museum writing a PhD dissertation in English literature.

Rodriguez learned to speak English and went on to acquire a liberal education. History, literature, science, mathematics, philosophy: these he studied and made his own. Rodriguez's story is of the cultural assimilation of a Mexican-American, but it is more than this, for by no means do all assimilated Americans conform to our image of a well-educated person. Rodriguez does because, to use the terms the philosopher R.S. Peters employs in his analysis of the concept of the educated man, he did not simply acquire knowledge and skill.[2] He acquired conceptual schemes to raise his knowledge beyond the level of a collection of disjointed facts and to enable him to understand the "reason why" of things. Moreover, the knowledge he acquired is not "inert": It characterizes the way he looks at the world and it involves the kind of commitment to the standards of evidence and canons of proof of the various disciplines that comes from "getting on the inside of a form of thought and awareness."[3]

Quite a success story, yet *Hunger of Memory* is notable primarily as a narrative of loss. In becoming an educated person Rodriguez loses his fluency in Spanish, but that is the least of it. As soon as English becomes the language of the Rodriguez family, the special feeling of closeness at home is diminished. Furthermore, as his days are increasingly devoted to understanding the meaning of words, it becomes difficult for Rodriguez to hear intimate family voices. When it is Spanish-speaking, his home is a noisy, playful, warm, emotionally charged environment; with the advent of English the atmosphere becomes quiet and restrained. There is no acrimony. The family remains loving. But the experience of "feeling individualized" by family members is now rare, and occasions for intimacy are infrequent.

Rodriguez tells a story of alienation: from his parents, for whom he soon has no names; from the Spanish language, in which he loses his childhood fluency; from his Mexican roots, in which he shows no interest; from his own feelings and emotions, which all but disappear as he learns to control them; from his body itself, as he discovers when he takes a construction job after his senior year in college.

John Dewey spent his life trying to combat the tendency of educators to divorce mind from body and reason from emotion. Rodriguez's educational autobiography documents these divorces, and another one Dewey deplored, that of self from other. Above all, *Hunger of Memory* depicts a journey from intimacy to isolation. Close ties with family members are dissolved as public anonymity replaces private attention. Rodriguez becomes a spectator in his own home as noise gives way to silence and connection to distance. School, says Rodriguez, bade him trust "lonely" reason primarily. And there is enough time and "silence," he adds, "to think about ideas (big ideas)".[4]

What is the significance of this narrative of loss? Not every American has Rodriguez's good fortune of being born into a loving home filled with the warm sounds of intimacy, yet the separation and distance he ultimately experienced are not unique to him. On the contrary, they represent the natural end point of the educational journey Rodriguez took.

Dewey repeatedly pointed out that the distinction educators draw between liberal and vocational education represents a separation of mind from body, head from hand, thought from action. Since we define an educated person as one who has had and has profited from a liberal education, these splits are built into our ideal of the educated person. Since most definitions of excellence in education derive from that ideal, these splits are built into them as well. A split between reason and emotion is built into our definitions of excellence too, for we take the aim of a liberal education to be the development not of mind as a whole, but of rational mind. We define this in terms of the acquisition of knowledge and understanding, construed narrowly.[5] It is not surprising that Rodriguez acquires habits of quiet reflection rather than noisy activity, reasoned deliberation rather than spontaneous reaction, dispassionate inquiry rather than emotional response, abstract analytic theorizing rather than concrete storytelling. These are integral to the ideal of the educated person that has come down to us from Plato.

Upon completion of his educational journey Rodriguez bears a remarkable resemblance to the guardians of the Just State that Plato constructs in the *Republic*. Those worthies are to acquire through their education a wide range of theoretical knowledge, highly developed powers of reasoning, and the qualities of objectivity and emotional distance. To be sure, not one of Plato's guardians will be the "disembodied mind" Rodriguez becomes, for Plato believed that a strong mind requires a strong body. But Plato designed for his guardians an education of heads, not hands. (Presumably the artisans of the Just State would serve as their hands.) Moreover, considering the passions to be unruly and untrustworthy, Plato held up for the guardians an ideal of self-discipline and self-government in which reason keeps feeling and emotion under tight control. As a consequence, although he wanted the guardians of the Just State to be so connected to one another that they would feel each other's pains and pleasures, the educational ideal he developed emphasizes "inner" harmony at the expense of "outward" connection. If his guardians do not begin their lives in intimacy, as Rodriguez did, their education, like his, is intended to confirm in them a sense of self in isolation from others.

Do the separations bequeathed to us by Plato matter? The great irony of the liberal education that comes down to us from Plato and still today as the mark of an educated person is that it is neither tolerant nor generous.[6] As Richard Rodriguez discovered, there is no place in it for education of the body, and since most action involves bodily movement, this means there is little room in it for education of action. Nor is there room for education of other-regarding feelings and emotions. The liberally educated person will be provided with knowledge about others, but will not be taught to care about their welfare or to act kindly toward them. That person will be given some understanding of society, but will not be taught to feel its injustices or even to be concerned over its fate. The liberally educated person will be an ivory tower person—one who can reason but has no desire to solve real problems in the real world—or else a technical person who likes to solve real problems but does not care about the solutions' consequences for real people and for the earth itself.

The case of Rodriguez illuminates several unhappy aspects of our Platonic heritage, while concealing another. No one who has seen Frederick Wiseman's film *High School* can forget the woman who reads to the assembled students a letter she has received from a pupil now in Vietnam. But for a few teachers who cared, she tells her audience, Bob Walters, a sub-average student academically, "might have been a nobody." Instead, while awaiting a plane that is to drop him behind the DMZ, he has written her to say that he has made the school the beneficiary of his life insurance policy. "I am a little jittery right now," she reads. She is not to worry about him, however, because "I am only a body doing a job." Measuring his worth as a human being by his provision for the school, she overlooks the fact that Bob Walters was not merely participating in a war of dubious morality but was taking pride in being an automaton.

High School was made in 1968, but Bob Walters's words were echoed many times over by 18- and 19-year-old Marine recruits in the days immediately following the Grenada invasion. Readers of *Hunger of Memory* will not be surprised. The underside of a liberal education devoted to the development of "disembodied minds" is a vocational education whose business is the production of "mindless bodies." In Plato's Just State, where, because of their rational powers, the specially educated few will rule the many, a young man's image of himself as "only a body doing a job" is the desired one. That the educational theory and practice of a democracy derives from Plato's explicitly undemocratic philosophical vision is disturbing. We are not supposed to have two classes of people, those who think and those who do not. We are not supposed to have two kinds of people, those who rule and those who obey.

The Council for Basic Education has long recommended, and some people concerned with excellence in education now suggest, that a liberal education at least through high school be extended to all. For the sake of argument let us suppose that this program can be carried out without making more acute the inequities it is meant to erase. We would then presumably have a world in which no one thinks of him- or herself as simply a body doing a job. We would, however, have a world filled with unconnected, uncaring, emotionally impoverished people. Even if it were egalitarian, it would be a sorry place in which to live. Nor would the world be better if somehow we combined Rodriguez's liberal education with a vocational one. For assuming it to be peopled by individuals who joined head and hand, reason would still be divorced from feeling and emotion, and each individual cut off from others.

The world we live in is just such a place. It is a world of child abuse and family violence,[7] a world in which one out of every four women will be raped at some time in her life.[8] Our world is on the brink of nuclear and/or ecological disaster. Efforts to overcome these problems, as well as the related ones of poverty and economic scarcity, flounder today under the direction of people who try hard to be rational, objective, autonomous agents but, like Plato's guardians, do not know how to sustain human relationships or respond directly to human needs. Indeed, they do not even see the value of trying to do so. Of course, it is a mistake to suppose that education alone can solve this world's problems. Yet if there is to be hope of the continuation of life on earth, let alone of a good life for all, as educators we must strive to do more than join mind and body, head and hand, thought and action.

Redefining Education

For Rodriguez, the English language is a metaphor. In the literal sense of the term he had to learn English to become an educated *American*, yet, in his narrative the learning of English represents the acquisition not so much of a new natural language as of new ways of thinking, acting, and being that he associates with the public world. Rodriguez makes it clear that the transition from Spanish to English represented for him the transition almost every child in our society makes from the "private world" of home to the "public world" of business, politics, and culture. He realizes that Spanish is not intrinsically a private language and English a public one, although his own experiences made it seem this way. He knows that the larger significance of his story lies in the fact that education inducts one into new activities and processes.

In my research on the place of women in educational thought I have invoked a distinction between the productive and the reproductive processes of society and have argued that both historians of educational thought and contemporary philosophers of education define the educational realm in relation to society's productive processes only.[9] Briefly, the reproductive processes include not simply the biological reproduction of the species, but the rearing of children to maturity and the related activities of keeping house, managing a household, and serving the needs and purposes of family members. In turn, the productive processes include political, social, and cultural activities as well as economic ones. This distinction is related to the one Rodriguez repeatedly draws between public and private worlds, for in our society reproductive processes are for the most part carried on in the private world of the home and domesticity, and productive processes in the public world of politics and work. Rodriguez's autobiography reveals that the definition of education as preparation solely for carrying on the productive processes of society is not a figment of the academic imagination.

Needless to say, the liberal education Rodriguez received did not fit him to carry on all productive processes of society. Aiming at the development of rational mind, his liberal education prepared him to be a consumer and creator of ideas, not an auto mechanic or factory worker. A vocational education, had he received one, would have prepared him to work with his hands and use procedures designed by others. They are very different kinds of education, yet both are designed to fit students to carry on productive, not reproductive, societal processes.

Why do I stress the connection between the definition of education and the productive processes of society? *Hunger of Memory* contains a wonderful account of Rodriguez's grandmother telling him stories of her life. He is moved by the sounds she makes and by the message of intimacy her person transmits. The words themselves are not important to him, for he perceives the private world in which she moves—the world of childrearing and homemaking—to be one of feeling and emotion, intimacy and connection, and hence a realm of the nonrational. In contrast, he sees the public world—the world of productive processes for which his education fit him—as the realm of the rational. Feeling and emotion have no place in it, and neither do intimacy and connection. Instead, analysis, critical thinking, and self-sufficiency are the dominant values.

Rodriguez's assumption that feeling and emotion, intimacy and connection are naturally related to the home and society's reproductive processes and that these qualities are irrelevant to carrying on the productive processes is commonly accepted. But then, it is to be expected that their development is ignored by education in general and by liberal education in particular. Since education is supposed to equip people for carrying on productive societal processes, from a practical standpoint would it not be foolhardy for liberal *or* vocational studies to foster these traits?

Only in light of the fact that education turns its back on the reproductive processes of society and the private world of the home can Rodriguez's story of alienation be understood. His alienation from his body will reoccur so long as we equate being an educated person with having a liberal education. His journey of isolation and divorce from his emotions will be repeated so long as we define education exclusively in relation to the productive processes of society. But the assumption of inevitability underlying *Hunger of Memory* is mistaken. Education need not separate mind from body and thought from action, for it need not draw a sharp line between liberal and vocational education. More to the point, it need not separate reason from emotion and self from other. The reproductive processes *can* be brought into the educational realm thereby overriding the theoretical and practical grounds for ignoring feeling and emotion, intimacy and connection.

If we define education in relation to *both* kinds of societal processes and act upon our redefinition, future generations will not have to experience Rodriguez's pain. He never questions the fundamental dichotomies upon which his education rests. We must question them so that we can effect the reconciliation of reason and emotion, self and other, that Dewey sought. There are, moreover, two overwhelming reasons for favoring such a redefinition, both of which take us beyond Dewey.

All of us—male and female—participate in the reproductive processes of society. In the past, many have thought that education for carrying them on was not necessary: These processes were assumed to be the responsibility of women and it was supposed that by instinct a woman would automatically acquire the traits or qualities associated with them. The contemporary statistics on child abuse are enough by themselves to put to rest the doctrine of maternal instinct. Furthermore, both sexes have responsibility for making the reproductive processes of society work well. Family living and childrearing are not today, if they ever were, solely in the hands of women. Nor should they be. Thus, both sexes need to learn to carry on the reproductive processes of society just as in the 1980s both sexes need to learn to carry on the productive ones.

The reproductive processes are of central importance to society, yet it would be a terrible mistake to suppose that the traits and qualities traditionally associated with these processes have no relevance beyond them. Jonathan Schell has said, "The nuclear peril makes all of us, whether we happen to have children of our own or not, the parents of all future generations" and that the will we must have to save the human species is a form of love resembling "the generative love of parents."[10] He is speaking of what Nancy Chodorow calls nurturing capacities[11] and Carol Gilligan calls an "ethics of care."[12] Schell is right. The fate of the earth depends on all of us possessing these qualities. Thus, although these qualities are associated in our minds with the reproductive processes of society, they have the broadest moral, social, and political significance. Care, concern, connectedness, nurturance are as important for carrying on society's economic, political, and social processes as its reproductive ones. If education is to help us acquire them, it must be redefined.

The Workings of Gender

It is no accident that in *Hunger of Memory* the person who embodies nurturing capacities and an ethics of care is a woman—Rodriguez's grandmother. The two kinds of societal processes are gender-related and so are the traits our culture associates with them. According to our cultural stereotypes, males are objective, analytical, rational, interested in ideas and things. They have no interpersonal orientation; they are not nurturant or supportive, empathetic or sensitive. Women, on the other hand, possess the traits men lack.[13]

Education is also gender-related. Our definition of its function makes it so. For if education is viewed as preparation for carrying on processes historically associated with males, it will inculcate traits the culture considers masculine. If the concept of education is tied by definition to the productive processes of society, our ideal of the educated person will coincide with the cultural stereotype of a male human being, and our definitions of excellence in education will embody "masculine" traits.

Of course, it is possible for members of one sex to acquire personal traits or qualities our cultural stereotypes attribute to the other. Thus, females can and do acquire traits incorporated in our educational ideal. However, it must be understood that these traits are *genderized*; that is, they are appraised differentially when they are possessed by males and females.[14] For example, whereas a male will be admired for his rational powers, a woman who is analytical and critical will be derided or shunned or will be told that she thinks like a man. Even if this latter is intended as a compliment, since we take masculinity and femininity to lie at opposite ends of a single continuum, she will thereby be judged as lacking in femininity and, as a consequence, judged abnormal or unnatural. Elizabeth Janeway has said, and I am afraid she is right, that "unnatural" and "abnormal" are the equivalent for our age of what "damned" meant to our ancestors.[15]

Because his hands were soft Rodriguez worried that his education was making him effeminate.[16] Imagine his anxieties on that score if he had been educated in those supposedly feminine virtues of caring and concern and had been taught to sustain intimate relationships and value connection. To be sure, had his education fostered these qualities, Rodriguez would not have had to travel a road from intimacy to isolation. I do not mean to suggest that there would have been no alienation at all; his is a complex case involving class, ethnicity, and color. But an education is which reason was joined to feeling and emotion and self to other would have yielded a very different life story. Had his education fostered these qualities, however, Rodriguez would have experienced another kind of hardship.

The pain Rodriguez suffers is a consequence of the loss of intimacy and the stunting of emotional growth that are themselves consequences of education. Now it is possible that Rodriguez's experience is more representative of males than of females. But if it be the case that females tend to maintain emotional growth and intimate connections better than males do, one thing is certain: educated girls are penalized for what Rodriguez considers his *gains*. If they become analytic, objective thinkers and autonomous agents, they are judged less feminine than they should be. Thus, for them the essential myth of childhood is every bit as painful as it was for Rodriguez, for they are alienated from their own identity as females.

When education is defined so as to give the reproductive processes of society their due, and the virtues of nurturance and care associated with those processes are fostered in both males and females, educated men can expect to suffer for possessing traits genderized in favor of females as educated women now do for possessing traits genderized in favor of males. This is not to say that males will be placed in the double bind educated females find themselves in now, for males will acquire traits genderized in their own favor as well as ones genderized in favor of females, whereas the traits educated females must acquire today are *all* genderized in favor of males. On the other hand, since traits genderized in favor of females are considered lesser virtues, if virtues at all,[17] and the societal processes with which they are associated are thought to be relatively unimportant, males will be placed in the position of having to acquire traits both they and their society consider inferior.

One of the most important findings of contemporary scholarship is that our culture embraces a hierarchy of values that places the productive processes of society and their associated traits above society's reproductive processes and the associated traits of care and nurturance. There is nothing new about this. We are the inheritors of a tradition of Western thought according to which the functions, tasks, and traits associated with females are deemed less valuable than those associated with males. In view of these findings, the difficulties facing those of us who would transform Rodriguez's educational journey from one of alienation to one of the integration of reason and emotion, of self and other, become apparent.

It is important to understand the magnitude of the changes to be wrought by an education that takes the integration of reason and emotion, self and other, seriously. Granted, when girls today embark on Rodriguez's journey they acquire traits genderized in favor on the "opposite" sex; but if on account of trait genderization they experience hardships Rodriguez did not, they can at least console themselves that their newly acquired traits, along with the societal processes to which the traits are attached, are considered valuable. Were we to attempt to change the nature of our educational ideal without also changing our value hierarchy, boys and men would have no such consolation. Without this consolation, however, we can be quite sure that the change we desire would not come to pass.

Toward an Integrated Curriculum

Just as the value structure I have been describing is reflected in our ideal of the educated person, so too it is reflected in the curriculum such a person is supposed to study. A large body of scholarship documents the extent to which the academic fields constituting the subjects of the liberal curriculum exclude women's lives, works, and experiences from their subject matter or else distort them by projecting the cultural stereotype of a female onto the evidence.[18]   History, philosophy, politics; art and music; the social and behavioral sciences; even the biological and physical sciences give pride of place to male experience and achievements and to the societal processes thought to belong to men.

The research to which I refer reveals the place of women—or rather the absence thereof—in the theories, interpretations, and narratives constituting the disciplines of knowledge. Since the subject matter of the liberal curriculum is drawn from these disciplines, that curriculum gives pride of place to male experience and achievements and to the societal processes associated with men. In so doing, it is the bearer of bad news about women and the reproductive processes of society. Can it be doubted that when the works of women are excluded from the subject matter of the fields into which they are being initiated, students of both sexes will come to believe, or else will have their existing belief reinforced, that males are superior and females are inferior human beings? Can it be doubted that when in the course of this initiation the lives and experiences of women are scarcely mentioned, males and females will come to believe, or else believe more strongly than ever, that the ways in which women have lived and the things women have done throughout history have no value?

At campuses across the country projects are underway to incorporate the growing body of new scholarship on women into the liberal curriculum. Such efforts must be undertaken at all levels of schooling, not simply because women comprise one half the world's population, but because the exclusion of women from the subject matter of the "curriculum proper" constitutes a hidden curriculum in the validation of one gender, its associated tasks, traits, and functions, and the denigration of the other. Supporting our culture's genderized hierarchy of value even as it reflects it, this hidden curriculum must be raised to consciousness and counteracted.[19] Introduction of the new scholarship on women into the liberal curriculum proper—and for that matter into the vocational curriculum too—makes this possible, on the one hand because it allows students to understand the workings of gender and, on the other, because it provides them with the opportunity to appreciate women's traditional tasks, traits, and functions.

In a curriculum encompassing the experience of one sex, not two, questions of gender are automatically eliminated. For the value hierarchy under discussion to be understood, as it must be if it is to be abolished, its genderized roots must be exposed. Furthermore, if intimacy and connection are to be valued as highly as independence and distance, and if emotion and feeling are to viewed as positive rather than untrustworthy elements of personality, women must no longer be viewed as different and alien—as the Other, to use Simone de Beauvoir's expression.[20]

Thus, we need to incorporate the study of women into curricula so that females—their lives, experiences, works, and attributes—are devalued by neither sex. But simply incorporating the new scholarship on women in the curriculum does not address the alienation and loss Rodriguez describes so well. To overcome these we must seek not only a transformation of the content of curriculum proper, but an expansion of the educational realm to include the reproductive processes of society and a corresponding redefinition of what it means to become educated.

The expansion of the educational realm I propose does not entail an extension of a skill-oriented home economics education to males. Although it is important for both sexes to learn to cook and sew, I have in mind something different when I say that education must give the reproductive processes of society their due. The traits associated with women as wives and mothers—nurturance, care, compassion, connection, sensitivity to others, a willingness to put aside one's own projects, a desire to build and maintain relationships—need to be incorporated into our ideal. This does not mean that we should fill up the curriculum with courses in the three C's of caring, concern, and connection. Given a redefinition of education, Compassion 101a need no more be listed in a school's course offerings than Objectivity 101a is now. Just as the productive processes of society have given us the general curricular goals of rationality and individual autonomy, so too the reproductive processes yield general goals. And just as rationality and autonomy are posited as goals of particular subjects, e.g., science, as well as of the curriculum as a whole, so nurturance and connection can be understood as overarching educational goals and also as the goals of particular subjects.

But now a puzzling question arises. Given that the standard subjects of the curriculum derive from the productive processes of society, must we not insert cooking and sewing and perhaps childrearing into the curriculum if we want caring, concern, and connection to be educational objectives? Science, math, history, literature, auto mechanics, refrigeration, typing: these are the subjects of the curriculum now and these derive from productive processes. If for subjects deriving form productive processes we set educational goals whose source is the reproductive processes of society, do we not distort these subjects beyond recognition? But then, ought we not to opt instead for a divided curriculum with two sets of subjects? One set might be derived from the productive processes of society and foster traits associated with those, with the other set derived from the reproductive processes of society and fostering their associated traits. Is this the only way to do justice to both sets of traits?

If possible, a replication within the curriculum of the split between the productive and reproductive processes of society is to be avoided. So long as education insists on linking nurturing capacities and the three C's to subjects arising out of the reproductive processes, we will lose sight of their *general* moral, social, and political significance. Moreover, so long as rationality and autonomous judgment are considered to belong exclusively to the productive processes of society, the reproductive ones will continue to be devalued. Thus, unless it is essential to divide up curricular goals according to the classification of a subject as productive or reproductive, we ought not to do so. That it is not essential becomes clear once we give up our stereotypical pictures of the two kinds of societal processes.

Readers of June Goodfield's *An Imagined World* will know that feeling and emotion, intimacy and connection can be an integral part of the processes of scientific discovery.[21] Goodfield recorded the day-today activities of Anna, a Portuguese scientist studying lymphocytes in a cancer laboratory in New York. Anna's relationship to her colleagues *and* to the cells she studied provides quite a contrast to the rationalistic, atomistic vision of scientists and scientific discovery most of us have. To be sure, some years ago James Watson made it clear that scientists are human.[22] But Watson portrayed scientific discovery as a race between ambitious, aggressive, highly competitive contestants while Goodfield's Anna calls it "a kind of birth." Fear, urgency, intense joy; loneliness, intimacy, and a desire to share: these are some of the emotions that motivate and shape Anna's thought even as her reasoned analysis and her objective scrutiny of evidence engender passion. Moreover, she is bound closely to her colleagues in the lab by feeling, as well as by scientific need, and she empathizes with the lymphocytes she studies as well as with the sick people she hopes will one day benefit from her work.

If scientific activity can flourish in an atmosphere of cooperation and connection, and important scientific discoveries can take place when passionate feeling motivates and shapes thought, then surely it is not necessary for science education to be directed solely toward rationalistic, atomistic goals. And if nurturant capacities and the three C's of caring, concern, and connection can become goals of science teaching without that subject being betrayed or abandoned, surely they can become the goals of *any* subject.

By the same token, if rational thought and independent judgment are components of successful childrearing and family living, it is not necessary to design education in subjects deriving from the reproductive processes of society solely around "affective" goals. That they can and should be part and parcel of these activities was argued long ago, and very convincingly, by both Mary Wollstonecraft and Catharine Beecher[23] and is a basic tenet of the home economics profession today.

Thus, just as nurturance and concern can be goals of any subject, rationality and independent judgment can also be. The temptation to institute a sharp separation of goals within an expanded educational realm corresponding to a sharp separation of subjects must, then, be resisted so that the general significance of the very real virtues we associate with women and the reproductive processes of society is understood and these virtues themselves are fostered in everyone.

Conclusion

In becoming educated one does not have to travel Rodriguez's road from intimacy to isolation. His journey of alienation is a function of a definition of education, a particular ideal of the educated person, and a particular definition of excellence—all of which can be rejected. Becoming educated can be a journey of integration, not alienation. The detailed task of restructuring an ideal of the educated person to guide this new journey I leave for another occasion. The general problem to be solved is that of uniting thought and action, reason and emotion, self and other. This was the problem Dewey addressed, but his failure to understand the workings of gender made it impossible for him to solve it.

I leave the task of mapping the precise contours of a transformed curriculum for another occasion too. The general problem to be solved here is that of giving the reproductive processes of society—and the females who have traditionally been assigned responsibility for carrying them on—their due. Only then will feeling and emotion, intimacy and connection be perceived as valuable qualities so that a journey of integration is possible.

Loss, pain, isolation: It is a tragedy that these should be the results of becoming educated, the consequences of excellence. An alternative journey to Rodriguez's requires fundamental changes in both educational theory and practice. Since these changes will make it possible to diffuse throughout the population the nurturant capacities and the ethics of care that are absolutely essential to the survival of society itself, indeed, to the survival of life on earth, they should ultimately be welcomed even by those who would claim that the loss, pain, and isolation Rodriguez experienced in becoming educated did him no harm.

Notes

[1.] Richard Rodriguez, *Hunger of Memory* (Boston: David R. Godine, 1982).

[2.] R.S. Peters, "Education and the Educated Man," in *A Critique of Current Educational Aims*, edited by R.F. Dearden, P.H. Hirst & R.S. Peters (London: Routledge & Kegan Paul, 1972); R.S. Peters, *Ethics and Education* (London: Allen & Unwin, 1966).

[3.] Peters, *Ethics and Education*, 9.

[4.] Rodriguez, *Hunger of Memory*, 47.

[5.] Jane Roland Martin, "Needed: A New Paradigm For Liberal Education," in *Philosophy and Education*, J.F. Soltis, editor (Chicago: University of Chicago Press, 1981): 37-59.

[6.] *Ibid.*

[7.] W. Breins and L. Gordon, "The New Scholarship on Family Violence," *Signs* 8, no. 3 (1983): 493-507.

[8.] A.G. Johnson, "On the Prevalence of Rape in the United States," *Signs* 6, no. 1 (1980): 136-146; B. Lott, M.E. Reilly & D.R. Howard, "Sexual Assault and Harassment: A Campus Community Case Study," *Signs* 8, no. 2 (1982): 269-319.

[9.] Jane Roland Martin, "Excluding Women From the Educational Realm," *Harvard Educational Review* 52, no.2 (1982): 133-148; and *Reclaiming a Conversation: The Ideal of the Educated Woman* (New Haven: Yale University Press, 1985).

[10.] Jonathan Schell, *The Fate of the Earth* (New York: Avon, 1982): 175.

[11.] Nancy Chodorow, The *Reproduction of Mothering* (Berkeley: University of California Press, 1978).

[12.] Carol Gilligan, *In A Different Voice* (Cambridge: Harvard University Press, 1982).

[13.] A.G. Kaplan & J.P. Bean, editors, *Beyond Sex-Role Stereotypes* (Boston: Little, Brown, 1976); A.G. Kaplan & M.A. Sedney, *Psychology and Sex Roles* (Boston: Little, Brown, 1980).

[14.] E. Beardsley, "Traits and Genderization," in *Feminism and Philosophy*, edited by M. Vetterling-Braggin, F.A. Elliston, & J. English (Totowa, NJ: Littlefield, 1977); Jane Roland Martin, "The Ideal of the Educated Person," *Educational Theory* 31, no. 2 (1981): 97-109; and Martin, *Reclaiming a Conversation*.

[15.] Elizabeth Janeway, *Man's World, Woman's Place* (New York: Morrow, 1971): 96.

[16.] Quite clearly, Rodriguez's class background is a factor in this judgment. Notice, however, that the form his fear takes relates to gender.

17. L. Blum, *Friendship, Altruism, and Morality* (London: Routledge & Kegan Paul, 1980).

18. This scholarship cannot possibly be cited here. For reviews of the literature in the various academic disciplines see past issues of *Signs: Journal of Women in Culture and Society.*

19. Jane Roland Martin, "What Should We Do With a Hidden Curriculum When We Find One?" *Curriculum Inquiry* 6, no. 2 (1976): 135-151.

20. Simone de Beauvoir, *The Second Sex* (New York: Bantam, 1961).

21. June Goodfield, *An Imagined World* (New York: Harper & Row, 1981); see also E. F. Keller, *A Feeling for the Organism* (San Francisco: W.H. Freemen, 1983).

22. James Watson, *The Double Helix* (New York: New American Library, 1969).

23. Martin, *Reclaiming a Conversation.*

Chapter 3

Introduction to Stephen F. Hamilton and Klaus Hurrelmann

Stephen Hamilton and Klaus Hurrelmann have examined the structure of American and German schools in an effort to determine how they effect student motivation. They argue that non-college bound German students were more motivated in schools than their American counterparts. Students in German vocational high schools, they report, understand the importance of what they learn since knowledge is linked clearly to making a good living. In sum, the goals of the German vocational high school are transparent and obvious. Nevertheless, this transparency has drawbacks. For example, it is virtually impossible in Germany to change from a vocational to a college preparatory school. On the other hand, this lack of permeability or flexibility so apparent in the German school is a defining quality of the American high school. Movement in the American high school from non-college bound to college bound is simple and even encouraged. To insure that we have permeability, American students are not encouraged to study for specific careers or vocational goals. Because our non-college bound students are not encouraged to choose career paths, they subsequently have trouble recognizing the relationship between schooling and subsequent jobs. The authors outline a plan whereby we can increase transparency while not losing permeability. Accordingly, we should increase the number of vocational schools in America while making it easier for these students to transfer to a college preparatory high school.

Americans have a high regard for school permeability since it is linked to equality of opportunity. To irrevocably tie high school students to a vocational track strikes us as being unfair. Students from poor families, they argue, should be given every opportunity to go to college. A structure that encourages early career planning smacks of discrimination toward minorities. The authors make a reasonable case that offers a synthesis of the seemingly conflicting criteria of transparency and permeability.

Consider the following questions when you read this article:

1. What would you make of the fact that about eighty-five percent of American vocational school graduates are not employed in their field of study or an allied field some five years after graduation?

2. Do our community colleges appear to be similar to the authors' career academies?

3. What objectives would minorities bring to career academies?

The School-to-Career Transition in Germany and the United States

by **Stephen F. Hamilton** *and*
Klaus Hurrelmann

Originally published in the *Teachers College Record,* Vol. 96, no. 2, (Winter 1994), pp. 329-344. Reprinted with permission.

This article compares the structure of the educational systems in the United States of America and the Federal Republic of Germany, with emphasis on organizational and curricular features of both school-based and work-based preparation for employment. The German and American educational systems have developed fundamentally different models for the transition from the educational system into the labor market. These differences, which are characterized as differences in the systems' transparency and permeability, affect young people's motivations for school achievement, their conceptions of work, and their future orientations. The article concludes with recommendations for improvements in both systems that could be achieved by borrowing from each other.

Fulfilling a campaign promise, President Clinton has launched a school-to-work initiative designed to create systems supporting successful entry into careers by young people who do not graduate from four-year colleges. This initiative recognizes that education and public policy in the United States have previously "forgotten" half or more of its youth and that new economic realities require better-educated workers.[1]   It seeks to create a form of education and training that scarcely exists in this country but is well established in others, most notably in Germany.

This article compares Germany's apprenticeship system with the United States's "nonsystem," in order to identify some of the issues that must be confronted in developing an American system. But it has a second purpose, consistent with the citizenship of its authors: We also point to ways in which the German system could be improved. Indeed, the first version of this article was published in a German journal.[2]   Simultaneously assessing both countries' systems suggests ways in which each can learn from the other.

Our central assumption is that the structure and organization of an educational system directly affects students' motivation to achieve. Specifically, we presume that a system will be more effective in motivating students if school performance opens attractive opportunities in the labor market.[3]   Young people who believe their engagement and effort in school will bring them closer to long-term career goals work harder and more intensively than those who believe that their future prospects are unrelated to what they do in school. This a key explanation for the wide gap in school performance between students competing for entrance in selective colleges and those who do not expect to continue their formal education beyond high school. Formulated more positively, when the organization of an educational system leads young people to believe that school achievement has a direct and significant impact on their future career path, they will engage seriously in education.[4]

The German and American educational systems have developed fundamentally different models for organizing their education and occupational training systems. In the following pages we will examine how the two systems construct the critical connections between education and career for people who do not earn four-year college degrees and what effects this has for young people's perspectives on work and orientations to the future in the two countries.[5]   As a next step, we will examine whether both systems might benefit from a reciprocal exchange of principles and practices, especially in view of some tendencies toward convergence that are already apparent.

Structural Principles of Transition Systems:

Transparency Versus Permeability

In the following pages, we shall refer to "school-to-work transition systems" rather than school systems. Our concern is with the connections between education (including employment training) and labor markets, or, if you will, education systems and employment systems. The phrase "school-to-work transition" can be misleading because young people participate simultaneously in both systems for many years rather than switching from being students to being workers in a single step. In Germany, this dual participation is a central feature of the apprenticeship system. In the United States, the vast majority of high school students are employed part-time in jobs unrelated to their education. Simultaneous participation will probably be even more common in the future as full-time or formerly full-time adult workers re-enroll in school to improve their earning prospects in a rapidly changing economy.

School-to-work transition systems can be conceived as what Bronfenbrenner called "meso-systems" (i.e., systems of systems). Our treatment of connections between school and work is consistent with Bronfenbrenner's hypothesis that human development is enhanced by connections between the different systems in which people function.[6]

Two key features of school-to-work transition systems are captured by the distinction between "transparency" and "permeability":

Transparency refers to how well young people can see through the system to plot a course from where they are in the present to a distant future goal. One indicator of a system's transparency is that many people are knowledgeable about how the system functions and where its multiple paths lead. They can readily explain how a person moves through the educational system into a particular career.

Permeability refers to ease of movement from one point in the system to another. In a permeable system it is relatively easy to move from one location to another, and to change direction at any time. Such changes are facilitated by the system's structure.

Comparing the structure and operation of the two countries' transition systems for people who do not earn four-year college degrees, we conclude that the American system is extremely permeable but rather opaque, while the German system is the opposite: quite transparent but also relatively impermeable. The German system is organized around career-related specialties. Examinations, certificates, and credentials play a central role; they serve as licenses authorizing movement from one location in the system to another. Their prevalence makes the system transparent by very clearly indicating how movement must occur. However, they also render the system relatively impermeable by preventing any movement outside the prescribed paths.

In the United States, in contrast, people have many possibilities to move from one place in the system to another. (Recall that we refer to education and employment at the subbaccalaureate levels, not, for example, to medical school or other highly selective postgraduate educational opportunities.) Connections between the educational and occupational systems are so loose that post-high school opportunities for either education or work are practically unconstrained by courses taken or by grades earned.

We turn now to a more detailed description of the two countries' school-to-work transition systems in order to elaborate this contrast between their transparency and their permeability.

The German System: Transparent But Impermeable

The "dual system" of work-based apprenticeship combined with related part-time schooling is the centerpiece of Germany's school-to-work transition system.[7]   It enrolls about two-thirds of the older youth population, including males and females preparing for white-collar and technical occupations as well as the skilled trades. Apprenticeship requires heavy investment by employers in the education and training of their future workforce and "social partnership" among employers, unions, and government.[8]

Apprenticeship combined with a wide range of full-time postsecondary vocational schools creates close connections between education and occupation, making the German system highly transparent. By their mid-teens, most German youth have rather specific career goals in mind and clear paths to follow in order to meet them. Most German adults can readily explain to a young person how to become an electronics technician, dental assistant, airplane mechanic, or office worker, because each occupation has an apprenticeship with clearly defined requirements and a qualifying examination.[9]

The tradeoff is impermeability. Training completion certificates are the tickets of entry for most desirable occupations. Only those who have completed an apprenticeship and passed the qualifying examination are allowed to enter one of the almost 400 apprenticeable occupations, most of which are legally reserved for certified completers. An auto mechanic in his third year of training cannot simply decide to become an auto body repairer. Rather, he must first find and then complete a new apprenticeship, including part-time vocational schooling, some of which is pure repetition. German workers who wish to change their occupation or whose occupation has been eliminated by new technology must in most cases seek retraining if they hope to find a new job at an equivalent level.

While German youth benefit from being able to see clearly what they are required to do in order to enter a specific occupation, the system's impermeability can be a disadvantage. Once a person has started toward an occupational goal, she or he has limited chances to change that goal without considerable sacrifice.

The American System: Permeable but Opaque

The balance between transparency and permeability is exactly the opposite in the United States. Few jobs in the middle and lower levels of the occupational hierarchy require formal credentials; workers move rather easily among employers, and from one type of work to another. Permeability can be an advantage to U.S. workers. It allows upward mobility, voluntary career changes, and adaptation to economic change. Auto mechanics become chefs. Laid-off factory workers become truck drivers. Hairdressers become receptionists.

High permeability matches employment practices and the individualistic ideology prevailing in the United States. Far more than in Germany, with its social democratic tradition, each individual is considered responsible for his or her own destiny. In the United States, requiring specific training and certification would be considered an infringement on the individual's freedom to choose an occupation and the employer's right to select freely among applicants, with the exception of health-related occupations and some trades such as electrician, which require licenses to practice. The tradeoff for this high permeability or freedom of movement is low transparency. Because the requirements for occupations are not spelled out clearly, a young person trying to plan for the future has a difficult time finding someone to tell her or him precisely what to do in order to prepare for a certain kind of employment. An opaque transition system or nonsystem undermines young people's motivation to perform well in school because it obscures the long-term purposes of school learning.

Trends and Reforms in the German System

Pressures imposed by rapidly changing technology, growing international competition, and widespread democratization—in the sense both of dramatic political transformation in the former East Germany and insistent demands for inclusion of women, people with disabilities, and non-Germans—have begun to move the German system toward greater permeability. This trend has several manifestations.

Changes in Schools

Impermeability in Germany's educational system begins quite early. Following four (or six) years of primary school (*Grundschule*), children enroll in one of three types of secondary schools: the lowest level "main school" (*Hauptschule*), the middle or technical school (*Realschule*), or the university preparatory school (*Gymnasium*). The separation of primary from secondary grades was initiated in the mid-1960s to allow time for children to demonstrate their capacity to perform schoolwork, thus increasing the school system's permeability.

In strictly legal terms, it is possible today to move back and forth easily among secondary school types, and the new comprehensive secondary school (*Gesamtschule*). However, empirical observations have found that few young people transfer among these school types. Investigators have established that pupils have a 90 percent probability of remaining in the same school type they entered at the completion of primary school. Among the sources for this continuing stability in enrollment are differences among curricula, distinctive cultures in the school types, and serious differences in achievement levels among students attending them.[10]

Notable steps have been taken in recent years toward increased permeability in the upper secondary grades. First, it is now possible to transfer into the upper grades of the *Gymnasium* by earning a qualified diploma from one of the other school types. Second, courses of study in vocational schools for apprentices (*Berufsschulen*) have been constructed to enable apprentices to enroll subsequently in higher education, including universities. Vocational schools can in this way fulfill the same purposes as the upper *Gymnasium* grades.

However, few *Berufsschulen* have integrated upper grades that encompass the occupational courses in the dual system as well as the full-time school-based courses leading to highly skilled careers and to qualifications to enter full-time postsecondary vocational schools or universities (i.e., *Fachhochschulreife* or *Abitur*). Transfers from the *Berufsschule* to the upper *Gymnasium* grades remain rare.

Formal changes designed to ease transfer among school types should render the distinctive secondary schools more nearly equal in desirability. However, steady increases in the proportions of young people enrolling in the *Gymnasium* indicate that equality has not been achieved. In contrast to the 1960s, when 75 percent of secondary school completers joined the dual system after grade 9 or 10, only about 50 percent do so now at that point, and the downward trend continues. Another warning signal is the high percentage of apprenticeship contracts being broken, which has climbed steadily in recent years and now stands at about 15 percent. This suggests a mismatch between the technical and social competence of youth and the working conditions and requirements they encounter in the dual system.

The number of students who choose the lowest-level elementary school, the *Hauptschule*, continues to sink rapidly. But this school form was originally conceived as the feeder school for the dual system.[11] If the historical balance between the strongly occupation-oriented educational path represented by the dual system and the science-oriented educational path through universities and postsecondary technical schools is to survive, then the dual system must be upgraded educationally. The dual system must not be allowed to be seen as a dead end that closes options for further education.

Strengthening of the dual system must begin in the lower secondary grades. Young people are increasingly inclined to select the *Gymnasium*, not primarily because they and their parents expect they will definitely enter the university later, but rather because they wish to hold open for the longest time the possibility of achieving the most highly valued diploma, thereby retaining the largest number of occupational prospects. With an *Abitur* indicating successful completion of the *Gymnasium*, they can always choose to enter the dual system or a full-time postsecondary vocational school. Upward transfer is much more difficult. Therefore, a primarily school-based alternative to the *Gymnasium* should be created in the first years after primary school, which will take up the tradition of the *Hauptschule* and *Realschule* and link their educational paths to the dual system and to postsecondary vocational schools.

Such an alternative would offer a distinctive independent occupational education program, which, from the beginning, would be more strongly oriented toward occupation and practice and for that reason more appropriate for those youth who think more practically (and more graphically) than the typical students of a *Gymnasium*. Such a step would also help secure the transparency of the German educational system, because the current multiple options of the secondary school system have definitely led to difficulty in comprehending the whole and thereby contributed to making the *Gymnasium* the most attractive school: There is no ambiguity about where this pathway leads.

Changes in Young People's Voluntary Behavior

A small but steadily growing minority of young people who qualify for university entrance by achieving the *Abitur* choose to become apprentices. Many enroll in universities after completing an apprenticeship and, upon graduation, become highly desirable employees because of their combination of academic and practical preparation. Although this group constitutes a small and privileged minority, they demonstrate that the old barriers between vocational "training" and academic "education" are no longer insurmountable. They are also significant because young people themselves have breached the barriers through their voluntary actions rather than waiting for the barriers to be cleared as a result of official policy.

Below the university level, a growing proportion of youth combine vocational training as apprentices with full-time postsecondary vocational schooling, achieving some of the same benefits of "double qualification" as those combining apprenticeship with university education.[12]   Combined with a trend toward remaining in secondary school longer than required (i.e., past grade 9 in most states, grade 10 in some), this practice has steadily increased the mean age of apprentices.

A small number of young people combine academic and vocational preparation by enrolling in higher education after completing an apprenticeship combined with *Berufsschule* enrollment and gaining work experience. The so-called second educational path—that is, enrollment in an evening *Gymnasium* as an alternative means of achieving the *Abitur*— has been available for many years, but the long hours of night school are daunting. More recently, other qualifications have been accepted as evidence of readiness for university entrance, including passing the examination as a master and completing other further education courses. Here too the traditionally firm boundaries between higher education and vocational training have been breached.

Changes in Work-Based Training

The attraction of work-based learning lies primarily in its contrast to school-based learning, which is characterized by didactic instruction. Work-based learning operates through the everyday requirements of the firm's operations. It becomes part of a firm's normal operating procedures. However, workplaces are not organized primarily as places for learning. They do not always respond to young people's needs for learning and development. For example, on initiation into the workplace an apprentice is often expected to conform without question to the constraints of work without being able to negotiate conflicts that might arise in a businesslike manner. In order to learn to treat apprentices as competent persons with legitimate interests, trainers need instruction in human resource management and conflict resolution, along with conflict mediation and supervision.

The conditions surrounding work-based learning must be improved along with schools if Germany is to evolve toward a more permeable system that still retains the advantages of transparency. Recent research demonstrates that young people today have much higher expectations of their future jobs than did earlier generations. While their parents hoped for secure jobs paying a living wage, today's youth expect to be able to work independently and creatively and wish to have the chance to develop personally at work and to be able to contribute their own competencies.[13] If training places and workplaces are to match these expectations, then the propensities of current employers must change. Work processes must be structured so that workers' multiple competencies can be flexibly deployed. Training firms must bring young apprentices quickly into all work processes. Contemporary principles of human resource management must be applied, and the old conception, at least among many small employers, that apprentices are essentially cheap labor must be rooted out. These changes would be in the long-term interests of employers, but some will see them as conflicting with their immediate interests.[14]

The consolidation of previously distinct occupations into larger and more inclusive clusters of related occupations is a structural modification that increases the permeability of the German school-to-work system.   This modification enables apprentices to delay specialization.   By selecting a broad occupational cluster, they postpone their choice of a specialty until they have had one or two years of training and experience.   They may also transfer more easily into a different but related occupation.   This increases mobility or permeability among related occupations.

The dual system's greatest advantage is that through it young people can acquire genuine occupational experience at the end of a ten-year period of schooling; they can see for themselves the social utility and productivity of their own actions, achieve a secure independent financial base, and take the role of an employed person.   In these ways, the dual system enables young people to acquire adult status much faster than the long and arduous path through the *Gymnasium* and higher education.   Notwithstanding this advantage, more and more German young people are concluding that the pathway through the dual system offers fewer possibilities and a less attractive future, perhaps even a dead-end street leading to uncertain employment prospects.

Learning from the United States

When we pose the question of which components of the American educational system could be adapted in Germany, the one that comes to mind first is the prevailing possibility of being able to move at each stage of education from one pathway to another.   Adapted to the German school-to-work system, such movement would require establishing distinct crossover points at which a change could be made from one path to another without losing credit.   A crossover point would not have to be available after every single year, as is possible in principle in the American system.   Perhaps such points could be more widely separated, for instance, at the completion of primary school, and after grades 8, 10, 12, and 13.   The principles and rules governing a change from one educational path or from one school type to another should be so clear and distinct that they provide the person making the change with good security.

The German school system, which is organized in principle around long-term occupational training, could be made more permeable than before by such a lateral structure of crossover possibilities without impinging on its good transparency.   The experience of the American educational system demonstrates just how inadequate excessive emphasis on only permeability is, because in the end it leads to a radically stratified system, in which students always think only of the next step, but are incapable of taking a longer time perspective. This is a valuable lesson, which definitely warns against too strong an organizational stratification of the German school system.

In order to strengthen the prestige of "nonacademic" education in the German school system, which has traditionally had a great impact on fixing the perspectives of less-accomplished students, higher standards should be developed and implemented, as many have already proposed and some in positions of authority have also foreshadowed. The values of this educational path can be strengthened by recognizing a completed apprenticeship in the dual system as equivalent in the realm of the *Gymnasium* and postsecondary schools. At the same time, the plurality of educational paths can be contained, which is a valuable characteristic of the German system of academic and occupational education. Strengthened recognition of already demonstrated effort should make possible an unbureaucratic and quick change from one educational and career path to another, as is possible in the United States.

Trends and Reforms in the American System

In international comparisons of young people's knowledge, the American educational system presents a puzzling contrast. Boasting what is generally recognized as the world's best and most inclusive system of higher education, the United States also consistently shows up poorly in comparisons of elementary and secondary student performance on tests of academic knowledge. No other modern industrial democracy has a rate of adult functional illiteracy that approaches the 50 percent claimed in a recent study.[15]

The only way these apparently contradictory facts can be reconciled is by pointing to the subtle but powerful stratification built into the American system. Although it purports to be democratic and comprehensive, that system is in fact characterized by dramatic differences among and within schools in what students are taught and what they are expected to learn. The problem is not that it is impossible for American children and youth to get a good education, but that only a small proportion receive the quality of education that gains them entrance and allows them to benefit from first-rate colleges and universities.

Those who do not expect to enroll in selective colleges and

universities, and even more those who do not expect to enroll in postsecondary education at all, are badly shortchanged. One reason for this gap is the opacity of the connections between school and career. High school students without aspirations to four years of higher education have no way of knowing how their current choice of courses and their performance in those courses will influence their further occupational and educational careers. These young people can see no connection between what they achieve in school and what will be expected of them later at work or in further vocational education.

While the American system maximizes permeability, which is desirable, it obscures at the same time the implications of each step in education and training for the next. Planning for the future is scarcely possible because young people cannot tell in advance what requirements they will have to meet to attain particular career goals. Most Americans are suspicious of "high-stakes tests" such as those taken by university applicants in Europe and Japan, preferring a number of smaller, less momentous decision points and always wishing to keep options open for "late bloomers." Unfortunately, the absence of clear decision points leaves young people without a sense of the connection between what they do in school and their later career opportunities. If no particular choice point is decisive, then none need be taken seriously.

This phenomenon can be highlighted not only by contrast with Germany but also by contrast with those American young people who—typically encouraged by well-educated parents—are oriented early in the course of their education toward selective colleges and universities. This is the group that is most highly motivated toward school achievement. They take the heaviest course loads and the most demanding courses. They do their homework and try to perform well on tests. Although they may have unformed career plans, they know that they are preparing for professional careers requiring at least four years of higher education and probably post-graduate studies as well. And they understand, as many children of less-advantaged families do not, that a degree from a prestigious college or university is far more valuable than one from a local or regional institution.

The system connecting secondary school performance, elite higher education, and high-status professional occupations is far more transparent than the system connecting secondary school with careers that do not require four-year degrees, but also much less permeable. Applicants with C averages are seldom admitted to Stanford. Graduates of state universities that were formerly teachers' colleges are not well represented at Yale Law School.

The recurring reciprocal relationship between transparency and permeability raises the question whether connections between high school and career can be made more transparent for students who do not receive four-year degrees without simultaneously reducing permeability to an unacceptable level. An American-style system of youth apprenticeship beginning with the secondary school years is a possibility that deserves exploration.

Youth Apprenticeship and Career Academies

Demonstration projects have already begun to experiment with "youth apprenticeship American-style" in several locations, including Pennsylvania, Wisconsin, Maine, Arkansas, Boston, Tulsa, and Broome County, New York. Siemens, the German multinational electronics firm, is seriously committed to adapting the kind of apprenticeships it sponsors in Germany to its plants in the United States, not only for youth but also as a means of upskilling adult workers. Most of these efforts place high school juniors in well-planned and closely supervised work-based learning programs that are related to academic and vocational courses either in their home high school or in a separate school organized solely for apprentices. All attempt to put young people on an educational path that extends beyond high school, usually through two years of a technical or community college. This entails enrolling in college preparatory or "Tech Prep" courses in high school and enables those earning an associate's degree to continue their higher education in a four-year college.[16]

A key component of these demonstration programs is orienting high school students to a career area to which they can relate their academic studies, in other words, increasing the transparency of the school-career connection. This is expected to increase the motivation of participants and future participants to perform well in school, including those whose school performance has previously been marginal.

Work-based learning is critical for this purpose. In youth apprenticeship programs, work-based learning is more formal and plays a larger role than in cooperative education programs, which are well established in secondary vocational education.[17] Students remain in the same program for as long as four years, rather than a semester or two. This provides for a much wider range of experiences and a greater depth of skill development. Furthermore, consistent with the use of the term *apprenticeship*, these programs at least aspire to awarding portable credentials equivalent in function to the journeyworkers' papers awarded to craft workers who have completed registered apprenticeships. Work-based learning in this sense has little in common with the type of work experience that is nearly universal among U.S. high school students: low-skill minimum wage jobs after school and on weekends that neither demand nor teach academic skills and often compete with school for students' time and commitment.[18]

Career academies also promise to improve the transparency of connections between school and work in the United States. Originally started in Philadelphia, career academies are "schools-within-schools" organized around a cluster of related occupations. Career academies have multiplied in California, where they focus students' academic study on occupational areas such as health care, electronics, communication, or transportation, demonstrating the relevance of schooling to subsequent employment.[19]   The Academies of Finance began in New York City with support from the American Express company and have since been established in several other cities with a range of sponsoring institutions. Students in career academies take a full load of required courses but add special courses in career-related areas. Visiting speakers from the industry help prepare students for summer jobs, providing a clear connection between school and work and a career perspective. Career academies can achieve greater flexibility in their schedules than ordinary schools, allowing time for field trips, work experience, and group projects.

Experience to date with career academies has been positive, demonstrating that high school students' motivation can be heightened by more clearly defining career pathways.   Better-defined career pathways are particularly beneficial to disadvantaged students. The moderate reduction in permeability introduced by these programs is more than offset by this gain in transparency. Indeed, many academies report greatly increased college enrollment by their graduates even though they were intended to serve, in part, as an alternative to college preparatory programs.

Youth apprenticeship programs and career academies can be found in only a few locations. Although small in scale and few in number, they have answered the fundamental question whether it is possible to implement in the United States the kind of school-related learning that lies at the heart of Germany's dual system. Furthermore, the presence of well-established cooperative education programs also demonstrates that work-based learning is feasible in the United States. The challenge posed by the Clinton administration's new initiative is to address the next question: Can this be done on a large enough scale to serve a substantial proportion of young people in the United States?

The Clinton initiative wisely enables states to begin their efforts at different points and to build on their own strengths. California, for example, will probably use its career academies as a base for creating "school-to-work opportunity systems." Many states have implemented Tech Prep programs linking occupational education at the secondary and postsecondary levels. Tech Prep programs, like career academies, can be strengthened by adding work-based learning.

If these approaches are to succeed on a large scale, young people will need preparation before entering them. Because all require a concentration on a particular career area, young people must be assisted in understanding, exploring, and selecting a career area much earlier than is normal in the United States. Various forms of career education have attempted to do this, but have languished in part because the time lag between education and vocational choice has been so great and in part because the methodology has been overly didactic. Career education is likely to be more effective when it is rooted in real-world experience, including field trips and classroom speakers, and in closer proximity to an important career-related decision, namely, applying for an apprenticeship.

Before selecting a career, high school students should have had a wide range of relevant experiences and information. Some of that may be simulated, as in classroom exercises or in school-based enterprises, even in the performance of needed work in and around the school. Many voluntary community service activities provide work-like experience. In the upper grades, trial apprenticeships lasting a week or two could give young people a more vivid sense of what awaits them and a firmer basis for making a choice.

Learning From Germany

What criteria should apply to the design of a "school-to-work opportunity system" as envisioned in the Clinton administration's new initiative and foreshadowed in these programs and demonstrations? Certainly the United States should not attempt to transplant the German system; it would not survive in a different educational and economic system. The goal should be to create a flexible system capable of performing some of the same functions as Germany's dual system but in a manner suited to the United States.[20]

One characteristic that can be borrowed is the duality of occupational education, the combination of school-based with work-based instruction. In addition, orientation of the education system as a whole toward occupational areas should be borrowed from the German system. However, we believe the United States should not reproduce the Germans' narrow definition of occupational areas. The U.S. labor market is too changeable and unstructured and the criteria for evaluation of school credentials are too uncertain. But defining required competencies for large occupational clusters would enable both schools and workplaces to organize learning opportunities for youth around the achievement of those competencies, providing young people with desirable and attainable medium-term goals for their education. Identifying target occupations and associated knowledge and skills would contribute significantly to increasing transparency in the American system. This is the goal of several projects currently underway to establish occupational standards.

As people in the United States experiment with these approaches, they should look to the most progressive aspects of Germany's system. Many reform efforts have been inspired by the dual system, but after gaining a reasonable understanding of that system, we should look most closely at its most current adaptations, at the way it is implemented in world-class firms and in locations where efforts are underway to increase its permeability.

Summary/Conclusions

Both countries should seek to achieve a good combination and mixture of permeability and transparency for their educational and employment systems in order to confront successfully the economic, technological, social, and political changes affecting education and employment. They must attempt to provide all segments of the younger generation with good and valuable opportunities for education in order to enable students to acquire social and occupational competencies, which are now required in all sectors of the economy. That educational system will be counted the best that most intensively develops the motivation and capacity of all young people within a democratic and just structure.

Notes ───────────────────────────

1. The William T. Grant Foundation Commission on Work, Family, and Citizenship, *The Forgotten Half: Non-College Youth in America: An Interim Report on the School-to-Work Transition* (Washington, DC: William T. Grant Foundation, 1988); idem, *The Forgotten Half: Non-College Youth in America: Pathways to Success for America's Youth and Young Families: Final Report* (Washington, DC: The William T. Grant Foundation, 1988); and National Center on Education and the Economy, *America's Choice: High Skills or Low Wages! The Report of the Commission on the Skills of the American Workforce* (Rochester, NY: National Center on Education and the Economy, 1990).

2. Stephen F. Hamilton and Klaus Hurrelmann, "Auf der Suche nach dem besten Modell fur den Ubergang von der Schule in den Beruf—ein amerikanisch-deutscher Vergleich" (The Search for the Best Model for the Transition from School to Work: An American-Germany Comparison), *Zeitschrift fur Sozializationsforschung und Erziehungssoziologie* 13 (1993): 194-207.

3. John H. Bishop, "Why the Apathy in American High Schools?" *Educational Researcher* 18 (1989): 6-10.

4. Cf. Helmut Fend, *Theorie der Schule* (Theory of the School) (Munchen: Urban, 1980).

5. The term *college* and the four-year time are both America. In Germany, the cognate, *Kolleg*, has a different meaning. Germany has no institution comparable to small liberal arts colleges. Students enter universities after thirteen years of elementary and secondary schooling. Having already taken "distribution requirements" equivalent to two years in most U.S. colleges and universities, they then take courses only in a major field of study. Their programs typically last six years or more and lead to what in the United States are considered post-graduate degrees. Future physicians, lawyers, and psychologists enroll immediately in programs leading to the terminal degree rather than first receiving an undergraduate degree and then enrolling in graduate or professional school. Comparisons between U.S. and German higher education make more sense if the basic German university degree is considered equivalent to a Masters rather than a Bachelors degree. Many courses of study found in U.S. colleges and universities (e.g., accounting, nursing) are relegated to postsecondary vocational schools in Germany, which are sharply distinguished from universities.

6. Urie Bronfenbrenner, *The Ecology of Human Development: Experiments by Nature and Design* (Cambridge: Harvard University Press,

1979): 215.

[7.] Stephen F. Hamilton, *Apprenticeship for Adulthood: Preparing Youth for the Future* (New York: Free Press, 1990).

[8.] Soskice, "Reconciling Markets and Institutions: An Interpretation of the Germany Apprenticeship System," in *The Privatization of Skill Formation: International Comparison* (Chicago: University of Chicago Press, 1991); and Wolfgang Streek et al., "The Role of the Social Partners in Vocational Training and Further Training in the Federal Republic of Germany" (Berlin and Bielefeld: CEDEFOP Research Project No. 1236/1968, Final Report, 1987).

[9.] Klaus Rodax et al., eds., *Struklurwandel der Bildungsbeleiligung* (Structural Change in Educational Participation) (Darmsatdt: Wissenschaftliche Buchgesellschaft, 1989); and Hans-Gunther Rolff et al., eds., *Jahrbuch der Schulentwicklung* (Yearbook of School Development) (Weinheim: Juventa, 1992).

[10.] Klaus Klemm et al., *Bildungsgesamtplan* (Comprehensive Educational Plan) (Weinheim: Juventa, 1991).

[11.] Jurgen Mansel and Klaus Hurrelman, *Alltagsstrep bei Jugendlichen* (Everyday Stress Among Youth) (Weinheim: Juventa, 1991).

[12.] Manfred Kaiser, Reinhard Nuthmann, and Heinz Stegman, eds., *Berufliche Verbleibsforschung in der Diskussion: Materialienband 1, Schulabganger aus dem Sekundarbereich I beim Ubergang in Ausbildung und Beruf* (The Debate Over Research on Career Persistence: Source Volume I, School Leavers from Secondary Level One at the Transition into Vocational Training and Occupation) (Nurnberg: Institut fur Arbeitsmarkt-und Beruffsforschung der Bundesanstalt fur Arbeit, 1985).

[13.] Mansel and Hurrelmann, *Alltagsstrep bei Jugendlichen*.

[14.] Wolfgang Lempert and Stephen Hamilton, "The Impact of Apprenticeship on Youth: A Prospective Analysis" (Manuscript submitted for publication).

[15.] Irwin S. Kirsch, Ann Jungeblut, Lynn Jenkins, and Andrew Kolstad, *Adult Literacy in America: A First Look at the Results of the National Adult Literacy Survey* (Washington, DC: Office of Educational Research and Improvement, U.S. Department of Education, 1993).

[16.] Hamilton, *Apprenticeship for Adulthood*.

[17.] U.S. General Accounting Office, Transition from School to Work: Linking Education and Worksite Training (HRD-91-105) (Washington, DC: General Accounting Office, 1991).

[18.] Ellen Greenberger and Laurence D. Steinberg, *When Teenagers Work: The Psychological and Social Costs of Adolescent Employment* (New York: Basic Books, 1986).

[19.] David Stern, Marilyn Raby, and Charles Dayton, Career Academies: Partnerships for Reconstructing American High Schools (San Francisco:

Jossey-Bass, 1992).

[20.] National Center on Education and the Economy, *America's Choice*; and Hamilton, *Apprenticeship for Adulthood.*

Chapter 4

Introduction to Seymour Sarason

At one time, Seymour Sarason believed that school reform failed because of the poor quality of teachers and teacher education programs. He felt that reform hinged on attracting better teachers with a liberal arts background. Liberal arts graduates, he concluded, were generally better students, and they did not suffer from a background in teacher education. Colleges of education, in fact, were dull and treated prospective teachers as adult children. Hardly the background for school reform. If schools could attract liberal arts graduates then the condition for reform would be set. Sarason soon discovered that liberal arts graduates were no better at reform than teachers with background in teacher education. This, he argues, suggests that neither the quality of student or their preparation were key elements in school reform. Reform, he speculates, rests with a far greater emphasis on the intellectual growth of teachers. We must pay far more attention to the working lives of teachers and how it is these variables might ultimately effect reform.

Within this context, Sarason argues that teachers should be granted sabbatical leaves. Professors have long escaped the rigors of teaching, research, and deadly administrative detail so that they can rest, explore, and develop perspective. Sabbaticals not only improve the working lives of professors but also help their students who profit from the intellectual vacations of their teachers. In sum, sabbaticals may be a factor in school reform since they reflect the view that school should exist for the twin purpose of the intellectual and moral growth of teachers and well as students. If we focus only on the growth of students, at the expense of teachers, then school reform will never happen.

Consider the following questions when you read this creative essay:

1. Would teachers use sabbaticals to enhance their income?

2. How would you evaluate the effects of sabbaticals?

3. Does Sarason hint that school reform is influenced more by the working lives of teachers than the motivation of students?

For Whom Do Schools Exist?

by Seymour B. Sarason

We can change power relationships, curricula, standards, the organization of the school day, the preparation and credentialing of school personnel, and the criteria for promotion and graduation. But to what ends? What are the aims of schools? The teacher in front of a class of students has not only immediate aims but also ones that are near and far term. I shall assume that no one would say that it is sufficient that a teacher's aims over the school year concern only the acquisition of information and technical skills. These aims are certainly important, but if we do not accept them as sufficient, it is because we intuitively feel that there is a difference between information and knowledge, just as we should not confuse facts with the truth. When the term "carnal knowledge" is used in the Bible, it does not refer to the facts or processes of sexual intercourse but to a comprehension that goes far beyond the factual, frequently in the context of morality and intrapsychic conflict. That is to say, the "know" in knowledge is not derivable only from the facts. There is, you might say, "know" knowledge and fact knowledge. To "understand" facts literally means to grasp what is "under" them: a context of meanings and relationships. I have never met anyone who denied the importance of that kind of understanding, regardless of how widely we differed on other educational issues. No one is comfortable with the imagery of children as fact machines. We want more for them, and if schools are generally uninteresting places to children, it is because they want more but rarely get it.

I must here avoid a trap into which almost all educational reformers have fallen. Indeed, it is no less the case for the public generally. I refer to the assumption, indeed it is one of those unverbalized axioms, that schools do and should exist primarily for students, that is, the aims of education are the aims we have for our children. If questioning that assumption seems strange, it is testimony to the strength of what is now a self-defeating tradition. Let me, therefore, explain how I came to question the tradition.

In the early sixties I directed the Yale Psycho-Educational Clinic, which was not a clinic in the usual sense that people could refer themselves for our services. We worked *in* classrooms and in nonschool settings that were nevertheless educational in their purposes. One of the reasons that clinic was started is wrapped up in the question: why do so many old and new settings fail of their purposes? And by *fail* I mean two things: they go out of existence, or they continue to survive even though they are not achieving their stated goals. It was not that they were not helping some people but rather that they were quite aware of the gulf between goals and performance. Those were the days when the term *burnout* gained currency as a way of accounting for poor staff morale, increase in staff turnover, or the fact that people were simply giving up and leaving the field. It is no less true today in education and the human services generally. Burnout is a complicated phenomenon that does not have a simple explanation. But there was one aspect of burnout and agency failure that I did think I understood and that had to be a major part of an explanation. That aspect was another one of those axioms: the setting exists primarily to serve others. *That* is its justification for existence. We are judged and we judge ourselves by how well we "foster growth in others who seek our help" encapsulates the axiom. In almost all instances I have studied, that axiom undergirded settings from their creation.[1]

Here is an example. If you, as I have, ask teachers (for example, in an elementary school) how they justify the existence of their school, the answer you get is that schools exist to further the intellectual and social development of students. Now, if you ask faculty members of a university how they justify the existence of the university, in one or another way the answer is that the university primarily exists to create and sustain those conditions that enable its faculty to learn, change, and grow. (You can have a university with few or no students.) The assumption is that if those conditions exist for faculty, it increases the chances that the faculty can create and sustain those conditions for students.

The two answers are polar opposites. The public school exists for students. Period. The university exists primarily for its faculty. Stated so baldly, that latter answer will strike some people as self-serving, narcissistic, or even antisocial. The imagery of university faculty paid to investigate the problems that interest *them*, to support them in their endeavors to contribute to knowledge in ways *they* choose, does not sit well with most people. The university, of course, does not publicly proclaim that its primary justification for existence is in furthering the development of its faculty, although in its most important internal forums for discussion that justification is taken for granted. What the university does proclaim is that creating and sustaining the development of faculty makes it possible for them to create that ambience for students. At the very least, the university exists equally for faculty and students.

I am aware that colleges and universities differ dramatically in their assignment of weights in this regard. What are by conventional criteria considered our "best" colleges and universities are those that have assigned equal importance to the development of both faculty and students. There are, unfortunately, many colleges and universities that give only lip service to the needs of the faculties and consider themselves "only" teaching institutions: they, like our public schools, regard the education of students as by far their most important function. In the scores of times I have visited such settings, I could count on hearing two things from their faculties: an expression of disappointment at the unwillingness or inability of the setting to support faculty development, and a recounting of the ways in which burdensome teaching loads and other duties over time erode satisfaction from teaching. In no less than our public schools the teachers have come to see that if conditions for their growth do not obtain, they cannot create and sustain them for students. And as in our public schools there were always a few faculty who managed somehow to keep their intellectual fires burning despite a nonsupportive institutional tradition. The fires in others had long been extinguished. In my opinion, it is extreme snobbery to judge these people as having second-rate intellects, as if institutional tradition and atmosphere have been insignificant variables in their lives. If these settings of lesser quality are impoverishing both for faculty and students, part (and only part) of the reason is the hold on the public's mind of the axioms that educational settings exist only or primarily for students, and that one can create the conditions for productive learning in students even though they do not exist for their teachers. Lest I be misunderstood: I am not saying that if, by a strange set of circumstances (the stuff of fantasy), educational settings were to accept the invalidity of the axioms and redress the imbalance, educational bliss would ensue. I am suggesting that redressing the balance increases the chances that more teachers and students will experience the sense of growth, without which life is a pointless bore.

Take the matter of sabbaticals. In our conventionally regarded "best" universities, sabbaticals are accorded to tenured faculty as a matter of course. Every seven years a faculty member may take a sabbatical at full pay for one semester or a full year at half pay. (At Yale you can take a semester off at full pay every three years.) The purposes of the sabbatical are two-fold and interrelated: to free the person from all teaching and administrative responsibilities and to encourage him or her to review past accomplishments, or to take stock, or to move in new directions, or to go somewhere to learn something new. It is intended to facilitate the recharging of one's mental and personal batteries—an opportunity to get out of a rut. It is explicit that sabbaticals be used to expand one's horizons in some way. The sabbatical is not a gift from the university. It is recognition that there has to be a time when you can take distance from your accustomed routine so that when you return there will be an infusion of new energy and new ideas. I am aware that there are people who use the sabbatical to do more of what they have been doing—that is, to have more time to complete a research or scholarly endeavor. Even so, it is testimony to the obligation of the university to create conditions that are intellectually productive. More often than not, however, the sabbatical is used for acquiring new experience and new directions.

But why is the sabbatical a matter of course in relatively few colleges and universities? The usual answer is that only a few universities have the financial resources to underwrite sabbaticals. Although this is true, it hides the fact that the tradition of the sabbatical was never built into most colleges and universities because they were regarded (that is, created) as teaching institutions, just as public schools were and are. As teaching institutions, their justification was in the education of students, not in the development of their teachers. My guess is that, if presented with a rationale for the necessity of the sabbatical in teaching institutions, the founders and sustainers of these institutions would have responded with staring disbelief. If one were to present that rationale to those heading these institutions today, I doubt that more than a few would comprehend its wisdom. Certainly, most of their faculty would comprehend and agree with that rationale, and not because they confuse a sabbatical with a vacation. They know their batteries are running low.

If only on this level of rhetoric, the sabbatical has an accepted, indeed treasured, place in higher education that is clearly not the case in our public schools. If my experience is any guide, the bulk of school systems make no provision whatsoever for sabbaticals. Some make it available to one or two teachers (and some of them require a financial sacrifice on the part of the teacher). It is discouraging that the significance and necessity of sabbaticals has never been a matter for discussion by educational reformers, either those inside or outside of our schools. This silence forces me to conclude that teaching is regarded as something you can do (and do well!) day in and day out, month in and month out, year in and year out without any decrease in motivation or change in style, satisfaction, patience, sensitivity, and sense of challenge. And this can apparently be done by all teachers regardless of where they teach, what they teach, and whom they teach. It should make no difference if the teacher does not experience any collegiality, has not role in decision making, is expected to be all things to all students, and regards him or herself as a member of the educational proletariat. I do not know of any set of expectations more invalid and defeating of the aims of reform. I do not say this because I believe sabbaticals should be at the top of any list of foci for reform, but because the silence about sabbaticals says a great deal about insensitivity to how the structure and culture of schools have the effect over time of subtly but powerfully undercutting the motivation, creativity, and professional-intellectual growth of educational personnel.

Sabbaticals are not vacations in that their purpose is not to "get away from it all" but rather to get a new perspective on "it all." There are few roles as demanding of one's energy, ingenuity, sensitivity, and patience as that of the classroom teacher. I have been in hundreds of classrooms and have interviewed even more teachers for one or another research purpose. It took me years to begin to understand why the majority of teachers seem to fall short of the criteria for what I consider a teacher should be. This is not to say that most were incompetent, although some were, but rather that they had settled into a routine that guaranteed that the classroom atmosphere would lack sparkle, buoyancy, challenge, and humor. These classrooms struck me as joyless, grim affairs, certainly for students end even for most teachers. Like that of most people, including educational reformers, my explanation (early on) gave prominent place to the quality of the minds of teachers—that is, generally speaking and by conventional test criteria, they were not as bright as those in other professions, such as law, medicine, or engineering. Therefore, a top priority for educational reform was to attract to teaching more bright people. This assignment of priority rested on two assumptions. The first was that by attracting those with higher test scores, one would be getting people who had a better and broader grasp of subject matter, if only because they were more likely to be found in colleges and universities that were more intellectually demanding than teachers' colleges. The second assumption was that there was a very high correlation between intelligence and achievement test scores, on the one hand, and creativity or imaginativeness, on the other hand.

Three things required a change in my thinking. The first stemmed from a sustained and intensive immersion in a teacher preparation program in a college that had only recently been changed from a teacher-training institution to a liberal arts one. More specifically, the immersion was in an undergraduate program that prepared special education teachers. The opportunity to participate was given to me by Burton Blatt, who chaired that small department and who is one of the most unusual people I have even known. It was through him that I learned about teacher preparation programs and began to understand how suffocating these programs could be for those seeking to become teachers. It was as if these students were adult children with no minds of their own, requiring that they be programmed like computers for their future role. However, if by conventional test criteria they were as a group unimpressive, they had the insight or maturity to conclude that their preparation was a very uninteresting, boring affair. (Indeed, one of the very few research findings in education that has withstood the test of replication is that most teachers judge their preparation to have been inadequate and irrelevant.)

The second experience that required a change in my thinking began in the early sixties, when the leadership of the New Haven schools made a valiant and successful effort to attract to teaching recent graduates from our "best" liberal arts colleges and universities. Attracting them was not very difficult because college campuses had many students eager to make a difference in those socially turbulent times. It was possible for those who wanted to become teachers to enroll in the summer in a teacher-training program, following which they became classroom teachers, taking a course or two during the school year. It was not unusual, given that teachers were in short supply, that some started to teach without any formal preparation. One of the things the Yale Psycho-Educational Clinic did was to initiate weekly seminars for these new teachers, the main purpose of which was to provide a forum where they could openly present and discuss whatever problems they were encountering.[2]

These new teachers were generally bright, lively, and engaged (especially in the early months in their new role). By the end of the year, one fact and one observation proved noteworthy. The fact noted was that the school systems provided no forums within the school and the system that in any way were regarded by these teachers as helpful. Each was essentially alone with his or her problems. The observation concerned the steady decline in morale among these teachers as they experienced their classrooms and their schools. The more they became aware of problems—their and their students—the more overwhelmed they became and the more they reluctantly lowered their sights. Although their energy level did not suffer, they found themselves seeking ways to defend themselves against passivity, bitterness, and an eroding sense of mission. I should note that these observations derived not only from the seminars but from our involvement in classrooms in several of the city's schools. They were not my observations alone but those of the score of clinic personnel who also were in classrooms and schools. And, it must be emphasized, these observations were no less true for new teachers who had completed an undergraduate teacher-training program in the local state college. In terms of culture shock, it made no difference where they had gone to college. It needs also to be said that those who lacked formal preparation did no worse or better than those who had such preparation. By the end of their first year, the soil I call the culture of the school had begun to sprout the weeds of burnout.[3] There were exceptions as always, but they were rare. I do not want to convey the impression that these new teachers had become wrecks or that they needed the services of psychotherapists. My message is contained in what one teacher said to me at the end of that first year: "I keep asking myself if I really want to be a teacher. Do I want to be alone all day with students who have scads of problems for which I have neither the time or knowledge? I am not blaming the kids, although some are impossible to reach or motivate, but, I keep asking myself, is this the way I will feel as the years go on? I feel so alone." What she said explains why in our book (Sarason and others, 1966) Murray Levine wrote a chapter titled "Teaching Is a Lonely Profession", which endeared us to many teachers who did not know us but who wrote to us.

During the sixties there were thousands of people from liberal arts colleges and universities who became "instant" teachers. I am not aware of any study that sought to determine what became of these people. Crucial here is how many left teaching and why? My observations, obviously based on limited experience, suggest that, on a percentage basis, more of them left teaching than was the case for those who had the usual formal preparation. We have statistics galore on many matters, important and not, concerning education. We have relatively few studies on what teaching in our schools does to teachers and other personnel. And what we have does not paint a favorable picture. Just as educational reformers have made recommendations about what they think can be done, not what needs to be done, those in the research community study what they can "measure," not what needs to be understood. There are exceptions, I know, but that is precisely what they are: exceptions. They are read but unheeded.

The third reason requiring me to alter my thinking goes back several decades to when I started a long-term research project in three very different school systems. I have to tell the reader that my formal training and experience were in clinical psychology. I mention that because training in any clinical profession (for example, medicine, social work, counseling) involves case conferences. Indeed, the amount of time spent in case conferences is best indicated in Murray Levine's advice that "all clinical installations need two staffs: one to go to meetings and the other to do the work." The case conference is the forum for sharing, discussing, and criticizing clinical tactics, conceptualizations, and goals. At their best, these case discussions forge and sustain collegiality and broaden horizons.

What startled me was that the tradition of the case conference did not exist in the schools. No teacher had a classroom lacking a child about whom he or she was puzzled; most of them had a disturbing number of such children, fewer than would be the case today. Even more startling was the stated reluctance of teachers to "refer" these children to anyone (for example, the principal, the pupil personnel department) for fear that it would be viewed as a sign of inadequacy. It was also true that many teachers did not make referrals either because "nothing will happen," or it would be weeks before someone "saw the child," or that when someone did see the child, no one would have a discussion with the teacher before or after. There was no forum where teachers and others with an obvious interest in or responsibility for the child could get together. Teachers were alone with their problems, theirs and their students. This was not only because of the pressures of time or lack of special services but also because the rationale for the case conference was not part of the school culture. By rationale I mean more than the potential benefits such a forum can provide for individual children. No less important is what it contributes to staff in regard to their learning, professional growth, collegiality, and sense of worthiness. It is a forum that says to staff: "You have knowledge, experience, or opinions that you are expected to articulate; you have a responsibility to yourself, your colleagues, your students, and your school." Case conferences are (usually) not decision-making affairs. They involve, among other things, ideas, actions, and values. At their best they are mind openers, forums one looks forward to—quite unlike faculty meetings described by one teacher as examples of man's inhumanity to man.

I am aware that time is a precious commodity in schools, and that schools do not have overflowing budgets. But I am also aware that considerations of time and money are clear indices of the scaling of aims, or values, or priorities. From their inception our public schools have never assigned importance to the intellectual, professional, and career needs of their personnel. However the aims of the schools were articulated, there was never any doubt that schools existed for children. If, as I have asserted, it is virtually impossible to create and sustain over time conditions for productive learning for students when they do not exist for teachers, the benefits sought by educational reform stand little chance of being realized.

The reader will encounter two obstacles to accepting what I have said. The first is simply in entertaining the possibility that schools should exist coequally for the development of students and educational personnel. It is a possibility that challenges long-standing beliefs held by these personnel and the public generally. One can point to examples in history (for example, women in relation to the world of work and ideas, the employment of children in the labor force, the absence of social security, national insurance for the elderly and others, the sixty- or seventy-hour work week, and so on) where challenges to what seemed right, natural, and proper were rejected out of hand. These and other examples are indirectly relevant but not particularly analogous because these challenges to customary thinking and practice rested primarily on moral grounds. These were challenges that had some grounding in our religious, legal, and constitutional history—that is, they essentially said that as a society we were not consistent with our fundamental beliefs, and that we were violating basic societal values of fairness, opportunity, and justice. Even so, it took decades of social turmoil and attitudinal change for these moral challenges to get reflected in our legal system. But morality is not the basis for my challenge to the unreflective belief that schools do and should exist primarily for children. Rather, the basis is that for our schools to do better than they do we have to give up the belief that it is possible to create the conditions for productive learning when those conditions do not exist for educational personnel.

Now to the second and, on the surface, more thorny obstacle. It is thorny because I have never had a serious, sustained discussion of this issue with anyone who, in the abstract, did not agree with my position. As one parent said to me: "That's a glimpse of the obvious, isn't it?" One can write human history as a saga of the inability to recognize the obvious. If my experience is any guide, the obvious is the bittersweet fruit of repetitive failures.

The second obstacle inheres in the recognition that the public generally and educators in particular are not "ready" to meet the challenge. It is easy to say that schools should exist coequally for students and educators. But what does that mean in practice? What are starting points? Neither question has clear answers. We are here not dealing with a problem that has a precise solution, as in arithmetic, a problem we do not have to solve again and again. In the realm of social affairs (societal, interpersonal, institutional), we are always dealing with problems we have to keep solving. Unlearning old attitudes, acquiring new ones, accepting new responsibilities, trying the new and risking failure, unrealistic time perspectives and expectations, limited resources, struggles as a consequence of altered power relationships—all this in a fishbowl into which are peering diverse groups whose understanding and support are as varied and complicating as they are necessary.

Of the two obstacles, the more difficult is the first one, because it requires us to change our view about whom schools are for. Such a change will not come about easily for several reasons (if it comes about at all). For one thing, such a change is so radical in its implications that most people will shrink from pursuing it. Second, there are no prescribed ways of overcoming this obstacle. Third, precisely because it is no less an obstacle for educators than for the general public, efforts to overcome it will be predictably conflictful, controversial, and both resisted and resented. Fourth, again precisely because it concerns our schools—in regard to which reform efforts have always been marked by the hard sell, unrealistic time perspectives, egregiously unsophisticated conceptions of the school culture, and confusion between appearance and reality—the efforts to overcome the first obstacle will be subject to similar mistakes. As I said earlier, educators and the public are not ready to confront, let alone think through, the thesis that schools must be coequally accommodating to the development of teachers and students. I am in no way suggesting, however, that we sit back and wait until that magical moment when public opinion polls tell us that people are "ready." That kind of argument is as ludicrous, insensitive, and ultimately self-defeating as when it was in earlier times presented to women, Blacks, and handicapped people.

There is one obvious and essential feature of readiness: the idea has to be in the marketplace, it has to have some currency, it has to have sellers seeking buyers. The obstacle I an discussing lacks these features. In light of that, it makes no sense to offer a prescription for what it would mean in practice for schools to exist coequally for students and teachers. I would have no difficulty coming up with such a prescription, but it would be the first and very brief chapter in a book detailing the operations of Murphy's and Sullivan's laws. (There are too many physicians who give prescriptions to patients without inquiring about their allergies, previous illnesses, and understanding of what is being given them, and, too frequently, without saying anything about possible side effects.) I trust that the reader will comprehend my reluctance to offer a prescription in regard to a problem that is not regarded as a problem! And that is the point of this chapter: the complete inability of educational reformers to examine the possibility that to create and sustain for children the conditions for productive growth without those conditions existing for educators is virtually impossible. If that is true, wholly or in large part, it is because we have so overlearned the standard answer to why and for whom schools exist that we have been rendered no less inadequate than our students in regard to critical thinking.

Contrary to what some readers might think, this chapter has not been an indulgence of fantasy. It is a direct outgrowth of coping with the intractability of schools to educational reform.   As soon as one takes intractability seriously—if only as a possibility deserving scrutiny—one is not likely to come up with explanations in terms of faulty legislation, inadequate budgets, impoverished curricula, lowered standards of performance, poor quality of personnel, or a society seemingly intent on going to hell. Although these explanations are not wholly without merit, they explain little or nothing about intractability. Intractability is the hallmark of problems for which customary assumptions and axioms are no longer valid, if they ever were. Intractability says: "The problem is not technical. Nor is it motivational. Nor is it moral. The problem inheres in your unreflective acceptance of assumptions and axioms that seem so obviously right, natural, and proper that to question them is to question your reality. Therefore, faced with failure after failure, having tried this, that, and almost everything else, you don't examine your bedrock assumptions.   Instead, you come up with variations on past themes—now with more desperation and anger, but less hope. Instead of stimulating discussion in which no assumption is sacred, no alternative automatically off limits, and arguments for practicality and the status quo are no inhibitors of envisioning alternatives, intractability has reinforced the repetition compulsion."

Let me illustrate the argument by analogy. Imagine that it is 1950 and you are at a national convention of the American Association on Mental Deficiency. In the midst of the proceedings someone gets up and says:

> I make a motion that this association go on record as being opposed to the institutionalization of mentally deficient individuals. These institutions are hellholes that are inimical to development and rehabilitation. They are warehouses for those our society rejects, does not comprehend, and isolates in institutions deliberately built in the middle of nowhere. There is no evidence whatsoever that they accomplish any purpose other than isolating these individuals.   In the middle of the nineteenth century, Dorothea Dix described to the Massachusetts legislature the inhumane conditions in our so-called humane institutions. These conditions continue today. When these conditions are exposed, there are frantic, well-intentioned efforts to improve these institutions. The clamor for reform subsides only to rise again when it is apparent that conditions changed but did not improve. It

has been noted at this meeting, with a good deal of alarm, that there appears to be a tendency for parents to use our courts in an effort to change and improve conditions. But no one is saying that we should rethink whether we need these institutions, whether it is possible truly to bring about and sustain desired change, whether it is both possible and necessary to maintain these individuals in their communities. Because we have these institutions is no excuse to use them as we have, to continue to fly in the face of their intractability to improvement.

The response to this impassioned speech would have been fourfold. First, the hat would have been passed for contributions to subsidize psychotherapy or institutionalization for the speechmaker. Second, there would be acknowledgement that these institutions were far from sources of satisfaction but that the task was to repair, not eliminate, them. Third, if they were in need of repair, it reflected the niggardliness of legislatures and the public generally—that is, an unwillingness to appropriate funds to do the job well. Fourth, granted that many residents did not need to be in institutions, the glaring fact was that society was not ready to accommodate to their needs in their communities.

Beginning in the fifties, and with increasing frequency, these kinds of institutions came under the jurisdiction of our courts. In 1969 Burton Blatt was invited by the governor to address the Massachusetts legislature on what these institutions were like, based on his studies of them in three states. He essentially repeated Dorothea Dix's address but with photographs. Ten years later he revisited these same institutions. The photographs indicate that conditions were "cleaner" but little else had changed despite efforts at repair. (Blatt, 1970a, 1970b).

It was correct to say that society was not ready for the deinstitutionalization of mentally retarded individuals. It was no less correct to say that there were citizens in that same society who came to see that these institutions were intractable to improvement. And it was these citizens, organized into groups, who in large measure (there were other factors) contributed to the speed of deinstitutionalization. But what should not be glossed over is the fact that the officials pressured into carrying out deinstitutionalization were not ready either in terms of knowledge of communities, or values, or realistic programming. Those charged with overseeing the process know institutions; they did not know communities. In truth, no one was really "ready."

Deinstitutionalization gathered momentum not because anyone was clear about the universe of alternatives that could or should be considered, but because it was powered by legal, economic, and moral pressures confronting the fact of intractability.   So if deinstitutionalization of the mentally retarded has been far from a success, it does speak to the issues of readiness.   If that is the case, the fact remains that no knowledgeable person will assert that we should return to creating or rebuilding the institutions of the past.   My imaginary 1950 speechmaker did not need psychotherapy or shock treatment because he challenged axioms undergirding the thinking of the times.   He was correct that the historical evidence supported a conclusion of intractability. He should be pardoned for not envisioning how lack of readiness on the part of everyone would inevitably produce very mixed results.   But lack of readiness is no excuse for inaction or silence. To wait for readiness is to wait for Godot. Understandably, we like to believe that our efforts at significant reform will accomplish our goals—soon, smoothly, unproblematically, no three steps forward and two steps backward.   If such hopes are understandable, they also betray a lack of understanding of what significant institutional and societal change entails.

In regard to my argument that schools are no less for the growth of staff than for students, I am in the same position as that of my 1950 speechmaker.   There is one difference, however.   Whenever and wherever I have presented my argument, I have gotten the sense that many people intuitively agreed with me.   It is by no means alien to my experience over the decades to have people tell me that I was wrong, egregiously or otherwise.   But in the past two decades when this argument was percolating in my head and I took advantage of countless opportunities to articulate it to others, no one has ever disagreed with what I said.   It has the ring of truth, a face validity.   But if no one has disagreed, it is also the case that no one considered the argument "realistic" or "practical," but rather one, like so many others, that requires a utopia for its spirit to be reflected appropriately in action. And so we are back to the lack of readiness! No one is ready.

We are beginning to hear much these days about the benefits to be derived from giving teachers a greatly enlarged role in changing and running schools. (If we are beginning to hear much, it says more about the ability of a few individuals to use or have access to mass media than it does about acceptance, which is minimal.   Nor should one underestimate the potential significance of the Illinois legislation that essentially lessens the decision-making power of all school personnel.) As indicated in an earlier chapter, these few sites are not being studied in a way (if they are being studied at all) that will permit us to draw conclusions about what has happened or is happening. Please note that I said study and not evaluate. To evaluate requires that we have as comprehensive a picture as is practically possible about the developmental processes of creation and implementation. *That* we do not and are not likely to have. But on the basis of some limited observations, less limited conversation with participants, and anecdotal reports in the mass media, one conclusion seems to emerge: there is agreement that the sole outcome by which these alterations in power are being and will be judged is what happens to the achievement test scores of students. That these alterations in power may have beneficial effects for the sense of worthiness and growth of staff is a desirable outcome only if it contributes to the elevation of test scores. That this elevation has not taken place (there are, apparently, the usual few exceptions) has had the predictable effect of a somewhat frantic, increased focusing on student performance. I am reminded here of my colleague Edward Zigler who helped initiate Headstart, was the first director of the federal Office of Child Development, and more than any other person, has helped protect that program from vicissitudes in the political arena. He relates that when he would go before a congressional committee in support of the program, which included meals for Headstart children, it was not sufficient to justify funds for meals on the basis that many children came to the program ill-fed and hungry. He had to justify it on the basis that the meals would contribute to improved learning. He, of course, knew better than that. Just as a full stomach stands in no direct relationship to productive learning, alterations in power relationships in no way ensure that the contextual ingredients that together stimulate and sustain student interest, curiosity, and perseverance will be altered. Alterations in power relationships—be they in favor of increased parental influence, or teachers, or of a new conglomeration of groups—are just that: alterations in power. Why these alterations? For whom are these alterations relevant? What is there about these alterations to suggest that they are intended to change the traditional classroom in ways no less significant for students than for staff? Should we not recognize and be concerned about the obvious fact that alterations in power are alterations among groups who differ very little in their thinking in regard to whom schools are for and how they should be judged? Alterations in power that are not explicitly intended to alter, among other things, the structure and atmosphere of the traditional classroom, will have little or no effect on student performance (which I do not equate with test scores). As I shall indicate in the next chapter, reform efforts have been stimulated by concern about inadequate test scores. They have not been stimulated by concern for lack of student interest and curiosity, except as such lacks are interpreted as reflecting low teacher expectations, a nondemanding curriculum, poorly educated teachers, the inadequate technical skills of teachers, family instability, and what I can only describe as the opposite of a shape-up-or-ship-out attitude of school personnel. *Whatever factors, variables, and ambience are conducive for the growth, development, and self-regard of a school's staff are precisely those that are crucial to obtaining the same consequences for students in a classroom.* To focus on the latter and ignore or gloss over the former is an invitation to disillusionment.

Notes

1. This and other themes in this chapter were taken up at length in the Creation of Settings and the Future Societies, published in 1972 by Jossey-Bass and reprinted in paperback in 1988 by Brookline Books, Cambridge, Mass.

2. Transcripts of some of these meetings can be found in S.B. Sarason and others, Psychology in Community Settings (New York: Wiley, 1966).

3. Without question, Farber's forthcoming (1991) book on teacher burnout is the most comprehensive, analytic, and instructive book on the topic, and I urge the reader to study it. He places the problem in the context of the culture of the school, enabling the reader to avoid the too frequent mistake of viewing burnout phenomena only in terms of an asocial individual psychology. And he does not refrain, if only because the literature is so compelling, from concluding that current efforts at educational reform are very likely to be disappointing. Indeed, his book contains a wealth of evidence for what I have said in these pages. His is truly a creative scholarly effort that, I predict, will stand the test of time. I wish to thank Professor Farber for allowing me to see his manuscript before it was published.

Chapter 5

Introduction to Martin Carnoy and Henry Levin

In this article, Carnoy and Levin suggest that schools constitute an "arena of conflict" because they are confronted with the dual roles of preparing both workers and citizens. They argue that these two opposing forces are not always in harmony with one another, and that within any historical period it is typical for one dynamic to rise above the other.

They indicate that during times when social movements are weak and business ideology is strong, schools tend to emphasize the production of workers for the workplace. On the other hand, when various social movements arise to challenge these practices, schools then tend to emphasize the matter of equalized opportunities and an expanded concern for human rights.

As an example, they point out that during the first three decades of this century the gains of big business over labor fostered social and educational inequalities that were out of line with the basic ideals of a democratic society. During the next four decades there came a backlash whereby strong social movements were founded as a means of "addressing the educational needs and deprivations of the economically disadvantaged blacks, females, handicapped, and linguistic minorities."

Much of the shift took place during a time of rapid economic expansion. However, as the expansion began to deteriorate, so too did the moneys and funding required for these social programs begin to disappear. This reduction in resources once again enabled the opponents of social, racial, and gender gains in both education and government to begin to re-establish their own priorities for the schools.

Our authors conclude that during the present decade, the "pressures for using the schools for the reproduction of the work force" have again gained dominance over the concerns for egalitarian reform. They assert however, that this dominance will be significantly weakened by certain factors which are constantly impacting upon educational strategies. These factors, according to the authors, "will include the false promises of technology, high unemployment, neglect of minorities and the poor, and the general trend towards participation in the workplace."

Questions:

1. What four major changes that occurred during the sixties and seventies significantly contributed to the economic difficulties of the time? What impact did these changes have upon education?

2. Two major reports during the eighties (*A Nation at Risk* and *Action for Excellence*) argued that most of the economic problems of the nation were products of weaknesses within the educational systems. What impact did these and other similar reports have upon prevailing educational practices?

3. Edson cites similarities in various educational reports during the history of our nation. What does Edson conclude from this "comparative analysis?" Do you agree or disagree with him?

4. Our authors suggest that we are now in a period whereby we are using our schools for the "reproduction of the work force." They suggest however, that certain factors will ultimately favor and reinforce the democratic dynamic of schooling." What are these factors, and to what degree do you feel that they are in fact capable of reestablishing the "democratic dynamics?"

The Potential and Limits of School Struggles

by *Martin Carnoy and Henry Levin*

Reprinted from SCHOOLING AND WORK IN THE DEMOCRATIC STATE
by Martin Carnoy and Henry M. Levin
with the permission of the publishers, Stanford University Press.
© **1985 by the Board of Trustees of the Leland Stanford Junior University.**

The schools are an arena of conflict because they have the dual role of preparing workers and citizens. The preparation required for citizenship in a democratic society based on equal opportunity and human rights is often incompatible with the preparation needed for job performance in a corporate system of work. On the one hand, schools must train citizens to know their rights under the law as well as their obligations to exercise these rights through political participation. On the other, schools must train workers with skills and personality characteristics that enable them to function in an authoritarian work regime. This requires a negation of the very political rights that make for good citizens.

That the educational system is charged with both these responsibilities creates within it the seeds of conflict and contradiction. The ensuing struggle between the advocates of two different principles for their objectives and operations tends to fashion schools that must necessarily meet the demands of both masters imperfectly.

Historically, tensions between these two dynamics have been set in the context of wider social conflict. Schools are part of a State that is both democratic and capitalist, and this dichotomy creates a major struggle in its own right. Since schools are situated within the State, they reflect that struggle. However, this is not to say that the influences of the two opposing forces are always in balance. To the contrary, in any historical period there is a tendency for one dynamic to gain primacy over the other. This can fuel a new round of opposition in which the opposing dynamic gains primacy, in a continuous and periodic cycle.

Schools are conservative institutions. In the absence of external pressures for change, they tend to preserve existing social relations. But external pressures for change constantly impinge on schools even in the form of popular tastes. In historical periods when social movements are weak and business ideology is strong, schools tend to strengthen their function of reproducing workers for capitalist workplace relations and the unequal division of labor. When social movements arise to challenge these relations, schools move in the other direction to equalize opportunity and expand human rights.

Such shifts in primacy are not a coincidence. Strong pressure in one direction creates contradictions that activate powerful social forces to shift the momentum in the other direction. For example, the gains of big business over labor in production and in the State (including education) during the first three decades of this century fostered social and educational inequalities that were contrary to the precepts of a democratic society. In the next four decades strong social movements were unleashed to address the educational needs of the economically disadvantaged, blacks, females, the handicapped, and linguistic minorities. Laws were passed providing these groups access to national resources, programs, and schools not available to them in the past.

Much of this shift took place, however, in a period of economic expansion during which personal income was rising. The State—because of its highly visible and positive role during the Depression and the Second World War—was able to get an increasing share of national resources after the war. Under the New Deal accords, labor and business could both see gain from economic growth and State arbitration of the growth process, and as long as the economy grew steadily, rising levels of taxation were viewed as a necessary cost of prosperity.

With the onset of lower growth rates, inflation, and falling real wages in the 1970's, however, this delicate arrangement began to deteriorate. A fiscal crisis of the State further constrained educational expansion. Social commitments to increased equity and equality became the subject of intense conflict, which was further exacerbated by the decline in school-age populations, especially among the middle class. Education seemed to lost its high priority as an increasing proportion of students came from minority and working-class backgrounds and as more older families had no children of school age.[1]

Moreover, many of the educational programs and commitments to greater equality and democratic participation incurred high economic costs, and others, such as busing for racial balance, were socially disruptive. The result was that public educational spending per pupil rose dramatically, but—faced by fiscal constraints—government had to curtail educational choices once taken for granted by most families. In that sense, the legal victories and legislation of the 1950's, 1960's and early 1970's, in which democratic and egalitarian ideals prevailed, contributed to and even stimulated the political backlash of spending cutbacks. The larger struggle between capital and labor over the resources controlled by the State during this period of economic crisis resulted in reductions of social spending on education, health, and other social services. The democratic dynamic so strong during the postwar period had been in part undermined by its own success: social problems had appeared soluble by expenditure of what for a time was a constantly growing source of public revenues generated by steady, seemingly unending economic growth. Once the economy stopped growing, however, the coalition that supported expanding social services broke down. The egalitarian dynamic thrives on a coalition of diverse groups. When the available resources for democratic reforms were curtailed, that coalition decomposed into divisive groups fighting for the shrinking pie. This conflict enabled opponents of the social, racial, and gender gains in education to begin to assert their agenda.

Social Policies in the Early 1980's

The U.S. economy in the 1970's was marked by business efforts to raise profits back to the "normal" levels of the mid-1960's and by labor's attempt to maintain real wages. In the arena of liberal government policy in which these demands competed, neither met with success. Growth and profit rates remained low, real wages continued to decline, unemployment rates and prices rose, and with inflation of nominal incomes, effective income tax rates increased.

This period witnessed a transformation in the structure of production, through four major changes that further contributed to economic difficulties. It appears that in the late 1960's and early 1970's, the implicit New Deal accord among capital, labor unions, and government to equate real wage increases to productivity increases began to disintegrate. With this breakdown, employers in manufacturing, where unionized labor is most prevalent, changed their investment policy from capital investment to raise productivity to attempts to reduce wages.[2] This tendency to invest in plant relocations in regions with lower labor costs and without unions (both inside and outside the United States) was not totally new, but it was sharply accentuated during the early 1970's. Although capital investment per worker in manufacturing increased rapidly after 1973, employment remained almost unchanged at 20 million wage and salary workers. Despite this increased capital per employee, productivity increases slowed and real wages fell. Outside of manufacturing, productivity increases and real wages also fell, but capital per employee fell and employment rose rapidly.

In both sectors, employers appear to have pushed for reduced wages rather than for higher productivity. In part, this effort shifted investment overseas and to nonunionized regions of the United States.[3] Another effect was to accelerate the already rapid incorporation of women into the labor force, as employers took advantage of the major untapped domestic source of low-paid workers.[4] The new investment pattern contributed to a slowdown in the growth of domestic employment in manufacturing and a gradual shift of that employment to the Third World, both through direct investment by U.S. manufacturers and through loans by U.S. banks to Third World governments and producers.[5]

The second major change that transformed the structure of production was the separation of capital accumulation from job creation. With the oil price increases of 1973 and 1979, profits from manufacturing, commerce, and services shifted to oil and gas companies and—as petrodollars reentered the United States—to banks. By 1980, about 45 percent of gross domestic private investment came from these two sectors, compared to 26 percent in 1966.[6] Yet these sectors accounted for less that 10 percent of employment. In contrast, the share of total domestic profits in commerce and private services remained approximately constant in the 1970's whereas the share of labor in those sectors rose slowly but steadily.[7] This change in the structure of production has persisted and characterizes the American economy today. It suggests that those sectors where employment is expanding most rapidly will have to turn increasingly for their investment capital to other sectors. The current period is historically distinct from others in that the economy no longer generates capital and employment in the same sectors as it did when agriculture and then manufacturing were dominant. The effect is to put much more emphasis on finance than on production itself.

The third major change was the rapid growth of high technology industry. Besides the employment and capital accumulation effects within the industry, its products could have significant effects—through robotization, computers, and automation—on productivity and employment in other industries, especially commerce and services. The effect would be to reduce employment in those other areas.

The fourth major change was increased foreign competition in markets traditionally dominated by goods produced domestically. Part of this competition came from foreign branches of U.S. firms, and another part was stimulated by U.S. banks and industries lending to foreign firms. But much of the competition also came from Japan and newly industrializing countries that were generating their own capital and competing directly against U.S. producers in the U.S. market. Technology transfer, both legal and illegal, accelerated, so that newer products such as microchips and video games were being produced by imitators in Asia only a year or two after being introduced in the United States.

One major effect of these changes in production has been the increased role of the State. The State is responsible for softening the impact of capital movements by providing unemployment insurance and welfare payments to the unemployed. It is the State that is called upon to retrain workers who are displaced by foreign competition and to expand formal schooling in times—such as the 1970's—of increasing youth unemployment (which has hovered at the 20 percent level or even higher in recent years). It is the State that helps stimulate high technology growth through military procurement and through research and development funding—primarily military and NASA. It is also the State that is called upon to come up with solutions to the low rate of growth, to inflation, and to the increasing rate of unemployment. Already in the 1950's and 1960's, the State, more than private employers, was the object of social movements' demands for reform. Even in their demands for equal wages, the civil rights and women's movements focused on the State rather than on private employers.

It is not surprising, then, that when growth rates slowed down, it was the State that became the site and focus of conflict. The structural changes that occurred in private production precipitated social conflicts that the State has been unable to resolve. In turn, those conflicts expanded and the State role as the arena in which they were played out. By the mid-1970's, as we argued in Chapter 3, middle-income families had become increasingly reluctant to pay the rising public costs associated with the changes in production that had increased the numbers of poor as real wages fell, that had increased unemployment as capital moved, and that had increased early retirement as fewer older workers were able to find jobs that paid well. Yet the victims of changes in production, the poor and unions, also contributed to the crisis. They seemed locked into demanding higher benefits from government and higher wages from employers—actions that were opposed by the middle class, and even by many employed, lowpaid, non-unionized workers because of the inflationary consequences of such demands. With such divisions among working people, the historic coalition that had been established in the 1930's began to founder, unable to respond cohesively to the new situation.

The election of a Republican government in 1980 was the logical answer to the Democrats' failure in 1976-80 to slow inflation, raise real wages (real wages did rise in 1976-79 but declined sharply in 1980), or meet increased foreign competition in both domestic and foreign markets. The 1980 election represented, by and large, not so much a rejection of the democratic and egalitarian gains of the previous decades as a demand for respite from their costs and a quest for economic growth and jobs with stable prices. The two are coupled because Americans seem to believe that economic growth is still the single biggest contributor to solving social problems.

After the Reagan victory, the majority of the population appeared willing to undergo a major austerity program if it would lead to the end of inflation and to economic recovery. The heart of the neoconservative appeal was its position against government spending and for individual initiative. There are deep roots in the American character that resonate to such an appeal. Deepest of all is the conviction that democracy and laissez-faire capitalism are inexorably linked—so linked, in fact, that we can measure the health of democratic ideals by how little government interferes in the economy. Thus, for many who voted for conservatives, democracy was very much an issue. But the Reagan Administration's response to this mandate was not a populist, democratic, conservative program. Instead it aimed almost exclusively at increasing profit rates and the income of the rich, on the assumption that only by income redistribution toward greater inequality could rapid growth be achieved—precisely the inverse of Keynes's view in the 1930's. According to the Congressional Budget Office (U.S. Congress 1982), income earners in the lowest income categories suffered net losses as a result of the 1981 tax and benefit cuts, whereas those in higher income categories received large gains. As part of this redistribution and as a way of cutting government spending, social programs—from government employment to welfare spending to health care and education—were all cut significantly in real terms. Yet, simultaneously, real military spending was increased.

Budget cutting was intended to reduce consumption, thereby reducing inflationary pressure and pressure on interest rates, to allow the Federal Reserve Bank to reach its goals early so that the economy could begin expanding on the crest of an investment boom to be stimulated by supply-side tax cuts. Once inflation and the expectations of inflation were curbed, capital investment and economic growth were to revive robustly.

This is the "economics" side of Reaganomics. But the investment stimulation was accompanied by attacks on social spending that had distributional and ideological purposes. The logic of the argument against social spending was as follows. If investment was to be stimulated, profit rates had to increase. Average corporate profit rates had fallen from the high rates sustained in the 1950's and mid-1960's, and this had presumably deterred productive investment. American industry was also suffering increasingly at the hands of foreign competition because of relatively high wages in the United States. Finally, the argument continued that one of the most important components of inflation had been wage settlements that had exceeded the slow growth of productivity. Both the market power of unions and the political power of labor had served to raise wages and improve working conditions, including workplace health and safety, beyond the capacity of the State and industry to support them.

To the Reagan Administration, the solution to all these problems seemed to lie in a two-pronged attack on labor. First came reductions in income-maintenance programs, the main intention being to reduce the rise in government spending, but another aim being to force increased numbers of people into the labor market. This in turn created additional unemployment and—especially among minimum-wage occupations—downward pressure on wages. The second, and more direct, attack on labor involved reducing the power of labor unions both through legislation and through support of legal challenges to the unions because non-unionized labor means less upward pressure on wages, less interference in the profit-making capability of private enterprise, and the undermining of a traditional source of support for the Democrats as well.

The major anomaly in Reaganomics occurs because of another aspect of its social program: militarism couched in virulent anti-Communism. This anomaly cannot be separated from Reagan's overall political economy—it is the sine qua non of postwar neoconservatism. And rightly so. If a Republican administration is going to increase average unemployment rates and also redistribute income to corporations and the rich, it must have an ideological stance that plays to mass political support. Making America the great military power it was back in the early 1960's is intended to do that.

Military spending is scheduled to climb from about 25 to more than 30 percent of a growing federal budget, from a total authority of $214 billion in 1982 to $400 billion in 1987. This includes building the B-1 bomber and the MX missile and refitting the Navy with new aircraft carriers and submarines. It does not include the booming U.S. arms export industry, like the AWACS Saudi-Boeing contract, now canceled because of falling oil prices. If our economy still had technology and production organization that were far ahead of the competition, and our only problem were underutilized capacity, military spending could serve to stimulate production, much as it did in the Second World War and Korea. But the conditions in the U.S. economy today are totally different: although industry is operating considerably below capacity, its two main problems are declining ability to compete effectively against imports and the high cost of credit.

Defense spending aggravates both these problems. Some years ago, in his book *Pentagon Capitalism* (1970), Columbia University professor Seymour Melman suggested that Defense Department contracting promoted built-in inefficiencies at the production end and built-in cost overruns. Melman also noted that military spending accounted for most of American industry's research and development and that the military-industrial sector employed many of the country's most able engineers and scientists. The utilization of these resources on military products means that they are *not* available to strengthen the civilian economy. These arguments have been largely confirmed in recent years.[8]

The enormous increase in military spending also has its financial impact in contributing to growing federal deficits. Deficits, in turn, create increased competition for private capital and put upward pressure on interest rates. This would not be so bad for America if the deficit were invested in new consumer goods technologies, in saving energy, or even in longer-range programs for reorganizing our transportation, health, and education systems. All these investments could create a healthier basis for the future long-term development of our economy and society.

The faith of conservatives in military spending can best be viewed as a social investment policy. In the main, this explains why the Reagan Administration is so wedded to it despite the "short-run" impediments it poses for the rest of Reagan's economic package. As a social investment policy, military spending rates Communist expansion as the single greatest threat to America's way of life. A precondition of such an economic/social policy has to be military preparedness and aggressive steps overseas to halt Soviet imperialism. Such steps can only be effective if the United States is clearly the world's strongest military power, willing to use that power whenever and wherever necessary to protect America's interests. Economic growth is meaningless if there is no security against the Communist threat. The revival of American capitalism does not make much sense if capitalism cannot protect itself on a world scale. In these terms, military spending is social investment. Within this framework, it is the very basis for ensuring the continuation of American institutions and therefore cannot be subject to compromise.

Military spending tends to keep interest rates high because of its contribution to large federal deficits without producing usable consumer and producer goods. It therefore hurts small businesses. It competes for engineers, technicians, and many other skilled labor categories, driving up the price of those types of employees. Many small businesses in technology-related industries are forced to pay higher wages for a whole range of skilled workers whose job alternatives lie in defense industry.

There are, however, two countervailing effects. Military spending also strengthens certain unions—such as the Machinists Union—that politically oppose Reaganomics and are powerful actors in the union movement as a whole. But, at the same time, military spending combined with cuts in government employment are a boon to small businesses, which are seeking qualified, non-technical, college-educated personnel—precisely the personnel not demanded by military contractors and released by government cuts. The Reagan Administration claims that the planned elimination of 300,000 Federal jobs will be offset by 1984 through an increase in defense industry employment. Yet the people who stand to lose their jobs from these cutbacks are not the ones being hired by defense contractors. Government employment primarily benefits professional women (both white and black), college graduates and professional minority men (about 50 percent of these two groups worked at all levels of government in the 1970's).[9]   Military contractors will hire some women and minorities, but few at the professional level. Large corporations have a dismal record on this score. It will be smaller, more competitive businesses that will have to employ these highly educated minorities and women, and at much lower wages than government paid them. Businesses in certain nonengineering industries and services could therefore benefit by the shift from direct government employment to military contracting.

The implications of shifting federal spending from social welfare to military contracts are clear for social mobility of women and minorities: much of this portion of the labor force is being forced into unemployment or into lower-paying, lower-skilled jobs. Military production tends to favor white, male, higher-skilled labor. The militarization of the economy relative to the expansion of other government services of even other private goods and services means greater discrimination in the labor force. In short, it represents increased sexism and racism. The principal employment for minorities in the military is as soldiers, although for low-skilled whites and minorities, military service is the single most important form of post-secondary-school vocational training.

The bottom line of Reaganomics is that it favors a small, already well-off minority of Americans at the expense of the bottom 60 percent of families on the income scale. The Reagan Administration has also put enormous resources at the disposal of large corporations in the form of accelerated depreciation, and has changed the conditions of using those resources by cutting enforcement of pollution controls, rolling back health and safety regulations, and siding with business against organized labor. Women, blacks, and Hispanics are losing the economic and cultural gains they made in the last two decades. Labor unions are more on the defensive than at any time since the 1920's. Reaganomics hopes to change the social conditions of U.S. production in order to raise profits and promote investment. All these sacrifices, it is argued, will result in higher growth and—in the long run—a trickle down of higher incomes and better jobs now going increasingly to the white upper-middle class.

By the summer of 1982, the results of combining supply-side tax cuts with monetarist high interest rates had important fractions of the business community moving against supply-siders. From the Wall Street point of view, the potential of huge federal budget deficits until 1989 or beyond portended either continued high interest rates or new rounds of inflation. Opposition in the business community aimed at increasing certain business and excise taxes and cutting military spending. Certain business groups also began opposing the Administration's severe attack on the public education budget. The specter of declining growth of engineers and scientists in an age of high-technology expansion brought business associated with that sector into the education-spending arena.

But the most important reaction to Reaganomics occurred among the groups most affected by its social policies. The coalition that had disintegrated in the 1970's came back together to elect liberal Democrats in the 1982 elections. Political resistance prevented cuts in Social Security and Medicare/Medicaid, and created a backlash against military spending increases. In the spring of 1983, despite signs of economic recovery, blacks and liberal whites elected a reformist black mayor in Chicago. As early as September 1981, the AFL-CIO—historically not the most militant of labor organizations—organized a mass demonstration against the antilabor, antipoor aspects of the Reagan program. Women's groups became increasingly anti-Reagan as the extent of the Administration's social policy's effects on women became clear. The increased politicization of labor, minorities, and women is a direct response to the Administration's attempts to reinforce the reproductive dynamic and permanently weaken the principal social organizations supporting the democratic dynamic. The political struggle we observe is one in which the two forces are vying for the power to develop society in a particular way, each exploiting the weaknesses and divisions in the other.

Educational Reforms of the 1980's

Nowhere is this struggle better reflected than in education. The educational thrust of the 1950's and 1960's was toward equality, but the economic crisis of the later 1970's and early 1980's served to shift the momentum to the efficient production of a work force that would respond to the needs of employers. Especially prominent was the charge to the schools to make U.S. industry competitive again through increasing the rigor of education and training. In 1983 and 1984 more than a dozen reports were issued by national commissions, business groups, political groups, educators, and citizen organizations.[10]   The two most important in terms of national sponsorship and dissemination were *A Nation at Risk* of the National Commission on Excellence in Education (1983),[11] a report to the U.S Secretary of Education, and *Action for Excellence* of the Task Force on Education for Economic Growth of the Education Commission of the States (1983).[12]   Both reports argued that much of the economic malaise of the nation was attributable to its educational weaknesses and recommended specific reforms for raising educational standards. This emphasis was in sharp contrast to the preoccupation of the previous three decades with educational equity, equality, and access.

The emphasis in most of the reports was on more required courses at the high school level, especially in sciences, mathematics, English, and computers, although one of the major reports[13] stressed writing and communications skills. Other recommendations included better teacher selection and retention through improved teacher training, evaluation, dismissal, and systems of merit pay; more time on instruction through longer annual school sessions and school days, the assignment of more homework, and more effective use of instructional time; and higher standards for high school graduation and college admissions.

These reports reflected the shift of commitment away from equity for bilingual, economically disadvantaged, racially isolated, and handicapped students in favor of a work force that would be more highly qualified to meet the needs of U.S. industry. Indeed, the reports make a point of justifying their recommendations on the basis of the crucial role that the schools must play in making the work force internationally competitive in a world of high technology. This movement away from equity was also reinforced by the reductions in federal grants for students with special needs and the shift to block grants, which permitted the states to determine how the funds would be used rather than targeting them to specific equity programs. At the same time, many conservatives, with the support of the Reagan Administration, pressed the case for public support of private schools through both educational vouchers and tuition tax credits. Educational vouchers would provide state-subsidized certificates that could be used to pay private school tuition. Tuition tax credits would enable parents to reduce their tax burden by some portion of tuition for each child enrolled in a private school.[14] The arguments were that such arrangements would improve educational standards through market competition for students[15] and that student achievement would be higher in private schools than in public ones.[16] Both of these arguments were challenged by other researchers.[17]

The educational response to the economic crisis was to reject the pattern of equality and democratization of education that had characterized the three previous decades in favor of shifting support to private schools and to the more advantaged students who were preparing themselves for college careers. This pattern was rationalized on two grounds. First, it would permit reductions in public expenditures by cutting commitments to the less-advantaged, thus freeing up resources for tax reductions and expansion of the military budget. Second, it would focus on the presumed needs for high skill levels in a high-technology work force to meet the new demands of a competitive international climate. There is a tacit assumption here that disadvantaged, handicapped, and minority students are less likely to be central to filling the educational needs associated with a high-technology economy. Rather, the focus on educational standards, computer skills, and assisting private-school constituencies took precedence over the democratic aspirations of education.

It is noteworthy that similar types of reforms have been recommended in times of earlier economic crisis. In the last three decades of the nineteenth century and the first decade of the twentieth, one of the most important educational reformers was Charles Eliot, president of Harvard University. In the depths of the serious economic crisis of 1893, Eliot issued his noted *Committee of Ten Report*. In comparing *A Nation at Risk* with the Eliot report of some 90 years earlier, Edson[18] found that their attitudes and the circumstances surrounding them were almost identical. Both recommend that high schools require four years of English, three years of history or social studies, three years of science, and three years of mathematics. The earlier report recommended four years of a foreign language, whereas the more recent one pushed for only two years of a foreign language, and a half year of computer science. Both reports recommended longer school hours and improvements in teacher selection, justifying their recommendations by dwelling on the superiority of schools among our main economic competitors in Western Europe and, in the case of the recent report, in

Japan.

Edson concludes that the social, political, and economic upheavals that preceded each of the reports led to a climate in which "individualism" and "survival of the fittest" were viewed as the path to stability and excellence. In both cases, such arguments were translated into educational terms that would simply ignore the needs of those who had to be "coddled" to be successfully integrated into the mainstream of American life. If the schools were to dawdle to assist the less fortunate, the nation would be threatened "by a rising tide of mediocrity that threatens our very future as a nation and a people." [19]

The states have also been pursuing the national agenda for reforms. Whereas the federal share of expenditures had risen from less than 5 percent of total expenditures on elementary and secondary schools in 1960 to almost 10 percent by 1980, the percentage dropped again to about 7 percent by 1984. Thus, the responsibilities for reforms have fallen on the states, many of which had established tax- or revenue-limitation measures. This meant that the states were seeking to implement the national recommendations for reform, often in the form of legislation, without adequate appropriations for satisfying the new requirements. For example, lengthening the school year and school day, alleviating teacher shortages, and retaining better teachers require hefty increases in school spending. But many of the states adopted the recommendations of the national reports without considering the costs of carrying out the changes. These costs were estimated at about $20 billion by Alan Wagner and Frances Kemerer at the State University of New York in Albany.

California is an important case in point, having passed Senate Bill 813 in 1983 without providing the necessary revenues to fund most of the new programs. Among the provisions called for in SB 813 were a longer school day and school year, improved classroom teaching, more demanding graduation requirements, increased teacher salaries and the establishment of a higher-paying category of "mentor teachers," and improved administration. Although these and other changes were expected to cost at least $1.5 billion to implement, less than $500 million in new funding was provided for the 1983-84 school year. Even with significant increases promised for 1984-85 as the state's economy improved, funding was not expected to meet the costs of the changes. California has over 4 million students in public elementary and secondary schools. The incentives to provide modest increases in the length of the school day and school year alone were estimated to cost over $250 million.

Hence, the reforms of the 1980's thus far are largely in the direction of greater efficiency in the educational system with respect to the particular outcomes considered important for economic vitality. The implicit message was that better education was a question not of more spending per pupil but of better "management," better teaching promoted by competition, and greater student discipline. Emphasis was placed on higher standards for preparing students for what was perceived as a workplace requiring higher and higher levels of skills for high technologies. Resources for funding the reforms were not adequate to the task, and the concern for equality in education and the democratic goals of schooling were relegated to a "benign neglect."

In this decade, the pressures for using the schools for reproduction of the work force have achieved primacy over those on the side of democratic and egalitarian reforms. Though much is said about the economy, little is said about democracy in pursuing educational change. What we wish to emphasize is that the struggle between the two forces is still very much alive, even though the present policy seems to favor capital accumulation rather than equity and popular participation. It is therefore instructive to point out the factors that will undermine the present strategies, ultimately reinforcing what we have called the democratic dynamic of schooling. These factors include the false promises of high technology; high unemployment; neglect of minorities and the poor; and the general trend toward participation in the workplace.

The advent of high technology has been held out as the driving force of our future economy. Although there is no single definition of high technology, the term is generally associated with computers, microelectronic devices, biotechnology, robots, and telecommunications. Firms involved in high technology are considered to have large investments in research and development and to employ relatively large numbers of persons with technical skills.[20] One of the assumptions of the national educational reforms is that traditional entry-level jobs in the economy will diminish, whereas highly skilled technical positions will increase to meet the expanding needs associated with microcomputers and other high-technology applications. Indeed, the view of many of the educational reports is that a lack of trained personnel for skilled positions is likely to place the nation at risk with respect to its competitive position in the world economy. At the same time it is assumed that low-skill jobs will disappear as the new laborsaving technologies make them redundant. The implications for students are that those with minimal education (such as completing high school) will face fewer job possibilities, whereas those with computer knowledge and other forms of scientific and technical training will have virtually unlimited opportunities.

Both the popular media and the schools have stressed this scenario, with the schools benefiting from the greater willingness of state treasuries to loosen the purse strings to finance education for a high-technology future. But the available evidence does not support this optimistic view of job development. Although jobs in many high-technology occupations are growing at a very rapid rate, the absolute number of increased jobs in these occupations is very small because they begin with a very small base. For example, the Bureau of Labor Statistics (BLS) of the U.S. Department of Labor estimated that between 1982 and 1995 the fastest-growing job category would be computer service technicians, with an increase of almost 100 percent in numbers of jobs over that period.[21] But since there were only about 55,000 such jobs in 1982, the increase would amount to only about 53,000 jobs. Although jobs for building custodians are expected to grow by less than 28 percent over that period, almost 800,000 new jobs are forecast for that occupation, or about 15 times as many jobs as for computer service technicians.

In fact, the occupations likely to experience the largest growth in terms of absolute numbers of jobs are heavily dominated by such low-level service occupations as building custodians, cashiers, office clerks, sales clerks, waiters and waitresses, and nurses' aides and orderlies.[22] Different studies of the job market are consistent in finding that relatively few new jobs will be created in high-technology occupations, and that most job growth will occur in service occupations that pay relatively low wages and require little education.[23] The BLS has estimated that only about 6 percent of all jobs will be in technologically oriented occupations in 1995,[24] and that of the 40 occupations expected to contribute the most jobs to the economy, only about 25 percent will require college degrees.[25] Not only does job growth favor low-skill jobs rather than the highly skilled ones that are the object of the educational reforms, but even many existing jobs are being transformed by technology into ones that require fewer skills. Traditionally, typists were required to have knowledge of document formats, letter-perfect typing skills, and strong spelling skills. However, word processors can correct typing and spelling errors automatically and provide appropriate document formats from memory, enabling operation by persons who have only the most rudimentary typing skills. Increasingly, powerful software packages permit highly sophisticated applications to broad classes of problems with only minimal programming skills. Many highly automated offices have no programmer at all, since all computerized tasks can be done through "user-friendly menus" of options. Similar stories can be told for computer and computerized-machine repair, data processing, auto repair, design, drafting, and many other occupations.[26] Whereas earlier forms of automation allowed the replacement of physical labor, the newer technologies displace mental labor, enabling jobs to be eliminated and reduced in terms of their skill requirements. The failure of high technology to deliver on its job promises will undermine the incentives of students to meet the new demands of the schools and will provide increasing calls by workers for government intervention in job markets. This phenomenon will be further reinforced by the relatively high unemployment rates that are likely to be maintained in the 1980's. With the rapid economic recovery in 1983-84 fueled by large federal deficits and enormous increases in military spending, unemployment rates were expected to fall from a high of almost 11 percent at the end of 1982 to about 7.5 percent by the mid-1980's. But such a rate would be—by far—the highest U.S. unemployment rate in "prosperous" times during the entire postwar period, with over 8 million unemployed at the height of recovery. Among all youth the rates were in the 20 percent range, and among nonwhite youth they approached 50 percent. These high rates of unemployment will not be brought down by educational changes, since they largely reflect an inadequacy of jobs relative to job-seekers.[27]

The neglect of minorities and the poor in the economy generally and the schools specifically will also serve to forge new social movements that will seek direct government intervention. The number of people in poverty in the United States rose substantially under the Reagan Administration, a result of policies accepting high levels of unemployment and promoting cutbacks in social programs. The fact that youngsters from economically disadvantaged and minority backgrounds have special educational needs that are ignored by the new educational agenda means that large numbers of such people will enter the labor market with little hope for social mobility. As long as such people can be relegated to the unemployed, employers may have little concern. But in some cities and regions minorities will represent a major share of the work force. In states such as California, it is expected that Hispanic students will become a majority in the public schools well before the turn of the century. And when school populations grow up, they become the new labor force. Thus, employers may join with these groups to push for greater equity in schooling, and there are likely to be new pressures on government by a broad coalition to promote greater equity in both labor markets and schools.

Finally, the general movement toward greater participation in the workplace associated with the overeducated worker (emphasized in Chapter 7) will also serve to undermine school reforms that ignore the democratic and egalitarian aspects of schooling. Groups that are dissatisfied with the present dynamic of schooling and the economy will likely join together with those concerned about the escalating military role of the United States, nuclear disarmament, conservation, energy, and many of the other dilemmas that have been created or exacerbated by present policies. Out of this political activity there will be new groups elected and pressures for new policies that support the broader-based concerns of a democracy, both inside the schools and in other parts of society and the economy.

Undoubtedly the most important message implied by our analysis is that democratic struggles are important for achieving the types of schools and economy that serve the broadest needs of our society and citizenry. Even under the present circumstances—when the quest for improved educational services for minorities, the poor, and the handicapped is under attack by conservative interests—it is the marshaling of social movements and democratic forces that places limits on retrenchment and makes the battle costly for the other side. But beyond this resistance, the struggle enables the tide of hegemony of the narrower interests of the wealthy to be countered in the courts, at the polls, in the media, and on the streets. Continuing struggle, together with the failures of existing policies to meet the larger concerns of a democracy, will increase the power of democratic coalitions for fairness, equity, and participation. Democratic struggles for just and meaningful schooling are effective counters to the economic forces that are attempting to gain primacy over American schools and the formation of our youth. A study of the past supports our optimism for the future.

Notes _____

1.   Michael W. Kirst and Walter I. Garms, "The Political Environment of School Finance Policy in the 1980's," in James W. Guthrie, ed., *School Finance Policies and Practices* (Cambridge, MA: Ballinger, 1980), 47-75.

2.   Martin Carnoy, Derek Shearer, and Russell Rumberger, *A New Social Contract: The Economy and Government After Reagan* (New York: Harper and Row, 1983).

3.   . Barry Bluestone and Bennett Harrison, *The Deindustrialization of America* (New York: Basic, 1982).

4.   Between 1960 and 1980, the total labor force grew by less than 50 percent, but the number of women in the labor force almost doubled (U.S. Dep't of Commerce, *Statistical Abstract of the United States: 1982-83*, 103d ed. (Washington, D.C.: G.P.O., 1982): 376.

5.   Direct investment abroad by U.S. investors rose 12 percent annually between 1972 and 1980, but U.S. bank loans increased by 43 percent annually in those same years (*Economic Report of the President* 1983: Table B-105). U.S. foreign investment in manufacturing increased from $61.2 billion to $90.7 billion (current dollars), or 48 percent, between 1976 and 1982 [U.S. Dep't of Commerce, *Survey of Current Business* 61, no. 2, (Feb., 1981): 59.]

6.   *Economic Report of the President 1983* (Washington, D.C.: G.P.O., 1983), Table B-83; *Business Week*, June 1, 1980.

7.   *Ibid.*, Tables B-83 and B-37.

8.   Robert W. DeGrasse, Jr., *Military Expansion, Economic Decline* (New York: Council on Economic Priorities, 1983)

9.   Martin Carnoy, Derek Shearer, and Russell Rumberger, *A New Social Contract: The Economy and Government After Reagan* (New York: Harper and Row, 1983), Chap. 6.

10.   J. Lynn Griesemer and Cornelius Butler, *Education Under Study* (Chelmsford, MA: Northeast Regional Exchange, Inc., 1983).

11.   National Commission on Excellence in Education, *A Nation at Risk: The Imperative for Educational Reform* (Washington, D.C.: Dept. of Education, 1983).

12.   Education Commission of the States, Task Force on Education for Economic Growth, *Action for Excellence* (Denver, 1983).

13.   Ernest L. Boyer, *High School: A Report on Secondary Education in America* (New York: Harper and Row, 1983).

14.   Thomas James and Henry M. Levin, *Public Dollars for Private Schools: The Case of Tuition Tax Credits* (Philadelphia: Temple U.P., 1983).

[15.] John E. Coons and Stephen D. Sugarman, *Education by Choice* (Berkeley, CA: Univ. of California Press, 1978).

[16.] James S. Coleman, Thomas Hoffer, and Sally Kilgore, *High School Achievement: Public, Catholic, and Private Schools Compared* (New York: Basic, 1982).

[17.] Henry M. Levin, "Educational Production Theory and Teacher Inputs," in Charles Bidwell and Douglas Windham, eds., *The Analysis of Educational Productivity: Issues in Macroanalysis*, 2, Chap. 5 (Cambridge, MA: Ballinger, 1980); *Sociology of Education* 55, nos. 2/3 (April/July, 1982); J. Douglas Willms, "Do Private Schools Produce Higher Levels of Academic Achievement? New Evidence for the Tuition Tax Credit Debate," in Thomas James and Henry M. Levin, eds., *Public Dollars for Private Schools* (Philadelphia: Temple U.P., 1983): 223-31.

[18.] Charles H. Edson, "Risking the Nation: Historical Dimensions on Survival and Educational Reform," *Issues in Education* (June, 1984).

[19.] National Commission on Excellence in Education, *A Nation at Risk: The Imperative for Educational Reform* (Washington, D.C.: Dept. of Education, 1983): 5.

[20.] Richard W. Riche, *et al.*, "High Technology Today and Tomorrow: A Small Slice of the Employment Pie," *Monthly Labor Review* (Nov., 1983): 50-58.

[21.] George T. Silvestri, *et al.*, "Occupational Employment Projections Through 1995," *Monthly Labor Review* (Nov., 1983): 46.

[22.] *Ibid.*, 45.

[23.] Richard W. Riche, *et al.*, "High Technology Today and Tomorrow: A Small Slice of the Employment Pie," *Monthly Labor Review* (Nov., 1983): 50-58; Russell W. Rumberger and Henry M. Levin, "Forecasting the Impact of New Technologies on the Future Job Market" (Stanford, CA: Stanford Univ., Institute for Research on Educational Finance and Governance, 1984).

[24.] Richard W. Riche, *et al.*, "High Technology Today and Tomorrow: A Small Slice of the Employment Pie," *Monthly Labor Review* (Nov., 1983): 50-58.

[25.] George T. Silvestri, *et al.*, "Occupational Employment Projections Through 1995," *Monthly Labor Review* (Nov., 1983): 44.

[26.] Henry M. Levin and Russell W. Rumberger, "The Educational Implications of High Technology" IFG Project Report 83-A4 (Stanford, CA: Institute for Research on Educational Finance and Governance, 1983); Henry M. Levin and Russell W. Rumberger, "Low-Skill Future of High Tech," *Technology Review* 86, no. 6 (Aug./Sept., 1983): 18-21.

[27.] Katherine G. Abraham, "Structural/Frictional vs. Deficient Demand Unemployment: Some New Evidence," *American Economic Review* 83, no. 4 (Sept., 1983): 708-24; Henry M. Levin, "The Workplace: Employment and Business Interventions," in E. Seidman, ed., *Handbook of Social Intervention* (Beverly Hills, CA: Sage, 1983): 499-521.

Chapter 6

Introduction to Jean Anyon

In this article Jean Anyon describes various processes and events which demonstrate how it is that "social manifestations of racial and social class status," when combined with one another, are capable of destroying even the most sincere efforts at meaningful school reform.

She points to three primary factors which when occurring within a "socially and economically isolated urban ghetto," can serve as powerful determinants of what ultimately happens to inner city schools as well as any efforts to improve them. These factors are:

- social cultural differences among participants in reform
- an abusive school government
- educators expectations of school reform

Anyon then goes on to illustrate the manner in which the above three factors, and others such as teacher's expectations of reform, teacher/student relations, and divergent dialects, have impacted upon efforts at improvement within one school in a large urban district in the northeast.

She then describes how it is that the "structural basis" for failure in inner-city schools is essentially a product of prevailing political, economic, and cultural conditions which must be changed before significant school reform can occur; and concludes by encouraging us to consider more radical political, economic, and cultural reforms in face of the continual and unremitting alienation of students, teachers, families, and cultures.

Questions:

1. Do you feel that meaningful educational reform will require major changes in political, economic, and cultural conditions? What might these changes consist of?

2. How might the existence of "divergent dialects" impact upon matters of student achievement as well as efforts at school reform?

3. To what degree do you feel that teacher expectations can impact upon student's perceptions of schooling?

4. How might various manifestations of racial and social class status combine to negate efforts at school reform?

Race, Social Class, and Educational Reform in an Inner-city School

by Jean Anyon

Originally published in the *Teachers College Record*, Vol. 97, No. 1, Fall 1995. Reprinted with permission.

Drawing on an assessment of reform efforts in one school in an urban ghetto in a large district in the Northeast, this article describes processes and events that illustrate how social manifestations of racial and social class status can combine to vitiate efforts at school reform. I argue that three factors—sociocultural differences among participants in reform, an abusive school environment, and educator expectations of failed reform—occurring in a minority ghetto where the school population is racially and economically isolated constitute some of the powerful and devastating ways that concomitants of race and social class can intervene to determine what happens in inner-city schools, and in attempts to improve them.

It has become increasingly clear that several decades of educational reform have failed to bring substantial improvement to schools in America's inner cities.[1]   Most recent analyses of unsuccessful school reform (and prescriptions for change) have isolated educational, regulatory, or financial aspects of reform from the social context of poverty and race in which inner-city schools are located.[2]   This article will discuss failed school reform from a somewhat different perspective. Drawing on an assessment of reform efforts in one school in an urban ghetto in a large district in the Northeast, the article describes processes and events that illustrate how social manifestations of racial and social class status can combine to vitiate efforts at school reform.[3]

I will first describe how sociocultural differences between reformers and the parents and teachers, and between reforms and the student population, created distrust among participants as well as inappropriate curriculum and instruction for the students. These sociocultural disjunctions made the successful implementation of change extremely difficult. A second factor I will discuss is the relationship between educators and students in the school. The lived professional culture of many teachers and the administrators in this school (for thirty years one of the poorest in the city) has deteriorated into a dehumanizing, abusive stance toward the student population, whose families lack the clout to ensure better treatment. This professional culture, and the students' active opposition to it, also contributed to the failure of attempted improvement projects. The final phenomenon to be discussed is the expectation of school staff that educational reform was not going to succeed. Almost all staff members felt that reform efforts were futile; most also felt that even if the reforms could be made to work, the resulting changes would have very little impact on the children's lives or futures.

I will argue that these three factors—sociocultural differences among participants in reform, an abusive school environment, and educator expectations of failed reform—occurring in a minority ghetto where the school population is racially and economically isolated constitute some of the powerful and devastating ways that concomitants of race and social class can intervene to determine what happens in inner-city schools, and in attempts to improve them.

Background

During the first two decades of the twentieth century, the schools in the city in which the research site is located (Newark, N.J.) were nationally recognized for their innovative attempts to serve an urban clientele, which included children of the industrial working class, the middle class, and the business elite as well as the poor.[4] However, in the early 1920s wealthy families began moving to the suburbs, followed in the next forty years by most of the city's middle class. Between 1917 and the early 1960s rural blacks, most of them with no financial resources and little formal schooling, moved up from the South and into the city. By 1961, the district schools were majority black and poor.

Until 1971, with the election of a black mayor and a black city council, the schools continued to be staffed by white administrators and teachers, and the city government was composed primarily of white ethnic personnel. No major educational initiatives were taken by government or educational leaders between 1922 and the 1971 election of the first black mayor. The system deteriorated. A 1940 assessment of the district schools noted that low achievement and dilapidated schools were common, and that measures to meet the needs of the city's poor (most of whom in 1940 were still white working-class ethnics) must be taken.[5] By 1968, a state-sponsored citizens' report found that the school system was in "advanced state of decay," and advised that the state run the city schools and provide massive assistance.[6] No such action by the state was undertaken.

The state did, however, begin to closely monitor the continuing decline of the schools in its largest city. A series of state-sponsored evaluations was undertaken, and in 1984 the state mandated that the district administration take action or the district would lose its accreditation.[7] In 1989, in response to a state threat of takeover, the district's leaders initiated a four-year program of reform in eight schools in the central section of the city, including the school that was the focus of the research to be reported here.

There were reasons to hope that this reform effort would bring some success: Millions of dollars had been donated by major corporations and foundations for projects in the eight schools (seven feeder schools and one high school). Twenty-five corporate, higher education, and local citizen groups provided plans and personnel.

Moreover, the reforms were organized and directed by representatives of the city's majority black population. In 1989 (as now), the superintendent was African-American, and the board of education was African-American and Hispanic; the assistant superintendent with responsibility for the reform initiatives (who is no longer with the district) was black, and her staff consisted of two blacks and a Hispanic. Then as now, African Americans were the majority of significant players at most levels of the school system and in the city government.

It was possible that local control by blacks would be a catalyst of change, making the schools more responsive to black students: The administration could, for example, choose reforms that empowered members of their own constituency—significant parent involvement if not community control could be a focus. A celebration of minority cultures could infuse the curriculum. Or the district could, given the studies that show black students' difficulty with standardized tests, present a serious challenge to government reliance on these tests as measures of achievement and funding.

The majority of classroom teachers in the district are African-American.[8] Perhaps these black educators could reverse commonly held low expectations for minority students from low-income households; perhaps they could understand and nurture their charges, laying the educational groundwork for academic success.[9]

However, and conversely, it was also possible that, as Edward Said, Albert Memmi, Frantz Fanon, and others studying oppressed minorities have shown, victims of race and class exploitation sometimes grow to mimic the behavior and attitudes of their oppressors, and themselves victimize others of their own group over whom they have power.[10] It becomes important, then to note here that some black educators, as products of past racial (and perhaps class) discrimination and exploitation, may have internalized beliefs about their students that mimic attitudes held by the white dominant society but that work to the detriment of children of color from poverty backgrounds.

Before proceeding further, I want to acknowledge the potentially controversial nature of statements by a white middle-class researcher concerning race and the possible effects of race on teaching, learning, and school reform. Perhaps it appears that I am stereotyping black teachers by asserting that some could excel with their students because they are black. Perhaps to expect a black administration to challenge the white power structure is to misplace the burden and is unfair. It is possible that these and other statements will be seen as racist.

It is important to remember, however, that the meanings or attributions of such terms as *race* (or gender, sexuality, or social class, for that matter) are not absolute. They are socially constructed. Groups and individuals develop from their experience and points of view denotations of these terms that make sense to them. I—as a white professional—discuss race in this paper in ways that may differ from the constructs others with other experiences might use. My interpretation of events, therefore, may differ from those of others: Where I will describe a black teacher, for example, as abusive of black students, others might see culturally sanctioned "strict discipline."

Moreover, I do not intend to disparage "all black teachers," "all white principals (or white teachers) in inner-city schools," "all low-income parents," "all middle-class consultants," or any other group, by inferring

that all members of any group act in the manner to be described here. I
report behaviors that I observed.

Marcy School

The research site, a K-8 school, will be called Marcy School.[11]
Marcy was considered by some personnel to be a good school ("It's a
happening school" [assistant superintendent]; "It's a very good
school—there aren't drugs all over it like in some of the other schools"
[drug counselor]). Others considered it to be "in the middle—not great,
not terrible; right at the mean" [school psychologist]. No teacher or
administrator considered it among the worst schools. As the principal
said, "We may have problems, but we're no way the worst."

The student body is 71 percent black, 27 percent Hispanic, and 2
percent Asian and white. All but 3 of the 500 students in the school
are from families with incomes below the poverty line, and qualify for
free lunch. (In the district as a whole, 63 percent of the students are
African-American, 26 percent are Hispanic, and most [78 percent] are
poor, and qualify for free lunch.)

The majority of the students at Marcy School live in nearby housing
projects. During the period of this study, the school had an official
homeless rate that fluctuated between 5 and 20 percent. A recent
psychological assessment of a random sample of forty-five Marcy
students found that they were plagued by the problems that result from
extreme poverty: chaotic lives, neglect and/or abuse, poor health
histories and chronic health problems, emotional stress, anxiety, and
anger.[12] Drug use and AIDS have claimed the parents of a large (but
uncatalogued) number of the students, and teachers comment that many
of their students are being raised by relatives and friends or, as a recent
newspaper article stated, are growing up "without any apparent adult
supervision."[13]

During the period of this study, the principal of Marcy School was a
white Italian male (a former shop teacher) and the assistant principal
was a Hispanic woman. Sixteen (64 percent) of the twenty-five
classroom teachers were black and a sizable minority of these stated in
interviews they had grown up in poor or working-class neighborhoods
of this or other cities. Six classroom teachers (24 percent) were
Hispanic, and three (12 percent) were white (almost all of both groups
are from working-class backgrounds; all but two now live in the

suburbs).

Most (61 percent) of the specialists and nonclassroom teachers in the school (basic-skills teachers, special education teachers, art and gym teachers, psychologist, social worker, learning disabilities specialist, etc.) were white. The rest were African-American. All the teacher aides in the buildings were black (with the exception of several Hispanic) women, and were parents of students or former students; all lived in the neighborhood, most in nearby housing projects. Perhaps half of the aides had themselves attended Marcy School. Almost all janitors and kitchen workers were black long-time residents of the city.[14]

Sociocultural Differences Between Reformers, Parents, and School Personnel

The following portions of the article discuss ways in which I see the racial-class histories and characteristics of participants in the reform process affecting attempts to change Marcy School. This section describes ways in which the sociocultural distances between reformers and parents and school personnel interfered with the implementation of several projects.

The assistant superintendent in charge of the reform, a black female Ph.D., called occasional meetings of her "collaborators"—twenty-five representatives from groups or agencies with projects in the eight schools. The collaborators included administrators and professors from three area colleges and universities (including me); executive directors of two regional philanthropic foundations; representatives of three statewide special-interest groups (Educate America, Cities in Schools, and One to One—a mentoring program started by a black congressman); the assistant director of a coalition of church groups; members of the city's chamber of commerce; an activist minister; representatives of three national financial corporations with headquarters in the city; the president and vice-president of a large consulting firm from a highly affluent suburb; and the director and representatives of the National Executive Service Corps, a group of retired white business executives who volunteer their services in city schools.

All who attended these meetings, and who took part in projects in the schools, were professionals; five (in addition to the assistant superintendent) were African-American and the other twenty were white. The field notes that follow are excerpted from a meeting that suggests how sociocultural differences between two of these reformers and low-income minority parents at Marcy School manifested themselves.

Two retired white executives from the National Executive Service Corps have been brought in by the assistant superintendent to advise parents at Marcy School on how to collaborate. The men are meeting with the Parent Corps in the library. Mrs. Betty Williams, a black woman of about sixty, former parent and student at Marcy, head of the Parent Corps, and a community leader in the housing projects where she and the four other parents (four black women and one Hispanic male) live, are sitting around a rectangular table. On the other, far side of the room, around a smaller table, sit the two executives, wearing expensive-looking suits, smiling across the room at the parents, and holding pencils above long yellow pads.

The five parents are seated so that only Mrs. Williams faces the two men across the room. At no time during the discussion does she or any of the other parents look at the executives.

One executive smiles broadly and asks the group: "We each had our own company. We've had a good deal of experience. What problems do you have that we—with our background—could help you with?"

Mrs. Williams responds, "Maintenance are our only problems. We've gotten everything done except the bathrooms. And we're fighting for equipment. I fought for two years to get a gym floor. I went to this school. We had all kind of equipment here. Now the kids don't have nothing to do in the gym. [Several parents nod.] We're going to send letters to parents so kids'll wear uniforms for gym. We go to the board meetings. The eighth graders don't know how to play kickball! We got taught that in gym. We were so amazed. They didn't know how to play kickball, so we teach them."

Retired white executive, "But [pause]—if there's anything we can do for you, we'd like your suggestions."

Mrs. Williams ignores his question and says to the parents, "I'm going to the dentist—to get me some teeth. And then I'm *really* going to eat!" (She then talks to the parents about an upcoming assembly in which she will give certificates to parent volunteers.)

Retired white executive intercedes: "What are your plans for getting more parents [referring to the fact that the Parent Corps has only eight parents]?"

Mrs. Williams says, "We *have* a lot of parents. We found that this is the way we get parents: In the morning I stand by the door and tell them they can talk to me about anything." [She again speaks to the group at her table about the upcoming assembly.] The retired executives look at each other, smile again at the parents, and stop asking questions. They sit quietly at the back of the room during the rest of the meeting and Mrs. Williams does not acknowledge them again.

The social gulf between the parents and the reformers that appeared to me to impair communication and joint planning at this meeting was never breached. During the subsequent months neither the white executives from the corporate world nor the black and Hispanic parents from the projects were able to utilize each others' skills. Commentators have long pointed to the fact that differences between social backgrounds and language can impair interaction and trust.[15] Other factors (such as inexperience) certainly contributed to the executives' lack of expertise in working with the parents, but even this lack of experience can be attributed in part to the enormous social and cultural gulf separating the two groups. Nothing came of the executives' attempted involvement in the parent group, and they terminated their visits after several months.

A similar social distance separated many teachers (most of whom, as noted above, were African-American, and who stated in interviews they had grown up in poor or working-class families) from the two consultants directing the largest reform project, "Training in Shared Decision Making" for school-based management. This project was run by two blond, expensively dressed consultants based in an exclusive suburb twenty-five miles away. In part because of their blond, suburban "look," the consultants were called by teachers "the all-American kids."

On several occasions these consultants complained to me that the teachers and administrators in this district "are just like the kids. They don't even know how to *talk* about collaboration. And they want immediate gratification. If they don't get it, they want to quit." The teachers also complained to me that they thought the two consultants were "too suburban": "They have no idea what city schools are like. They don't know what we're up against." "They don't know the kids!" A number of teachers complained to the assistant superintendent that the consultants were racist, and had made racist comments. The assistant superintendent told me she had agreed with the teachers, but that she had counseled the teachers, "We have to work with them despite the racism. They have a lot to teach us [about cooperation]."

The professional development project was resisted by both teachers and administrators as "too abstract," and "not geared to city schools."[16] In part because of teacher complaints of racism and the perceived inappropriateness of the consultants for the city's schools, the board of education rescinded permission for the consultants to continue the project in shared decision making after the second year, and it was never fully implemented in the eight schools.

Middle-level management employees (both black and white) from the nearby headquarters of two national corporations in town participated in a tutoring program at Marcy and two other elementary schools. In two schools the administration refused to cooperate with them, saying they were not equipped "to deal with the kids." In Marcy School the tutors quit because they said "nobody was interested in the students getting any tutoring" from them. Referring to middle- and upper-middle-class helpers in the reform effort (such as the groups of executives, as well as graduate students from a university in New York City), a Marcy teacher stated: "They come in the schools and they can't handle the kids. We have to train them and monitor them. It takes too much time." Another said, "They have no idea of the *situation* we have here! They just get in the way."

As these examples indicate, social distance arising in part from lack of mutual experience and knowledge of each other in people of different class and racial backgrounds can impair communication, trust, and joint action between reformers and school personnel, can foster an incompetence that arises in part from this lack of knowledge, and can in these and other ways hamper the implementation of educational improvement projects. In the examples presented here, teachers and parents resisted the efforts of reformers, and several improvement projects were vitiated.

Sociocultural Differences Between Reforms and the Student Population

I asked the assistant superintendent who had decided which projects would be part of this reform effort. She said that she, members of the board of education, a union representative, and a parent representative had taken a weekend retreat together in June of 1989 and had chosen the projects that would be attempted. I asked whether what she and they chose differed in any way from what the state had mandated in recent regulations. "No, we chose the exact same things," she said. "We chose what is raising scores across the country: school-based management, ungraded primary, all-day kindergarten, departmentalization of the middle grades, programs like whole language and cooperative learning. We ordered all new textbooks in math, science, reading, phonics, and a whole language series."

I asked if any of the reforms responded to the fact that most of the school children were African-American. "No," she said, "although the superintendent and I are black nationalists—well, I was a pan-Africanist, but we chose what was fundable." I asked if any of the reforms responded to the poverty of the children. "No," she stated again, "just the parent forums [informational meetings]. A lot of our parents are young, and disenfranchised." I then inquired if any of the reforms had anything to do with the students' black dialect (or, more accurately, "inner-city dialect," since all the students seem to speak it—blacks, Hispanics, and the few poor whites as well). "No—but that does get in the way. They can't express themselves."

I press, "Why not choose reforms that respond in some way to the children—at least a multicultural focus to curriculum, for example?" She responds, "It wouldn't be politically do-able. Education is as much about politics as it is about kids. You have to be aware of the larger bureaucratic system you're working in. The old-boy network, they're white men, and that's where the money is! You have to go to them for money to do things. What you do has to be acceptable to them."

What I would like to suggest is that these and other reforms that were chosen (see below) have little if anything to do with this district's students and the cultural and economic realities of their lives, and in part because of this sociocultural inappropriateness, the reforms actually impede the students' academic progress and thereby preclude reform success.

One of the reforms initiated by the board of education in 1989 was an attempt to enforce teacher accountability by mandating that instruction be based on the new textbooks, and that these texts were to be used "on grade level"—for example, fifth-grade texts used with all fifth-graders, despite the fact that the majority of students in most classrooms are reading and computing well below grade level. A recent state report directed district teachers to adhere closely to those texts. Both state and district mandates include directives that teachers are to reteach and retest students on any skills not passed on the quarterly tests devised by the publishers of the reading and math series.[17]

Teachers complain bitterly about the "on-grade-level" policy, stating that it is impossible to teach students from textbooks they cannot understand. "They can't read the books and they're labeled failures before they even try!" was a typical complaint.

There are additional ways in which this reliance on mainstream texts and workbooks to teach students marginalized by poverty and race interferes with their achievement. An examination of the texts revealed that despite an occasional story featuring a minority character, the texts are a microcosm of white middle-class interests and situations. Teachers state that the stories in the reading and language series, for example, "have nothing to do with the kids, they hate them, they think they're boring and stupid." Exclusive use of these texts and the continual testing and retesting of the skills in them mean that there is no room for (for example) curriculum about black and Latino history (although the district has produced excellent curriculum guides in this area). No teacher of the twenty-four in the school I queried supplements the written curriculum with black studies in a systematic way except—to varying degrees—during black history month. Two years ago high school students at two city high schools demonstrated (unsuccessfully) to get a black studies curriculum in use at their schools.

The children I interviewed at Marcy School knew very little about black history. I interviewed twenty-five nine- to thirteen-year-olds at the school, and only eight knew who Martin Luther King, Jr. was. Of these, five stated they had heard about him or other figures in black history from family members. More knew about Malcolm X because of the recent movie ("they have T-shirts and hats about that," said one twelve-year-old).

However alienating a curriculum that does not concern them may be to students, and however frustrating trying to study a book that is too difficult for them may be, there is another way in which the curriculum impedes the progress of the students. This is the fact that the texts are written in standard English, a dialect that, because of their extreme marginalization and isolation from the mainstream, almost none of the students speak.[18] As Joan Baratz argued in 1970, the fact that the texts continually reject nonstandard dialect as inferior provides a continual insult to nondialect speakers.[19]

Not only is the standard English in written materials an insult to nonstandard dialect speakers; according to a large body of research it also interferes in important ways with reading achievement.[20]   This interference is caused in part by the subtlety of the differences between standard English and nonstandard English.   Joan Baratz and others demonstrated that it is extremely difficult to learn to read a language you do not speak, and that reading achievement can be significantly retarded by a reliance on texts whose syntax and phonetic structure differ from the structures of one's own language.   Conversely, reading comprehension increases significantly when one learns to read from texts printed in one's native tongue.[21]

In 1987, Eleanor Orr demonstrated fundamental ways black dialect can interfere with mathematical thinking in educational contexts, where mathematical thinking is governed, in textbook and in most pedagogy, by standard English language and forms of thought.[22]   She argues that not only do the subtlety of differences and the lack of familiarity with terms impede mathematical understanding, but that outright conflicts of black dialect terms with standard English terms also interfere.   Orr demonstrates that the grammars are distinct, the lexicons overlap; and—significantly—the unconscious rules that govern syntax in black dialect often conflict with and cause interference with standard English, which uses different rules.

One of the many kinds of mathematical problems encountered by the black dialect speaker involves the conflicts among standard and nonstandard English expressions used to compare parts of objects or amounts (partitive comparative expressions):

Standard English	*Nonstandard English phrases used to express the standard English expression*
half of	two times less than
half as large as	two times smaller than twice as small as half as small as
half as much as	half less than

half as fast as   twice as slow as
                                   half as slow as

In some cases, the terms in which black dialect speakers think are the inverse of what they read in the math textbooks. For example, in an expression like "half as much as," the expression is in the vocabulary of both languages—the students' language and the language of the texts—but with opposite meanings. The confusion that can occur is substantial. Orr demonstrates how such confusion over the meanings of standard English mathematical expressions can also affect scientific reasoning:

> In a chemistry class a student [who speaks nonstandard dialect] stated that if the pressure was doubled with the temperature remaining constant, the volume of a gas would be "half more than it was." When I asked her if she meant that the volume would get larger, she said, "No, smaller." When I then explained that "half more than" would mean larger, one and a half times larger, indicating the increase with my hands, she said she meant "twice" and with her hands indicated a decrease. When I then said, "But 'twice' means larger, two times larger," again indicating the increase with my hands, she said, "I guess I mean 'half less than.' It always confuses me."[23]

When the teacher attempting to teach speakers of nonstandard dialect from books written in standard English is also a speaker of nonstandard dialect, as many teachers are in the district under discussion here, the confusion can be compounded.[24]

Despite the curricular reforms—new textbooks, departmentalization, mandated instructional changes, and state and district regulations that attempt to align instruction with basals and other textbooks—the children's achievement scores have not increased. The standardized scores of the students at Marcy School (and at the other seven schools in this, one of the poorest wards of the city) are (as they have traditionally been) among the lowest in the district, and they declined between 1988 and 1992. District achievement scores are among the lowest in the state, and are considerably below national medians.[25]

The teachers, black and white, are in the unenviable position of being asked to impart a white, middle-class curriculum, written in a language that differs from and interferes with the students' (and many teachers') own language and that in most cases is presented to students in textbooks that are too difficult for them to fully comprehend. The situation certainly fosters student failure, and—consequently—the failure of reform to raise achievement. Moreover, the frustration engendered by the students' low achievement has the potential to worsen classroom relations between teachers and students.

Relations Between Teachers and Students

Teachers face an extremely difficult pedagogical situation at Marcy School. In addition to the curricular and instructional mandates and circumstances discussed above, teachers confront classrooms full of anxious and angry students. The desperate lives most of the children lead make many of them become restless and confrontational; many are difficult to teach, and to love. This section first discusses interactions I observed between black personnel and students, and then those of white staff.

It was apparent to me that some black teachers care deeply about their students: For example, one young teacher at Marcy School prays over her class every morning and evening, and prays each day for each of her students. Another teacher in the building takes homeless students home to live with her whenever she can. Another coordinates a clothing drive in the spring, and food baskets at Thanksgiving.

Most African-American teachers I interacted with during my work in the school also, however, expressed deep frustration in dealing with their students. Perhaps fueled by this frustration, these black teachers are—to varying degrees—abusive of their students. (I will argue below that most white teachers also exhibit—to varying degrees—systematically abusive behavior toward their students.)

During the ten months in which I spent a full day each week working with teachers and their classes, I heard a tirade from black teachers of what seemed to me to be verbal humiliation and degradation, directed at students. For example: "Shut up!" "Get your fat head in there!" "Did I tell you to move [talk; smile]?" "I'm sick of you." "He's not worth us wasting our time waiting for." "Act like a human being." "I'm going to get rid of you!" and "Excuse me!" said with what sounds like withering contempt. I heard one particularly abusive black male teacher teacher tell a girl her breath "smelled like dog shit," and her clothes "smelled like stale dust." A sampling of other, not atypical, comments

I overheard includes:

You're disgusting; you remind me of children I would see in a jail or something. (Black teacher to her class of black and Hispanic first-graders.)

Shut up and push those pencils. Push those pencils—you borderline people! (Black teacher to his class of black and Hispanic sixth-graders.)

Your mother's pussy smells like fish. *That's* what stinks around here. (Black teacher to black fourth-grade girl whose mother is a prostitute.)

Janice Hale-Benson argues that a cultural norm of harsh discipline exists among African-Americans, and thus verbal expressions that a white observer might perceive as abusive are not so perceived by African-American teachers or students.[26] As one black teacher explained to me, "It's what they're used to. They wouldn't listen to us if we didn't yell and put on a mean face. They know it's only our school voice." An older black teacher explained, "You can't treat these kids nice. They don't deserve it." Then, referring to a beginning teacher who had taken her class to the museum and had been asked to leave because the students were "touching everything," the older teacher said, "Why did she take them on a trip? They don't deserve to go to the museum! They don't know how to act!"

On eight occasions when I was working with teachers in their classrooms I saw black teachers, none of whom was considered an unusually harsh disciplinarian, smack a student with some force on the head, chest, or arm as if it were a routine occurrence. On numerous occasions I saw teachers grab students by the arm and shake them. No one reacted to these actions. I also witnessed two severe beatings by parents or guardians while a teacher or the school disciplinarian was present and did nothing to stop the beating.

My experience at Marcy School leads me to believe that the treatment of students by many black adults at this school goes beyond any tradition of harsh discipline that would be culturally sanctioned among African Americans, and represents, instead, aspects of a lived professional culture that characterizes the behavior of both black and white teachers, and that systematically degrades the children.

Thus, I found many white personnel to be just as verbally abusive as the black teachers discussed above. The following comment is from the white male gym teacher, who refused to give a fourth grade their scheduled gym class because "they're too rough. They throw the ball, it could kill you!": "If I had a gun I'd kill you. You're all hoodlums." Other white staff:

Stop picking in your ear. Go home and get a bath. (White basic-skills teacher to a black boy.)

Why are you so stupid! I'm going to throw you in the garbage. (Other white basic-skills teacher to a black boy.)

Don't you have *any* attention span? You have the attention span of cheerios! (White principal trying to quiet a class of black and Hispanic fourth-graders.)

This ain't no restaurant, you know—where you go in and get what you *want*! [pause] You have no sense! You have no sense! (White teacher reprimanding three African-American girls in the hall outside his door.)

As if in explanation for the way he treated his students, a white teacher stated during a meeting, "When you realize who they [the students] are, you laugh, and you can't take it [teaching] seriously." Two white teachers expressed fear of confronting their students. One stated: "I don't talk to them like I used to. They'll challenge you now, and you might not win." I did not see any white teacher strike a student, perhaps out of cultural norms that do not sanction it, or perhaps out of fear of retaliation. As one white male teacher said, "They all have social workers, and the social workers tell the girls don't let any man touch you. One girl accused me of touching her on the knee—her mother told her to do it, to get [her] out of my class. And it worked."

The school psychologist alleged that abuse by teachers is "common" in this school. The school social worker told me that she thinks there is less teacher abuse in the last four to five years because the Department of Social Services is "more diligent." However, the district—which serves only 4 percent of the state's students, but which itself is 89 percent minority and 78 percent poor—reports over 40 percent of the institutional child abuse reported by school systems to the state.[27]

Each school is required by the board to post "inspirational sayings" on walls and bulletin boards around the building. The purpose of the sayings is to motivate the students. The following are sayings the principal and a teacher posted:

If you have an open mind, chances are something will fall into it.

The lazier we are today, the more we have to do tomorrow.

The way to avoid lieing [*sic*] is not to do anything that involves deception.

It is easier to think you are right than to be right.

Don't pretend to be what you don't intend to be.

If you can't think of anything to be thankful for, you have a poor memory.

These "motivational" sayings are also instantiations of a lived professional culture that degrades the students at Marcy School. The school staff's abusive, implicitly sanctioned attitudes and behaviors have evolved over time in a situation in which the student population is extremely poor, racially marginalized, of low academic achievement, difficult to motivate educationally, and from families that have little or no social power. The lived culture of the teachers combines with the alien curriculum described above to create a hostile, rejecting situation for the students.

The students in turn describe their reactions. Following are representative quotes from eight of the twenty-five students I interviewed. The students are African-American, unless otherwise noted.

"Tell me about your class," I say to a fifth-grade girl during her interview. "My class stupid. They mentally depressed. They don't want to learn." "Why not?" "They don't like the teachers." "Why not?" "Well, Miss Washington, she assigns all this homework, and she never collect it. Lots of parents puts in complaints about Mr. D., but they don't do nothin." "Do you have many friends in your class?" I ask. "No," she responds, "I'm lonely. I'm a nerd." When asked to explain why her teachers and the principal act the way they do, this girl said, "When they need a low place to come to [teachers and principals] they come here. That the only place they get a job." (Eleven-year-old girl who attempted suicide twice during the year I knew her)

During another interview a boy tells me, "Teachers throw kids out, say 'I don't want you in my class.' They throw us on the floor and be grabbin us. Teachers too mean. They lie on people." "So what do you do?" I ask. "We make him mad." "How?" "Talk, laugh and have fun." (Eleven-year-old boy)

I ask a boy to "tell me about the teachers in this school." He responds, "Most teachers here don't teach us." "Why not?" "Because of the kids. They runs the halls and makes the teachers upset." "Why do they do that?" "Um, they think [teachers] just doin the job for money, they don't care." (Ten-year-old boy)

A boy tells me, "Most of the kids here don't do well." "Why?" I ask. "They fight too much and they don't feel like going to school." "Why not?" "They don't like school. They want to hang out." "And then?" "Then they'll drop out." (Eleven-year-old boy)

When I ask a girl why some kids don't do well at school, she says, "Kids don't want to learn. They be playin in the halls. They don't study." "Why not?" "It's boring and they get mad at the teachers." "How do you think the teachers feel about that?" "They don't care. [pause] If we don't learn, the teachers still gets their paycheck." (Thirteen-year-old girl, one of the three white students in the school)

I ask a ten-year-old girl, "Why don't some kids here do well at school?" "It's they fault. Because Mr. Thompson—you saw him teach—he's crazy, but he's a good teacher. The kids that don't learn don't want to learn." "Why not?" "They don't like school. They don't like Mr. Thompson. They playin so much in school they don't have time to learn." [At this point the principal comes over, and pinches her hard on her cheek leaving a red mark. He

says, "Mr. Thompson knows what to do with *you*, doesn't he?]
(Ten-year-old Hispanic girl)

"Tell me about your teacher," I request of a boy. "He says we're
animals. Hooligans. He said we should be in a zoo. I feel bad
when he say that. I get kinda sad." "So what do you do?" "I put
my head down." (Nine-year-old boy)

A boy walking past us as we sat talking in the hall added, "He
treats us like we're toys. So we make him mad." "What do you
do?" "We run around. [pause] Watch!" This ten-year-old boy
proceeded to do forward and backward cartwheels, flipping high in
the air off a desk that was in the hall. Several other boys who were
wandering the halls gathered around and cheered him on.

Almost all of the students I interviewed seemed to be in an
oppositional stance to their teachers; most were aware that they are in a
situation in school that is hostile and aggressively rejecting of them.

McDermott argued several years ago that black children who have
white teachers may "achieve" failure by rejecting the oppressive
definition of them they perceive their teachers to hold, and
concomitantly rejecting the teachers' and schools' definition of
success.[28] The black and Hispanic children I interviewed apparently
feel oppressive rejection on the part of both black and white teachers.
In this regard, almost all of the interviewees said it did not matter
whether you had white or black teachers ("They all the same"). One
student stated that his aunt told him, when he complained about his
teacher, "Just be glad you got a black teacher," but another black child
said it was better to have a white teacher, "as long as it's a lady."

It may be that the hostile social situation in which teaching,
learning, and testing occur in this school has important consequences
for achievement on the standardized tests given the students every
quarter and every spring, which are the benchmark of success in
educational reform. Ernest Haggard demonstrated in 1954 that the
social situation made a significant difference in how the 671 black
inner-city children he studied performed on IQ tests. The attitude of the
student to the tester was the most important aspect in determining how
students did on these tests. Significantly, the attitude of the student
toward the tester was more important than the content—for example,
identifiable cultural bias—of the test items.[29]

Teachers and administrators at Marcy School wonder aloud why the students "can do all the things in the street they won't do for us. Did you ever see a drug dealer who couldn't make change? They're walking spread sheets!" In the face of intense district pressure on teachers to "get the scores up," teachers convey to their students angry, desperate hopes that students will perform well on the tests. I suspect that, although some children may not be intellectually capable of learning what the school asks, one effect of the hostile atmosphere in the school is that many students may simply refuse to comply. The assistant superintendent told me that one of her biggest problems in the high school was "to get the students to take the [standardized] tests seriously."[30]

The result of student opposition to the academic demands of the school could be devastating for reform. Standardized tests are almost always the criterion that defines success in inner-city schools. As long as testing takes place in a hostile, oppressive situation, and measures a curriculum that is culturally and linguistically unsuited to the students, I suspect the scores will not rise.

Expectations For Reform

Most school personnel appear resigned to the failure of current reform efforts in the eight schools. The principal of Marcy School stated that "nothing will happen. This school was built over a hundred years ago. They just replaced the [original] windows five years ago! With the decades of neglect in this ward, it'll take years to fix it up." Teachers agree: "Nothing will be left when the money goes home." "The first year was nice—we were treated like professionals; the second and third year? Nothing." One teacher stated, when asked what she thought would come from the reform projects: "Maybe I'll get them [her students] from 'very low' to 'low' on the [achievement] tests." Then she added, "But even if they do learn to read and write, there are no jobs."

A consequence of this resignation is that it is much harder to garner the enthusiasm and energy to carry out improvement projects that most people are convinced will fail. Indeed, most personnel imply that they accept the present situation as "the best that can be expected." I heard over and over again, "We're doing the best we can" and "This is the best that can be done with what we have."

Many of the district's administrators, teachers, and principals, as well as the majority of the participating parents (e.g., classroom aides), grew up in the city. They and their children attended the city's schools. Due in large part to a diminished industrial base (and resulting insufficient employment opportunity) and nine decades of political patronage in the city bureaucracies, the board of education is the largest employer in the city. For the people who work in the schools, this is "their" system; the system provides their jobs, and despite the system's faults, they defend and support it.

Even I, an outsider, after several months of intense work with the students and teachers, began to think of the school as a good urban school, and I hoped the state evaluators in an upcoming evaluations would see it that way also. From my field notes:

I was very negative about the school when I arrived. Now I find myself thinking, "This is a good urban school," and hoping the state people will feel that way too. I feel many of the teachers work very hard, and actually teach. I go through the halls—with the doors slamming, adults going in and out of classes, kids roaming the halls, the intercom blaring and crackling, and the teachers shouting and angry—and I have to remind myself that this is an incredibly noisy and distracting place for studying. It is beginning to sound normal to me. So is what goes on in the classrooms. ("Good" is, of course, relative. If I were in [an affluent district in which I have done several district evaluations] what happens here would signal crisis/breakdown of the system. It would never be considered "good." I must be part of the system now; those who are in an institution have a hard time seeing it from the outside.

Several days later I write in my field notes:

After being in Marcy yesterday where chaos filled the halls, and teachers tried angrily and in vain to get the children to go back in their rooms, I went to my daughter's class today. [She is in third grade, in a public school in another city in a "model" school. The parents are, for the most part, professionals; 40 percent of the students are minority, but only 10 percent of them are low-income students. It is widely known as a very good school, occasionally being written up in the *New York Times*.]

The contrast was overwhelming. The kids were sitting, doing various activities, all over the room, on the floor, at tables—one black boy was curled up on top of a low book shelf, reading a book. The children were reading, making Father's Day presents from brightly colored materials; they were working with manipulables of various kinds. Materials, books, and supplies were everywhere, and in abundance; the children's work was on display on the walls, hanging from the ceiling, and in the hall. Murals and papier-maché projects decorated the back of the room. The T-shirts they had tie-dyed and silk-screened for their "Olympics" day the next day were hanging from rope across the room drying. The children were working easily, absorbed, in little clusters. Chatter filled the air, and smiles; and—most importantly—they seemed involved and interested in what they were doing. They seemed happy to be there!

It seemed unbelievable to me, how wonderful it was. It made me realize how far I had gone toward accepting the starkness of Marcy's bare and vacant rooms, the angry, wounded-looking children, and the resentful, hostile teachers—as acceptable.

Conclusion

The foregoing discussion delineates some of the ways blackness and whiteness, extreme poverty and relative affluence, cultural marginalization and social legitimacy, come together—and conflict—within a school to affect educational reform. The events and behaviors I have described take place when people of low social status—for example, impoverished people of color—comprise the student and parent population and do not have the power to prevent them. Such events occur when the rage and resignation of those in a community and school are so great that no good deeds can overcome them.

Such tragedies occur in a school and district when administrators from an oppressed group (for example) mimic, in educational policy choices, their oppressors, and when teachers from an oppressed group (for example) devalue students of their own group, as does the dominant culture and teachers of that culture. Perhaps most of all, such tragedy occurs when people in a community and a school confront the workings of a racist, class-biased system without sufficient resources and without hope.

What is to be done? Are the children in our ghettos doomed? I predict that educational change in schools like Marcy will require fundamental alteration of the social situation. First, we must create an alliance of blacks and whites in political struggle to eliminate poverty. A broad redistribution of social and economic resources must take place. In this city, an arts center whose initial cost is estimated at over $104 million is under construction downtown, less than a mile from Marcy School.[31] The art center is touted as destined to draw suburban residents to its performances and nearby businesses, thus "revitalizing" the downtown area. However, if the history of Detroit, Philadelphia, Boston, and Baltimore (among other cities that attempted "revitalized" downtown areas) is any indication, this art center will do little if anything for the residents of the surrounding ghettos.[32] It would be better to spend money to create meaningful long-term jobs in the locality, to train people for those and other well-paying jobs that may already exist in the locality, to provide adequate health care and housing, and, ultimately, to improve the schools.

Adequate health, personal finance, and social resources bring people a freedom of choice that poverty denies, and bring an end to the debilitating dependency that poverty enforces. A population can then feel hope; and people can feel a sense of agency, rather than unproductive rage and resignation. Students who are less oppressed are easier to teach, and teachers can then more easily excel.

I am suggesting that the structural basis for failure in inner-city schools is political, economic, and cultural, and must be changed before meaningful school improvement projects can be successfully implemented. Educational reforms cannot compensate for the ravages of society.

In the interim, before poverty and racial marginalization can be eliminated, I foresee three possible courses of action, none of which appears to me particularly viable. One possibility is metropolitan-area desegregation, as Gary Orfield and Jonathon Kozol have recommended.[33] For example, schools in this city could be closed, and students and teachers integrated into wealthier nearby suburban school systems—the students to get a better education, the teachers to participate in a professional culture that does not systematically devalue children. Such a solution, however, although it might provide an educational alternative, would not by itself overcome the deleterious effects of the students' returning each night to the ghetto—to poverty and desperate situations. Unless metropolitan-area school desegregation were accompanied by (at a minimum) substantial housing and job desegregation, metropolitan-area school desegregation would be a partial and ultimately unsuccessful solution.

A second possibility is that the state "take over" and run the city district (as it runs two other districts). Given the fact that many of the reforms attempted by the district in Marcy and the other pilot schools were actually mandated by the state department of education, it is not likely that the reforms the state would attempt in the district's other schools would be different. Moreover, the reforms described in this article, as well as other, administrative, reforms, have already been introduced by the state in two nearby low-income minority urban districts when state personnel took control of those districts in 1989 and 1991. So far, little if any academic progress has been made in these cities' schools, and insufficient numbers of students have passed recent state standardized tests to certify the districts.[34]   According to news reports concerning the two districts under state control, some administrative mismanagement of funds by prior officials has been stopped, so that more classrooms have textbooks, paper, and other supplies, but several state personnel administering the larger district are themselves under indictment for misuse of school funds.[35]

A third eventuality that should be considered is that personnel in the district described here will themselves ultimately effect significant improvements in the schools—with time, perhaps, and with larger infusions of money and more or better assistance. It should be noted in this regard that the district has unsuccessfully attempted continual reform initiatives since 1984. Moreover, the numerous improvement projects of the 1970s also failed to raise students' achievement.[36] While poverty and racial despair have escalated in this city since the 1970s—as in other cities—so has educational alienation and failure.[37]

Given the persistent historical correlation between poverty and school failure; given the resiliency of lived professional cultures such as that of school personnel described in this study; and acknowledging the power of the social and cultural distances between racially/economically marginalized school populations and the educational "help" they receive, it is unlikely that educators in ghetto schools will be successful in making substantial, long-term changes in their schools.

Thus, I think the only solution to educational resignation and failure in the inner city is the ultimate elimination of poverty and racial degradation. The solution to educational failure in the ghetto is elimination of the ghetto. This prescription seems extremely difficult to implement. I acknowledge this, but urge you to view its assumed improbability differently. As James Baldwin suggests in *The Fire Next Time*,

> I know that what I am asking is impossible. But in our time, as in every time, the impossible is the least that one can demand—and one is, after all, emboldened by the spectacle of human history in general, and American Negro history in particular, for it testifies to nothing less than the perpetual achievement of the impossible. . . . If we do not now dare everything, the fulfillment of that prophecy, recreated from the Bible in song by a slave, is upon us: GOD GAVE NOAH THE RAINBOW SIGN, NO MORE WATER, THE FIRE NEXT TIME! [38]

I would like to acknowledge the valuable comments by Janet Miller, Lois Weis, and Julia Wrigley on earlier versions of this paper. I could not have completed the article without the crucial advice given to me by Roslyn Arlin Mickelson.

Notes

[1.]   See, for example, Jonathan *Kozol, Savage Inequalities: Children in America's Schools* (New York: Crown Publishers, 1991)1 and Gary Orfield and Carole Ashkinaze, *The Closing Door: Conservative Policy and Black Opportunity* (Chicago: The University of Chicago Press, 1991). See also, among others, Lauro Cavazos, "National Assessment of Educational Progress," *Education Week* 7 (1990):1, 21; Seymour B. Sarason, *The Predictable Failure of Educational Reform: Can We Change Course Before It's Too Late?* (San Francisco: Jossey-Bass, 1990); and Robert Rothman, "Obstacle Course: Barriers to Change Thwart Reformers at Every Twist and Turn," *Education Week* 10 (February 1993): 9-12.

[2.]   See, among others, Sarason, *Predictable Failure*; Richard F. Elmore and Associates, *Restructuring Schools: The Next Generation of Educational Reform* (San Francisco: Jossey-Bass, 1990); Michael Fullan (with Suzanne Steigelbauer), *The New Meaning of Educational Change* (New York: Teachers College Press, 1991); George A. Goens and Sharon I.R. Clover, *Mastering School Reform* (Boston: Allyn and Bacon, 1991); Dwight W. Allen, *Schools for a New Century: A Conservative Approach to Radical School Reform* (New York: Praeger, 1992); Ann Bradley, "Education for Equality," *Education Week* 11 (1994): 28-32; Peter Schmidt, "Urban School Results Linked to Funding Woes," *Education Week* 11 (1994): 3; Patricia Wasley, *Stirring the Chalkdust: Tales of Teachers Changing Classroom Practice* (New York: Teachers College Press, 1994); and Ann Lieberman, ed., *The Work of Restructuring Schools: Building from the Ground* Up (New York: Teachers College Press, 1995). But see Kozol, *Savage Inequalities*, and James Comer, *School Power* (New York: Free Press, 1980), who consider more than most the contributions of race and poverty to the success or failure of educational reform.

[3.]   I will call on the concept of "ghetto" to highlight the extreme poverty and destitution of children in America's inner cities. The definition of ghetto that I will use throughout the article is that recently proposed by William Julius Wilson: A ghetto is an inner-city neighborhood in which more than 40 percent of the inhabitants are poor. Most inhabitants of such neighborhoods are black (with increasing percentages of Hispanics) and are economically, culturally, and politically isolated from the mainstream, despite their usual proximity to city hall and downtown shopping districts. The school that is to be discussed in this article exists in such a neighborhood, or ghetto. Census data from 1990 show that, in the census tract in which the school is located, 45 percent of all persons have incomes below the poverty level; of female-headed householder families with related children under eighteen years, 66 percent are below the poverty level; of female-headed householder families with related children under five years, 82 percent are below the poverty level. According to the 1990 census, the per capita income in the census tract in which the research site is located was $7,647. (The per capita income in 1990 in the city was $9,437. Per capita income in the State was $24,936, which was 33 percent higher than the national average. New Jersey, the state in which the school is located, was in 1990 the nation's second wealthiest state.)

(See William Julius Wilson, "Public Policy Research and The Truly Disadvantaged," in *The Urban Underclass*, edited by Christopher Jencks and Paul E. Peterson [Washington, DC: The Brookings Institution, 1991], 460-82; and idem, *The Truly Disadvantaged: The Inner City, the Underclass, and Public Policy* [Chicago: University of Chicago Press, 1987].)

4. David B. Corson, "Some Ideals and Accomplishments of the Newark School System," National Education Association Proceedings and Addresses (1921): 707-13; and idem, "Leading School Systems of New Jersey: The Newark System," *New Jersey Journal of Education* 13 (March 1924): 1ff.

5. George D. Strayer et al., *The Report of A Survey of the Public Schools of Newark, New Jersey* (New York: Bureau of Publications, Teachers College Columbia University, 1942).

6. State of New Jersey Governor's Select Commission of Civil Disorder, *Report for Action: An Investigation into the Causes and Events of the 1967 Newark Race Riots*, February, 1968 (New York: Lemma Publishing Corporation, 1972) 170-71.

7. *Report to the Acting Executive Superintendent, Newark School District*, from the State of New Jersey Department of Education and the Commissioner of Education, Trenton, August 13, 1984.

8. According to New Jersey Department of Education data, in 1992-93, 51 percent of the certified full-time teachers in the city were black, and 8.5 percent were Hispanic (New Jersey Department of Education, 1992-93 Certified Full-Time Staff Report by District, Position and Race [Trenton: Department of Education, 1994]): 1374. According to an informant in the Bureau of Research at the city's Board of Education, the percentage of African-American teachers cited in the state statistics is low. According to this informant, the percent of African-American teachers in the city is much higher, due to the relatively high number of teachers in the district who are not certified, and who are part-time (long- or short-term substitutes). Almost all part-time teachers in the district are African-American.

Although statistics could not be obtained from the district, observation reveals that in schools (such as the research site) where black children are the majority, there are more black teachers than at district schools where the majority of the children are Italian or Portuguese. As noted below, 64 percent of the classroom teachers at the site were African-American.

According to state figures, in 1992-93, 43.3 and 7.7 percent of district administrators were black and Hispanic, respectively. Fifty percent and 5.8 percent of special-services personnel in the schools were black and Hispanic, respectively (p. 1374).

9. Sabrina Hope King, "The Limited Presence of African-American Teachers," *Review of Educational Research* 63 (1993): 115-50.

10. Albert Memmi, *The Colonizer and the Colonized* (Boston: Beacon Press, 1965 and 1991); idem, *Dominated Man* (Boston: Beacon Press, 1968); Frantz Fanon, *Black Skin, White Masks* (New York: Grove, 1967); Paulo Freire, *Pedagogy of the Oppressed* (New York: Herder and Herder, 1970); and Edward Said, *Orientalism* (New York: Pantheon, 1978).

11. I participated in the reform during 1991-1993 primarily as staff developer. I carried out workshops in cooperative learning in several of the eight target schools and subsequently assisted teachers in their classrooms. I carried out the workshops at Marcy School between January 1992 and February 1993, and worked at least one full day a week during the ten school months in teachers' classrooms, providing coaching in the new methods (see Jean Anyon, "Teacher Development and Reform in an Inner-City School," *Teachers College Record* 96 [1994]: 14-31, for further description of one portion of this work).

In addition to the more than 200 hours spent with teachers in their classrooms, I also attended reform team meetings during school years 1991-1992 and 1992-1993, and spent numerous hours talking with teachers at these meetings. In my year at Marcy School I spent approximately half (21) of the lunch periods "hanging out" with the students in the cafeteria and on the asphalt yard; I also chatted with them frequently in classrooms and halls. I became wee acquainted with the assistant superintendent responsible for the reform, commuted on the train with her on numerous occasions, and often discussed the reform efforts with her, and with members of her staff. Between 1991 and 1993 I formally interviewed the assistant superintendent, her staff, twenty-four of the twenty-five classroom teachers at Marcy School, the members of Marcy School's school-based support team, both Marcy School administrators, the school's drug counselor, fifteen parents, and twenty-five students. I read numerous school and district reports and other documents (such as state reports) pertaining to the schools and the reform initiative. I examined all curriculum materials—those in use and those prepared by the district but not much used.

12. Mun Wong et al., "Under Siege: Children's Perception of Stress" (Paper presented at the annual meeting of the American Psychological Association, Washington, DC, August 1992).

13. "For Idle Young in Newark, Pride in a Theft Done Right," *New York Times*, August 11, 1992: A1.

14. The analysis of adults in the school reported in this article is based on

my observations and interactions with African-American and white employees, and statements about teachers are confined to members of these groups. As far as I could tell, the relatively few Hispanic employees (six classroom teachers, several aides, and the vice-principal) did not differ in substantive ways from their white and black colleagues. However, with the exception of one teacher and the vice-principal, the Hispanic staff were (unofficially) isolated from the rest of the school in a bilingual program, and the time I spent with them was limited.

15. See David D. Laitin, *Hegemony and Culture* (Chicago: University of Chicago Press, 1986); and Russell Hardin, *Collective Action* (Baltimore: Johns Hopkins University Press, 1982).

16. See Jean Anyon, "Inner City School Reform: Toward Useful Theory," Urban Education (in press), for further description of the Professional Development Project. See also idem, "The Retreat of Marxism and Socialist Feminism: Postmodern and Poststructural Theories in Education," *Curriculum Inquiry* 24 (1994): 115-34, for a discussion of the theoretical import of this and other reforms.

17. New Jersey Department of Education, *Newark Public Schools, Level III External Review* (Trenton: Author, April 16, 1993: Education Programs): 13, 15.

18. Examples of black dialect (gathered in classrooms of Marcy School) follow. (See also Geneva Smitherman, *Black Language and Culture: Sounds of Soul* [New York: Harper & Row, 1975].)

STUDENTS:
"They lookin at us paper." [at our paper]
"He ain't ax you." [didn't ask you]
"I'm is the girl you want." [I am]
"When my sister take my baby sister toys she be in school."

19. Joan C. Baratz, "Beginning Readers for Speakers of Divergent Dialects," in *Reading Goals for the Disadvantaged*, edited by J. Allen Figurel (Newark, DE: International Reading Association, 1970): 77-83.

20. *Ibid.*; Morton Wiener and Ward Cromer, "Reading and Reading Difficulty: A Conceptual Analysis," *Harvard Educational Review* 37 (1967): 620-43; William Labov, "Some Sources of Reading Problems for Negro Speakers of Non-standard English," in *Teaching Black Children to Read*, edited by Joan Baratz and Roger Shuy (Washington, DC: Center for Applied Linguistics, 1969); Joan Baratz, "Teaching Reading in an Urban Negro School System," in *Teaching Black Children*: 92-116; and Bernice E. Cullinan, *Black Dialects and Reading* (Urbana, IL: National Council for Teachers of English, 1974).

21. See Cullinan, *Black Dialects and Reading*; Figurel, *Reading Goals for*

the Disadvantaged; and Baratz, "Beginning Readers." For studies of children speaking other nonstandard dialects (Native American, Appalachian, Hawaiian), see, among others, Barbara Z. Kieler and Johanna S. DeStefano, "Cultures Together in the Classroom: 'What You Saying?'" in *Observing the Language Learner*, edited by Angela Jaggar and M. Trika Smith-Burke (Urbana, IL: National Council of Teachers of English, 1985).

[22.] Eleanor Wilson Orr, *Twice as Less: Black English and the Performance of Black Students in Mathematics and Science* (New York: W.W. Norton, 1987).

[23.] *Ibid.*, p. 171.

[24.] I estimate that most of the African-American teachers at Marcy use dialect with their students at least some of the time (mixing it with standard English). I estimate that approximately one-third use dialect all the time with their students. Examples follow:

TEACHERS:
"What does a sentence begins with?"
"When I be out they has a good time!"
"You didn't do nothin' yet."
"You wrong!"
"Take your crayons—we can't get no more."
"Have anyone seen Shawana?"

I estimate that approximately the same fraction, one-third, of the principals I talked with at reform team meetings also consistently spoke black dialect. According to the assistant superintendent, these men speak dialect "most of the time."

PRINCIPALS:
"He have a parent who . . ."
"Many people have came here."
"He don't never come to school."

[25.] Newark Board of Education, *Restructuring Urban Schools in Newark, NJ: An Evaluation of the Cluster Program* (Newark, NJ: Author, 1992).

[26.] Janice E. Hale-Benson, *Black Children: Their Roots, Culture, and Learning Styles*, rev. ed. (Baltimore, Johns Hopkins University Press, 1986).

[27.] New Jersey Department of Education, Newark Public Schools, Education Programs, p. 68. The phrase "institutional abuse" as used by the New Jersey Department of Education refers to emotional, physical, or sexual abuse of students by public school employees.

A conversation I had early in my work at Marcy School is of interest here.

During one of my first few weeks in the building, the child study team (psychologist, social worker, learning disabilities specialist) invited me to lunch. They seemed eager to tell me about the school. The following is from my field notes:

> We are discussing the enormous problem the team sees "getting anything done" at Marcy School. "We're part of the problem, you know," the psychologist says, "I mean, jailors and prisoners are the same." The social worker adds, "This district has enormous problems—the mayhem of the system itself is a big problem. But the children's lives are the biggest problem." "Yes," agrees the psychologist, "We should be teaching them [the students] who they are in the system, and what the system does to them. We need a diagnosis like they have in Europe—of economic and social victimization—that's what these kids are—victims."
>
> "What about the teachers," I ask. "What are they like?" The psychologist states, "There is a lot of teacher abuse of the students—it's common here. The children have desperate lives, and the teachers distance themselves from that by abusing them, by separating themselves from the children, even though they're [the teachers are] black, too. But you know, most of these teachers are one paycheck away from welfare themselves."
>
> "And you," I ask, "how do you deal with the children and the system?" They say they blame the system. "Contradictory initiatives on the part of the board; disarray at the board," says the learning disabilities specialist. And he blamed the state. "The state is weak; it has no money to monitor the system, and couldn't afford to take over [the city's schools]." "Even your project," says the psychologist, referring to my work teaching the teachers to use cooperative learning. "We've seen it all before. We did cooperative learning in the early 1970's—the open classroom, curriculum integration, there's nothing new being done now, it's all been tried before." "Yes," I say. "But maybe this is how *we* distance ourselves from the problems. We say, 'there's nothing we can do, it's all been tried before.'" "Maybe," said the psychologist.

28. Ray McDermott, "Achieving School Failure: An Anthropological Approach to Literacy and Social Stratification," in *Education and Cultural Process: Anthropological Approaches*, 2nd ed., edited by George Spindler (Prospect Heights, IL: Waveland, 1987): 82-118.

29. Ernest A. Haggard, "Social Status and Intelligence: An Experimental Study of Certain Cultural Determinants of Measured Intelligence," *Genetic Psychology Monographs* 49 (1954): 141-86. See also, among others,

Courtney Cazden, "The Neglected Situation in Child Language Research and Education," in *Language and Poverty: Perspectives on a Theme*, edited by Frederick Williams (Chicago: Markham, 1970); and Geneva Smitherman, *Talking and Testifying: The Language of Black America* (Boston: Houghton-Mifflin, 1977).

[30.] See also Herbert Kohl, *"I Won't Learn from You": The Role of Assent in Learning* (Minneapolis: Milkweed Editions, 1991).

[31.] "In Newark, a Prologue to a Performing Arts Center," *New York Times*, January 1, 1995, p.A9.

[32.] Orfield and Ashkinaze, *The Closing Door*; Norman Fainstein and Susan Fainstein, *Urban Policy Under Capitalism* (Beverly Hills: Sage, 1982); and Dennis R. Judd and Todd Swanstrom, *City Politics: Private Power and Public Policy* (New York: Harper Collins, 1994).

[33.] Orfield and Ashkinaze, *The Closing Door*; and Kozol, *Savage Inequalities*.

[34.] Mathew Reilly, "Report Says Jersey City Schools Need Two More Years Under State Control," *The Star Ledger*, June 21, 1994, p. 19. See also Kimberly J. McLarin, "Education Board Extends Takeover of Jersey City Schools," *New York Times*, September 8, 1994, p. B6; and idem, "Schools in Paterson Lagging on Standards, Report Says," *New York Times*, November 4, 1994, p. B6.

[35.] Robert J. Braun, "Top School Officials Fired in Jersey City," *The Star Ledger*, July 6, 1994, p.1; and idem, "Klagholz Details 'Loose' Fiscal Policies Found in Jersey City Audit," *The Star Ledger*, July 7, 1994, p.16.

[36.] As assessment detailing the fact that the city's student achievement scores were well below national levels in the late 1970s stated, "In both reading and mathematics Newark has attempted to improve pupil performance during the past ten years by resorting to a staggering variety of new programs. Indeed, one of the consistent criticisms voiced is that too many programs have been tried with too little effective evaluation of them" (Paul Trachtenberg, "Pupil Performance in Basic Skills in the Newark School System since 1967," in *1967-1977: As Assessment*, edited by Stanley B. Winters (Newark, NJ: New Jersey Institute of Technology, 1978): 235-43.

[37.] Orfield and Ashkinaze, *The Closing Door*, idem, "Public Policy Research"; and Andrew Hacker, *Two Nations: Black and White, Separate, Hostile, Unequal* (New York: Charles Scribner's Sons, 1992).

[38.] James Baldwin, *The Fire Next Time* (London: Michael Joseph, 1963 [Reprinted: Random House, 1992]), 119-20.

Chapter 7

Introduction to Patricia Malone and Norman Benson

In this essay, Patricia Malone and Norman Benson argue that the ongoing debate over the liberal interpretation of American history has the potential for revolutionizing the teaching of American history.

They begin by pointing to two important events which ultimately led to a reexamination of the policy of "liberal universalism." These were:

1. At the end of World War II increasing numbers of minority groups enrolled in graduate programs with a resultant proliferation of historical studies dealing with marginalized minority groups.

2. These new studies led to a re-examination of the traditional "liberal universalistic" narrative accounts of American history, an account that portrayed our past simply as the story of one people held together by a common understanding of political equality.

Within the context of these two factors, the authors review two traditional perspectives ("socialization" and "counter-socialization") of the goals of social studies programs. This review clarifies the relationship of these views to the perspectives of "liberal universalism."

Malone and Benson argue that theorists who favored "socialization" goals typically approved of non-critical accounts of United States history, whereas theorists who favored "counter-socialization" objectives in the social studies were more interested in helping students "to deliberate and compare our actions with our political ideals."

They then go on to suggest that although a "new synthesis which integrates the histories of various groups has yet to be developed -- teachers are not thereby precluded from offering analyses of various group interactions and contributions."

Malone and Benson conclude by recommending that social studies educators consider Thomas Bender's approach to historical synthesis which "focuses on the formation of an evolving public culture, and which strives to incorporate minority social groups in a manner which emphasizes a pluralistic ideal of strong political equality."

Questions:

      1. In what ways is the immigrant nation of the United States being redefined by the cultural influences of its newer immigrants?

      2. Do you feel that multiculturalism should permeate the social studies curriculum? Why? Why not?

      3. What were some of the major factors that led to a re-examination of the policy of "liberal universalism?"

      4. Why might the older version of "liberal universalism" no longer be a defensible basis for a social studies curriculum?

Contemporary Theories and Research on Schooling and Work

by *Patricia Malone* and *Norman Benson*

Originally published in the *Journal of Thought* Volume 30,
(Summer 1995), pp.8 - 18 Reprinted with permission.

Popular assumptions about the relationship between schooling and work in America have usually been predicated upon the belief that there is a simple and direct relationship between one's educational attainments and his/her vocational mobility. To a large extent, these assumptions reflect a corollary belief that one's educational achievements are primarily contingent upon one's academic ability and personal commitment to educational goals and thus relatively unaffected by either race, gander, or social class. This conventional understanding of the relationship between the two institutions considered the criteria for successful schools to be their success in preparing individuals to compete for existing jobs in the workplace and thus did not imply a need for substantial structural change in either institution.

Despite the continuing prevalence of the conventional view of schools in the public at large, educational and social theorists have continually debated both the existing and the ideal relationship between schooling and the workplace since the early years of this century. They have disagreed about the amount of correspondence which exists in this relationship in a democracy. To a lesser extent, the debate has focused on the relative importance of one's social class and race in the articulation of a theory which explains the effect of schooling on an individual's work outcomes. A small group of theorists has contended that gender has a significant role in structuring both educational and workplace experiences. To date, this group has not had a significant impact on the main body of social and educational theory which has developed around this important debate.

This essay will describe both mainstream and alternative theories of the schooling/work relationship and also the most recent critique of that literature which calls for a revision of those theories which have equated male experiences in schools and in the workplace with universal experiences.

One of the early contributions to the dialogue about schools and society is contained in the work of the early Progressives. John Dewey believed that educational practices could eventually reform the workplace. He wrote about an ideal school where students would learn not only about the essential unity of thought and work, but also about the proper relationships with others.[1] Thus, Dewey not only believed that schools enjoyed an essential degree of autonomy but he also believed that the understandings gained through educational experiences could transform the workplace when students acted on their understandings as adult workers.[2]

Some of the later Progressives shared Dewey's conviction that schools were sufficiently autonomous to become successful in developing curriculum and instruction which did not reflect the fragmented work organization of the industrial sector. They focused their attention on schools which they viewed as racist, dehumanizing, and overly conformist in their expectations of students. Writers such as Holt believed that, despite the similarity between practices of the schools and the negative aspects of the workplace, the schools could somehow be improved.[3] Critics of the late Progressives have contended that Goodman was one of the few writers of that period who actually confronted the contradictory implications of their own analysis.[4] Others failed to ask how schools which were so much like the workplace in reproducing its unjust features could be expected to become more just and humane.

An alternative analysis of the school/society debate did not ignore the similarities between the organization and practices of the schools and the hierarchical divisions of the workplace. In fact, the correspondence which the Progressives largely ignored in formulating their analysis became the cornerstone of two conceptual frameworks based on the structural correspondence. One of these consists of an economic analysis which contends that the structure of schools in America has always been designed to reproduce the social stratifications of the workplace.[5]

In *Schooling in Capitalist America*, Bowles and Gintis point to the mechanisms within school which mirror the social relationships of the private economic sphere. In schools there are vertical authority lines from administrators to teachers and students. Students are motivated to perform their work through the use of grades rather than through the intrinsic interest of the work itself. Competition among students is also fostered in schools. Students of different social classes are socialized by both the curriculum and the teaching methods to accept, as natural, the kind of authority which they will be expected to recognize when they become part of the workforce, which is also segmented according to social class distinctions.

Students from high socio-economic classes are exposed to teaching methods which encourage self-direction, and which foster an ability to manage others through their training in analysis and problem solving. The curriculum and instruction of lower socio-economic groups accustoms them to accept fragmented work where one needs little understanding or problem solving ability, but instead requires one to be able to complete simple tasks under close supervision.

The economic analysis of schooling offered by Bowles and Gintis has served the important function of challenging the meritocratic assumptions about schooling and work which have dominated popular beliefs and also much of the academic mainstream writing. However, the ensuing debate was followed for the most part by arguments based on a cultural analysis of schools. Many cultural theorists focused on those processes in schools which produced a consciousness among students that was not totally shaped by the values of the dominant social class. They contend that the reproductive mechanisms described by Bowles and Gintis are never quite complete since they are always met with some resistance from both teachers and students.[6] In *Education Under Siege*, Giroux contends that the failure of the structural theorists to address the power of human actors to influence their own destiny is yet another example of an historical failure of educational theory for decades to address the dual existence of reproductive mechanisms and resistance forces within teachers and students.

Apple has written of the ambiguity which this duality has created when students are exposed to pre-packaged curriculum units that have enjoyed increasing popularity in American schools.[7] These curricula severely curtail the autonomy of both students and teachers. He believes that they also foster a consciousness which is overly competitive and individualistic. However, Apple stresses that domination of students' consciousness is far from inevitable. It is possible that the use of this curriculum will engender opposition from teachers or students. Apple contends that the important issue in judging the effect of this curricular organization for students is their eventual choices about work. Willis has also called attention to the variety of vocational choices which may result from students' resistance to the culture of the dominant classes.[8] His study of English working class students demonstrates that students' own culture may appear to put them into opposition with the school culture. However, their resistance to school culture may not prevent their eventual choice of jobs which correspond to their social class origin. In his study, male working class students rejected the school culture, but substituted cultural values of their own which led them to value the very jobs that were "suitable" for their class in the segmented workplace.

Fuller has also demonstrated the ambiguous nature of student resistance to school cultures.[9] Her study of black, female high school students in England demonstrated that students were able to maintain some of their own cultural identity while simultaneously conforming to both school culture and to other subcultures within the school. These black, female students were convinced of the importance of education in their lives, but were also aware of the norms of black male students which discouraged being perceived as openly conforming to teacher expectations. The result of these conflicting values was a pattern of behavior which outwardly appeared to resist teacher expectations in daily performance in classrooms (they did not appear to be eager, obedient students who handed in assignments readily), but which actually consisted of completing the curriculum requirements so that they could achieve passes on British academic examinations.

As stated above, the structuralist interpretation of the schools and society relationship contained in the economic interpretation of the best known correspondence theorists, Bowles and Gintis, was one of two analyses of this type. The second structural analysis not only pre-dated the economic functional analysis, but overshadowed it in subsequent influence on educational theory. The structural functionalist analysis has dominated educational sociology in both the United States and England for thirty years. Sociologists of education have generally accepted the thesis that society is a consensual whole with general needs that are properly met by its major institutions.[10] One of the fundamental prerequisites of an advanced industrial society is the development of attitudes and skills which will promote economic growth.   In this view of society, it is acceptable and desirable for schools to meet the needs of the industrial sector of society.

A third conception of the school/society relationship rejects both the progressive view that schools are fundamentally autonomous institutions and the structuralist analysis which presumes that schools are primarily mirrors of the industrial system.   Carnoy and Levin contend that the most useful analysis of the relationship is a dialectical one in which changes within one of the two sub-systems result in changes in the other.[11]   They further contend that there are fundamentally two forces operating in schools in a democratic state. One is reproductive of existing inequalities and the other favors democratic change.

Several circumstances may contribute to the dominance of one of these forces at any particular period of history.   Changes occurring in schools and the workplace as a result of these shifting emphases may have unexpected results in both sectors.

In developing their dialectical analysis of schooling and society in *Schooling and Work in the Democratic State*, Carnoy and Levin first offer an important critique of the consensual view of society that has dominated educational writing for decades.   This critique contends that the consensual view of the state implicit in the mainstream analysis of schools is based on the erroneous conception of the individual as the basic unit of economic and political analysis. It views the individual as a basic unit of economic and political analysis, and it ignores the connections of individual views expressed collectively through the state with the social relations in the family and in the private economy.

Another error of the consensual view of society is the assumption that the state represents the common good. When the common good theory is combined with a belief that the free market system is just and socially efficient, the result is an avoidance of issues concerned with economic and political power, the lack of class mobility, and the effect of class division on the control of the state. They contend that the most relevant paradigm for the analysis of schooling and work is a dialectical one which is based on a social conflict theory of the democratic state.

In the dialectical model of the school/state relationship, changes within schools and changes within state agencies in response to demands of under-represented social groups, produce reactions and counter-reactions in both the schools and other social institutions, particularly the workplace. According to this view of the state, the state bureaucracy sometimes acts somewhat independently. This happens when classes and sub-groups within classes lose power as they fractionalize over their competing interests. However, the state is most often the scene of conflict as various groups seek to influence state policy. Since there is no consensus within the state as to how to deal with these attempts to control state policy, there are necessarily conflicts and contradictions within the state bureaucracy itself. Although the state attempts at specific times to reproduce class divisions of labor and also the social relations of production through its control over school policy, social movements outside the dominant class frequently demand more resources and more control over state policies, and thus often diminish the influence over state policy enjoyed by the dominant classes. Examples of the influence of subordinate groups on state policy are legislation enacted to make schools more responsive to the needs of women, minority groups, and the educationally disadvantaged during the 1970's.

In the Carnoy and Levin analysis, the struggle between dominant and subordinate groups for the control of state policy may result in educational changes that have direct and significant consequences for the management of the workforce. An example of this is the "overeducation" of the workforce which occurred in the sixties and seventies because schools were responsive to demands of groups who wanted more access to educational institutions. This "overeducation" phenomenon which originated in the schools had important consequences for the economic system since managers began to employ highly educated workers demanding more autonomy and more interesting work. New workers were also less responsive to the traditional exercises of authority in the workplace. However, Carnoy and Levin contend that industrial managers may have several possible reactions to the presence of more highly educated workers. They may respond by changing the social relationships of work, thus giving employees more control over their work, while at the same time advocating tighter admission standards at four-year colleges and a focus on emphasis on vocational rather than academic courses at the community college level.

When employers in the United States were faced with the "overeducation" phenomenon in the 1970's, in combination with a declining rate of productivity, some turned to management strategies which gave workers more control over their work, such as autonomous work groups and workers' councils. However, Carnoy and Levin contend that managers' responses were also influenced by national events such as union movements. Such factors are always an important constraint on changes in the workplace.

Carnoy and Levin's analysis also allows them to describe some probable outcomes in schools which may follow reforms in the workplace. They argue that, because of the economic hard times of the 1970's, schools in the eighties will probably be more influenced by the reproductive tendency (the mirroring of business practices) rather than by the democratizing forces, since economic downturns tend to make business the reference point for decision making in the United States. Since large businesses have utilized autonomous work groups and workers' councils to improve the management of the workforce, schools which are reacting to pressure for change may develop school reforms which parallel workforce reforms. This may include changes in instructional methodology emphasizing more student autonomy and cooperation such as group work and peer tutoring. The governance of schools may change to reflect less hierarchical control in the management of both schools and individual classrooms.

The dialectical model of the changing relationship between schools and the workplace is rich and complex, and thus represents a valuable contribution to the longstanding educational debate over the role of both structure and human agency in the schools. However, Carnoy and Levin, like the majority of their predecessors, have left out gender as a significant factor in their analysis of both schools and the workplace.

Anyon contends that Carnoy and Levin's statements about the stronger democratic tradition in schooling than in the workplace in the United States illustrate their failure to recognize the scholarship demonstrating the uniqueness of female experiences in schools.[12] They assert that schools have been provided more opportunity for participation than has the workplace. Anyon notes that until recently schools have been far less accessible for female rather than for male students. They assert further that the outcomes in schools are more equitable than they are in the workplace. Anyon reminds us that, despite the fact that girls have always done better than boys in school, the outcomes have been far less equal for women than men. Finally, she notes the omissions included in their statement over the workplace in regard to governance. She stresses that schools as workplaces for women have afforded them little equality with superiors.

It is also clear that Carnoy and Levin have not considered gender a significant factor in their analysis of the workplace. They describe a segmented American workforce which contains three groups separated by different entrance requirements, wage levels, and promotion patterns. Furthermore, there are discriminatory patterns within the workforce based on race, social class and gender. They note that there is a close relationship between racial and ethnic discrimination and social class discrimination. Carnoy and Levin make a brief reference to the fact that discrimination against women cuts across social classes. However, they make no attempt to elaborate on this statement about the particularity of female experiences in the American workforce despite the existence of research on both gender discrimination and the sex-role typing of jobs which have contributed to women's economic history.[13]

MacDonald argues that research on women's education has demonstrated that schooling produces both classed and sexed subjects.[14] Moreover, this scholarship contains, in her opinion, an inherent challenge to current theories of schooling which have glossed over or ignored the sexual division of labor within the school and its impact on shaping the relations between the family, the schools, and the labor processes. She provides an analysis of how this new scholarship challenges major bodies of theory about the relationship between schooling, the family, and work processes. One of these is the work of Bowles and Gintis.[15] MacDonald maintains that their analysis of the secondary labor market is incomplete since Bowles and Gintis include women simply as another minority group in this market which is characterized by low wages, little unionization, low job security, and little chance of promotion and training. MacDonald believes that the inclusion of discrimination against women with racial and ethnic discrimination contributes to their failure to address patriarchal power structures which are an integral part of capitalist social organization in the United States. She contends that Bowles and Gintis have also ignored the sexual division of labor in the primary labor market where women are in an inferior position with regard to wages and training prospects. Research concerning the relationship of racism and sexism in the workplace to practices which materially benefit employers is also absent from their analysis. Another significant factor that must be included in any theory of the relationship between schooling and the workforce is the dual position of women as both domestic and wage laborers. MacDonald demonstrates that the employment of women causes a dilemma for employers. Women who work outside the home may be less effective in their domestic work as wife, mother, therapist, etc., and thus the reproduction of the workforce may be threatened. However, women are desirable as employees since they are not expected to pay the full costs of the household and can, therefore, be paid less than men for their waged labor.

Class differences among the female workforce also need to be a part of theories about schooling and the workplace, in MacDonald's view. While some women have only their own labor to sell in the workforce, upper class women may benefit indirectly from family wealth and may not have to work at all. A few women have even become owners of capital and thus are part of the management and control structures of the labor force.

Current theories of schooling have also failed to integrate research demonstrating the significant differences which characterize the routes females take through the educational system. An important factor in this difference is the pervasive variation in the interaction between teachers and their students based on the gender of pupils. Research has shown, for example, that teachers pay more attention to boys than to girls.[16] Although more of this difference exists in disciplinary exchanges than for instructional messages, the difference cannot be dismissed as due to the fact that boys' more aggressive behavior patterns demand more of the teacher's time and energy. It has been demonstrated that girls who exhibit problem behavior do not receive more attention from teachers than girls in general.[17] It is clear from these studies that what counts is not the behavior but who is performing the behavior. What boys do matters more to teachers than what girls do, in her view.[18]

Girls' and boys' behaviors are also differentially reinforced in many classrooms. Boys receive more negative responses for disruptive behavior, while girls are more likely to receive negative teacher comments for the quality of their work. When boys perform poorly on academic tasks, teachers attribute the performance to lack of motivation much more frequently for boys than they do for girls.[19] Moreover, two-thirds of all negative evaluations received by girls in this study concerned the quality of their work, whereas two-thirds of the negative assessments given to boys involved non-intellectual tasks such as behavior. Boudreau contends that these patterns may account for the pattern of sex differentiation in regard to expectancies for future success found by many researchers.[20] Studies have shown that, based on objective ability measures, males tend to overestimate their future success relative to their ability level, while females tend to underestimate their future chances of success. Moreover, while these differences in expectancies are not found in preschool children, they become stronger with the number of years spent in school.

Boudreau also notes the tendency for teachers to reinforce female students for good behavior. In combination with the high frequency for negative academic evaluations for girls, these reinforcements may lead girls to stake their sense of self-worth more on conformity than on personal competency. Research demonstrates that when people are rewarded for behavior which is unrelated to personal effectiveness, they are likely to become dependent on evaluation from others.[21] It is clear that girls' socialization toward social approval can become dysfunctional in situations where independence and assertiveness are required. While more research is needed to explain the decline in girls' performance relative to boys, as they move through the junior and senior high school (girls continue to do well but their superiority over boys in elementary school declines in certain subjects), Boudreau contends that sex role socialization experiences within the schools are the key to explaining the differing value orientation and future occupational plans.

The important differences in sex role socialization evident in elementary schools are frequently perpetuated in the experiences of women as they move through the system up to and including the graduate school level. Studies of college classrooms have shown that professors frequently pay more attention to male students by calling on them more frequently and by paying more attention to what male students say.[22]

In a study of letters of recommendation written for applicants to doctoral programs, it was found that professors exhibited more sexual bias against women students than they did against women students applying to master's level programs.[23] In letters for doctoral applicants, women were pictured as more able and mature, but men were depicted as being more committed, more self-directed, and as having more background knowledge. Women were depicted as having pleasing personality in 39 percent of the recommendations, while this was mentioned as characteristic of only 19 percent of male students. Finally, 63 percent of women applicants were characterized as making good graduate students while 44 percent of males were so characterized. As future scholars, only 37 percent of women were so recognized, while 56 percent of the men were recommended on this basis.

It is far from clear whether research on women's education and on the differential experiences and outcomes for women in the workforce will bring about a reassessment of current theories of the schooling/work relationship. A recent review of the status of three alternative bodies of theory which have challenged the dominant Western analysis of schooling, namely the existentialists, neo-Marxists, and the feminists, contends that these three voices of dissent have not received an even response from American educational theorists who have mainly taken into account only the first two of these three alternative views.[24] She notes that, even though feminist writings are appearing in professional journals and on conference programs, they frequently are regarded as papers by women and for women. She believes that the quality of feminist pedagogy requires a presence in the other liberation theories of educational philosophers.

If a dialectical model of education and work is a reliable tool for analysis, one can assess the future impact of scholarship on women on educational theory by looking to both the national political arena and also to the workplace itself for guideposts. The success of the women's movement in demanding political recognition of equity claims in legislation together with the favorable resolution of equity claims in the industrial workplace may contribute to a reassessment of educational theory with gender included as a significant variable for analysis.

Notes

[1.]   William Kilpatrick, "Dewey's Influence in Education," in *The Philosophy of John Dewey*, edited by P. Schlipp, (The Library of Living Philosophers, vol. 1) (Evanston, IL: Northwestern University Press, 1939): 462-463.

[2.]   Arthur Wirth, "Exploring Linkages between Dewey's Educational Philosophy and Industrial Reorganization," *Economic and Industrial Democracy* 2, no. 2 (1981): 121-140.

[3.]   John Holt, *How Children Fail* (New York: Pitman, 1964). See also Paul Goodman, *Compulsory Mis-Education* (New York: Horizon, 1964); and Edgar Friedenberg, *Coming of Age in America* (New York: Random House, 1963).

[4.]   Martin Carnoy & Henry Levin, *Schooling and Work in the Democratic State* (Stanford: Stanford University Press, 1985).

[5.]   Samuel Bowles & Herbert Gintis, *Schooling in Capitalist America* (New York: Basic Books, 1976).

[6.]   Henry Giroux & Stanley Aronowitz, *Education Under Siege* (South Hadley: Bergen & Garvey, 1985).

[7.]   Michael Apple, "Curricular Form and the Logic of Technical Control: Building the Possessive Individual," in *Schooling, Ideology and the Curriculum*, edited by L. Barton, R. Meeghan, & S. Walker (Sussex: Falmer Press, 1980): 11-27.

[8.]   Paul Willis, *Learning to Labor* (Lexington, MA: Heath, 1977).

[9.]   Mary Fuller, "Black Girls in a London Comprehensive School," in *Schooling for Women's Work*, edited by R. Deem (London: Routledge & Kegan Paul, 1980).

[10.]   David Reynolds & Michael Sullivan, "Toward a New Socialist Sociology of Education," in *Schooling, Ideology and the Curriculum*, edited by L. Barton, R. Meeghan & S. Walker: 160-195.

[11.]   Carnoy & Levin, *Schooling and Work*.

[12.]   Jean Anyon, [Review of *Schooling and Work in the Democratic State*] *Teachers College Record* 89, no.1 (1987):158-161.

[13.]   Julie Matthaei, *An Economic History of Women in America* (New York: Schocken Books, 1982).

[14.]   Madeline MacDonald, "Socio-cultural Reproduction and Women's Education," in *Schooling for Women's Work*, edited by R. Deem (London: Routledge & Kegan Paul, 1980).

[15.]   Bowles & Gintis, *Schooling in Capitalist America*.

[16.]   J.E. Brophy & T.L. Good, *Teacher-Student Relationships: Causes and Consequences* (New York: Holt, Rinehart & Winston, 1974).

[17.] Philip Jackson, *Life in Classrooms* (New York: Holt, Rinehart & Winston, 1968).

[18.] Frances Boudreau, "Education," in *Sex Roles and Social Patterns*, edited by F. Boudreau, R. Sennott & M. Wilson (New York: Praeger, 1986).

[19.] C.S. Dweck, W. Davidson, S. Nelson & B. Enna, "Sex Differences in Learned Helplessness: The Contingencies of Evaluative Feedback in the Classroom, An Experimental Analysis," *Developmental Psychology* 14, no. 3 (1978): 268-276.

[20.] Boudreau, "Education."

[21.] J. Marolla & D. Franks, "Efficacious Action and Social Approval as Interactive Dimensions of Self-Esteem," *Sociometry* 39 (1976): 324-341.

[22.] R.M. Hall, "The Classroom Climate: A Chilly One for Women," in *Project on the Status and Education of Women* (Washington, DC: Association of American Colleges, 1982).

[23.] F. Boudreau & W. Newman, "An Analysis of Letters of Reference for Graduate School Applicants," (Unpublished manuscript, 1977).

[24.] Glorianne Leck, Review article "Feminist Pedagogy, Liberation Theory, and the Traditional Schooling Paradigm," *Educational Theory* 37, no. 3 (1987): 343-354.

Richard B Lyons
25 MALLARD Rd.
Needham, MA 02492